AUTO RECIPE 300
KENMORE MICRO/CONVECTION COOKING

SEARS

Home Economics Director: Virginia Peterson
Senior Home Economists: LuAnne Dugan, Thelma Pressman, Alice Stoltzner, Betty Sullivan

Editor: Naomi Galbreath
Project Manager: David P. Stefani
Art & Design: Thomas C. Brecklin
Graphic Artist: Barbara Schwoegler
Typography: A-Line, Milwaukee
Food Stylists: Carol Peterson, Jean Carey
Photography: Teri Sandison, Los Angeles

USER INSTRUCTIONS

PRECAUTIONS TO AVOID POSSIBLE EXPOSURE TO EXCESSIVE MICROWAVE ENERGY

(a) DO NOT ATTEMPT to operate this oven with the door open since open-door operation can result in harmful exposure to microwave energy. It is important not to defeat or tamper with the safety interlocks.

(b) DO NOT PLACE any object between the oven front face and the door or allow soil or cleaner residue to accumulate on sealing surfaces.

(c) DO NOT OPERATE the oven if it is damaged. It is particularly important that the oven door close properly and that there is no damage to the:
- (1) DOOR (bent)
- (2) HINGES AND LATCHES (broken or loosened)
- (3) DOOR SEALS AND SEALING SURFACES

(d) THE OVEN SHOULD NOT BE ADJUSTED OR REPAIRED BY ANYONE EXCEPT PROPERLY QUALIFIED SERVICE PERSONNEL.

Library of Congress Catalog Card Number: 85-070396
ISBN: 0-87502-146-8
Published by The Benjamin Company, Inc.
One Westchester Plaza
Elmsford, New York 10523
Printed in Japan
10 9 8 7 6 5 4 3 2 1
13048

CONTENTS

What's It All About?

You are about to enter an exciting new world of automatic cooking. You can now cook using the incredible speed of microwaves, the efficiency of convection, or a combination of both methods with micro/convection — all in a single cavity unit. In addition, there is an important plus: here, for the first time, is a micro/convection oven that has an entire cookbook preset in its computer memory. You don't have to calculate cooking time or select the proper cooking method for any of the 300 recipes in the book. The oven will automatically change from one system to another, to provide the best cooking techniques required for each recipe.

A Cooking School

We have selected both traditional and new recipes that will show off this oven to its best advantage. But before you try a recipe, please read these introductory chapters carefully. You will find a complete "cooking school" with how-to pictures and illustrations to guide you. There is nothing complicated about using this oven. All you need is a little understanding of the special possibilities it offers. Just take a few minutes to read the instructions and acquaint yourself with the principles and techniques involved in micro/convection cooking.

– *Chocolate-Cherry Bundt Cake (page 193) is just one of the 300 recipes stored in this oven's computer.*

How Does It Work?

First, let's look at convection. Convection cooking isn't new. Restaurant kitchens have enjoyed the advantages of this cooking technique for years. It is an energy-efficient cooking mode and is similar to your conventional oven in operation. Unlike conventional ovens, convection ovens have a fan that assists circulation of the heated air. This constant movement of heated air strips away the cooler air that surrounds food, again and again. Heat sources at the top and bottom of the oven provide a hot, dry environment for items like soufflés, bread, angel food cakes, cookies, pizza, and heat-seared meat and fish. No changes are required to adapt your favorite oven recipes to convection cooking. All heatproof cookware may be used in convection cooking. The notation *"Oven cooks: convec"* indicates convection-only cooking.

In microwave cooking, microwaves travel directly to the food without heating the air. Ordinary electrical current is converted into high frequency microwaves, just like radio and television waves. A stirrer-fan distributes the microwaves evenly throughout the oven. Microwaves are waves of *energy*, not heat. They will do one of three things: they will be reflected by metal surfaces; they will pass right through certain materials; or they will be absorbed.

When the convection or micro/convection cooking methods are used, hot air (red) is circulated constantly. Microwaves (blue) are also used with the micro/convection method. The oven is hot when both methods are used.

Glass, pottery, paper, and most plastics allow the waves to pass through. The see-through panel in the oven door is made of a specially prepared material that contains a metal screen. The metal screen reflects the microwaves, yet enables you to observe the food as it cooks. The waves cannot penetrate the screen.

The moisture in food absorbs the microwaves and creates friction through the movement of the molecules. This molecular motion generates heat somewhat the way heat is generated when you rub your hands together rapidly. Cooking begins from the outside and the interior then cooks by conducted heat, in much the same way conventional cooking operates. The microwave method is the best choice for preparing sauces, vegetables, poached eggs or fish, and for reheating, defrosting, or sautéing. No metal cookware may be used but glass, paper, and most plastics can be used. The notation *"Oven cooks: micro"* indicates microwave cooking.

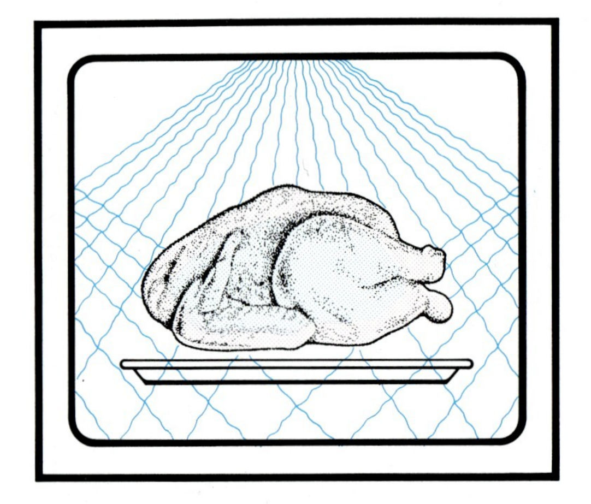

Microwaves bounce off oven walls and are absorbed by food. The oven is usually cool in microwave cooking but may be hot if another method was used recently.

In combination cooking, the convection and microwave systems contribute their best features in cooking the food. The convection system heats, browns, and dries the surface of the food for crisping. The microwave system speeds cooking and prevents dehydration. Combination cooking is best for roasting poultry, for quiches, some pies, and other food. Special considerations apply in selecting cookware; see pages 15-19. The notation *"Oven cooks: micro/convec"* indicates combination cooking.

Look What You Can Do!

Now you have an oven that can do just about everything. Here is an array of food that illustrates the results provided by the wide range of cooking techniques available with this oven. The recipes for all the dishes illustrated are in the book. You'll find that each method — microwave, convection, or micro/convection — has its own specialties. Let's take a look.

□Angel food cake and cookies are scrumptious and use the hot, dry convection method. □That old-time favorite, Apple Pie, uses the convection method. Hot air cooks the crust to flaky perfection. □Convection gives Pineapple Baked Alaska its mellow goodness. □Candies of all kinds are easy-to-make delights provided by the microwave method. □Smell that bread baking! A shortcut is provided for proofing with the microwave method while convection gives just-right baking.

☐Micro/convection cooking gives Roast Duckling a delicious, crisp skin and it's easy, yet elegant. Oven-Fried Chicken is also ready in a flash the micro/convection way and it will be perfectly crisp. ☐Steak is sure to become a favorite when it is cooked using the convection method. ☐You'll love to cook breaded or baked fish by convection for a crisp outside texture and a tender, moist inside. Reheat fish (or chicken) by convection, too, to retain that just-cooked crispness. ☐Bacon and scrambled eggs are cooked by the microwave method with no splatter to clean and with bacon as crisp as you like. Eggs are so fluffy and moist, there'll be no more breakfast-skipping at your house!

☐Hot appetizers can be ready as needed and are quickly cooked. Stuffed Mushrooms are stars of the microwave method and Sausage Rolls are brown and crisp, thanks to convection. ☐Now, even for the beginner, soufflé success! Spinach/Cheese Soufflé — cooked to perfection by convection. An impressive presentation for family or friends. ☐Basic White Sauce, flavored with cheese, shows off the ease and speed of microwave sauce preparation. No double boiler needed, a simple glass measure is all you need.

☐The most glamorous vegetable presentation: garden vegetable medley is full of color and nutrition, cooked by the microwave method and served in the same dish. Serve it with cheese sauce for a filling treat.

☐There's no need to turn on a big oven to heat a small pot pie, a turnover, or a pizza. Use the convection method for the hot, dry environment needed to crisp these crusts. ☐Heat soup, chili, and beverages right in the serving cup, mug, or bowl. The microwave method makes it possible. Heat a snack in just about two minutes. ☐Cut preparation time by melting butter and chocolate and softening cream cheese the microwave way.

Now that you have some idea of what this exciting oven can produce for your table, let's take a look at what you need to know to start cooking!

Here's What You Need to Know

Read this basic information and look at the accompanying illustrations — they're important! They will help you derive the maximum benefit from this oven's unique qualities. Whenever you have a question about a cooking term or method, you can refer back to this guide. It will tell you why some foods cook faster than others, which cooking method is best for certain foods, and what cooking utensils are appropriate to use. It will also provide you with basic information about timing and temperature.

You will be introduced to microwave cooking, convection cooking, and micro/convection cooking — and learn the basic principles of each method. Once you understand these basics, you'll find the transition to microwave and convection cooking easy.

Your new oven is suited to every cooking style. The 300 recipes we have preset for you provide the speed and simplicity we all value. In addition, your family favorites can be easily and quickly prepared. And if you are an innovative cook, you'll find this oven versatile enough to answer your every need. We encourage you to enjoy your oven in all these ways.

Knowing the basic principles of microwave and convection cooking will be helpful, even if you intend to cook only with our 300 preset recipes. If you follow the preset recipes exactly, you will get excellent results. But there will be times when your ingredients may vary somewhat from the preset recipe. A few ounces of difference in a cut of meat can require an adjustment in cooking time, particularly when the microwave method is used. While an adjustment in timing may also be necessary for micro/convection or convection cooking, timing is somewhat less critical with those methods. In addition, the information that follows will prove useful, whether you choose preset recipes, family favorites, or your own new dishes. In any event, study now can eliminate frustration later. Let's go to school.

ABOUT TIMING

Temperature settings and timings given for conventionally cooked recipes are meant to be guides to good cooking. This is also true for microwave, convection, or micro/convection cooking. Don't be afraid to use your instinct and judgment. Cooking is always a matter of observation and taste, no matter what appliance is used. However, timing for the microwave method is of particular importance because one minute can make the difference between a perfect sauce and one that is overcooked. A dish that requires one hour of cooking time in a conventional oven usually requires only one-quarter of that time when the microwave method is used. Since just one minute can make an important difference, microwave cooking requires a somewhat different approach to timing. Therefore, you will find that most cookbooks give microwave recipes with probable minimum-maximum cooking times, such as "Cook 2 to 3 minutes." The "Cooking Guides" or charts in this book use that same procedure. Stop cooking at the minimum time suggested and check for doneness. Then cook longer if necessary. (This procedure is not necessary for the preset recipes unless the ingredients are changed.)

The same precautions about timing apply to micro/convection cooking. However, when combination cooking is used, the microwave portion cycles on and off and therefore timing is somewhat less critical.

Convection cooking does not call for any more attention to timing than conventional cooking. You can use your conventional oven recipes without changes in the timing or temperature settings.

Cooking times for all preset recipes are precise. However, if your ingredients are changed in any way, timing will be affected and you must check as the food cooks. You may also want to adjust timing in some preset recipes to reflect your preference regarding doneness.

Why such variances in cooking times? Precise cooking times could only be provided if a way were found to guarantee that a given type of food would always be exactly the same, if the utilities would guarantee not to vary power (there are frequent changes in the voltage levels that reach our homes), and if our tastes were all alike. But the fact is that food varies in density, moisture or fat content, shape, weight, etc. And, some of us like our eggs soft-scrambled, while others prefer them firm. Even the temperature at which food is placed in the oven can affect cooking time. Therefore, the cook must be ready to adjust to these differences and be flexible. This applies even when you are using one of the 300 preset recipes. All of them have been meticulously kitchen tested by expert home economists. You will rarely find that the timing must be altered. However, as with all fine cooking, the recipes will benefit from your personal touch. (The preset timing and cooking method are presented in italics with each recipe.)

CHARACTERISTICS THAT AFFECT TIMING

Many characteristics of food, such as quantity, shape, density, and starting temperature affect timing. Understanding them will help you become an expert microwave cook.

Quantity

The larger the volume of food there is, the more time is needed to cook it. One ear of corn in the husk cooks in about 3 minutes; 3 ears may cook in 8 minutes. Therefore, if the quantity in a recipe is changed, an adjustment in timing is necessary. Many of the preset recipes have such timing changes automatically calculated for you. They are identified with this symbol ⊞ throughout the book. Consult the Use & Care Manual for details.

When changing the quantity of a microwave or micro/convection recipe on your own, follow this general rule: When doubling a recipe, increase the cooking time approximately 50 percent. When cutting a recipe in half, reduce the time by approximately 40 percent. Treat quantity adjustments for convection just as you do for conventional cooking.

Shape and Size

Thin cuts of food cook faster than thick cuts and small pieces cook faster than large. This common-sense observation leads to special treatment in cooking with microwaves. Because of the distribution pattern of microwaves, food next to the rim of the dish cooks faster than food in the center. To ensure even cooking, place thick pieces by the rim

Always consider the cooking method and desired results when deciding which cooking position to use. Vegetables retain color and texture cooked by microwave on the ceramic tray (upper left). Crescent Rolls (page 78) are flaky and brown when cooked by the convection method with the wire rack on the oven bottom (upper right). Fresh Pear Pie (page 185) baked by micro/convection with the wire rack in the lower position has a flaky crust enclosing perfectly cooked fruit (lower left). Steaks and chops (Guide, page 85) have heat-seared flavor and appearance when cooked by convection with the wire rack in the upper position (lower right).

of the dish and thin pieces in the center. For best results, cook pieces of similar size and shape together.

Height

For heat-seared flavor and appearance, use the convection method, with the wire rack in the upper position. When cooking microwave or micro/convection, more care is needed, especially with tall food. The microwave energy source is at the top (as is one of the heat coils) and some food may require turning to promote even cooking. Otherwise, the portion of the food nearest the top of the oven could be overdone before the rest is cooked.

Density

Dense food like potatoes, roast beef, and carrots take longer to cook than porous food such as cakes, ground beef, or apples. Not such an important consideration for convection cooking, but it does take longer for microwave energy to penetrate the denser texture. For example, a 2-pound beef roast will take longer to cook (microwave) than a 2-pound meatloaf.

Starting Temperature

As in conventional cooking, the temperature of the food when it is placed in the oven affects cooking time. More time is needed to cook food just out of the refrigerator than food at room temperature. For example, it takes longer to heat frozen green beans than canned green beans. Also, hot water from the tap will start boiling sooner than cold. Recipes in this book assume that food is at refrigerator temperature if that is its usual storage environment.

Moisture Content

In microwave and micro/convection cooking, food with a high moisture content cooks faster than dry food because the microwave energy is more easily absorbed by the moisture in the food. For example, 1 cup of sliced zucchini will cook faster than 1 cup of carrots because of the higher water content of the zucchini.

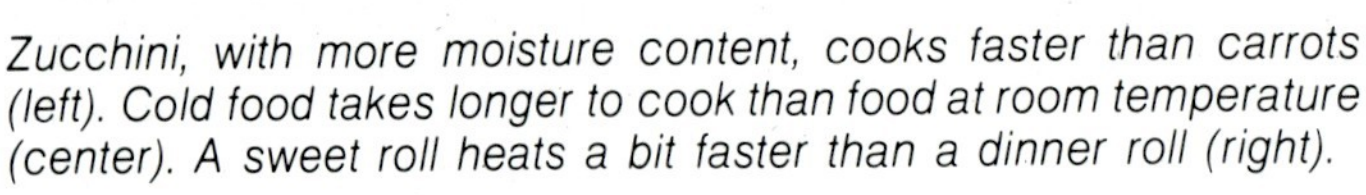

Zucchini, with more moisture content, cooks faster than carrots (left). Cold food takes longer to cook than food at room temperature (center). A sweet roll heats a bit faster than a dinner roll (right).

Delicate Food

This term is used to refer to ingredients that cook so quickly by the microwave and micro/convection methods that they can overcook, causing them to toughen, separate, or curdle. This includes mayonnaise, cream cheese, eggs, cream, and dairy sour cream. Other food, such as snails, oysters, and chicken livers, may "pop." Using lower power settings (microwave) and reduced temperatures (micro/convection and convection) will prevent this. It's the same principle as reducing the heat on a gas or electric burner when food is cooking too fast. When delicate ingredients are mixed with other food, higher settings may be used. The increased volume slows down the cooking.

Sugar and Fat Content

Food high in sugar or fat heats more quickly when the microwave method is used because the energy is attracted to these areas. For example, the fruit or cheese filling of a sweet roll heats faster than the pastry itself.

ABOUT UTENSILS

There's no need to retire any of your favorite cookware to use this oven. Nor is it necessary to acquire anything new, although there are some unique items that can make the microwave method even more satisfying. Simply put, the cooking method or methods used will determine the type of cookware. Convection cooking needs no special equipment: cookware is the same as that used in conventional ovens.

Microproof Cookware

For microwave cooking, we have created a new term, *microproof*. It means that an item is safe and recommended for microwave cooking. Since we're accustomed to the term "heatproof" for conventional cookware, it shouldn't take long for us to accept *microproof* as a just-as-familiar friend. Much heatproof cookware is also microproof. The most distinguishing feature of microproof cookware is that it is never, even partially, made of metal.

When selecting a new piece of cookware for microwave use, first check the manufacturer's directions. Also review the "Materials Checklist" on page 17 and "A Guide to Cookware" on page 19. If you are still in doubt, here is a test you can make to see if it is microproof. Place the item on the ceramic tray with a measuring cup full of water alongside. Cook (micro) on HI 45 seconds. If your dish feels hot, it is absorbing microwave energy and should not be used. If it feels barely warm, it has limited microproof capability and may be used for brief periods (warming food). If it remains cool, it is microproof. Keep in mind that metal cookware, or items trimmed with metal are not used for microwave cooking. Not only do they reflect microwaves and prevent them from reaching the food, but they can cause sparks, a static charge, known as arcing. Arcing is

A wide variety of bundt pans, muffin pans, ring molds, cooking dishes, bacon racks, roasting racks, and glass utensils have been invented or improved in microproof form for microwave use and some are also heatproof (top left). Most paper, plastic, and woodware items are microproof (top right). Metal utensils of all kinds are used in convection cooking without reservation and can be used in micro/convection cooking only when they are placed on the ceramic tray (above right). At left is an assortment of heatproof cookware that can be used for microwave cooking, for micro/convection cooking, or for convection cooking.

not harmful to you, though it will deface the oven. Oh, did you know that paper products are microproof? They are!

Micro/Convection Cookware

For micro/convection cooking, the general rules are fairly easy: (1) cookware must be *both* microproof *and* heatproof whenever it is to be placed on the wire rack; (2) cookware needs to be only heatproof when it is to be placed on the ceramic tray (metal is acceptable).

Selecting Containers

Containers should accommodate the food being cooked. Whenever possible use round or oval dishes, so that the microwaves are absorbed evenly into the food. Square corners in cookware receive more concentration of energy than the rest of the dish, so the food in the corners tends to overcook. Some cake and loaf recipes call for ring molds or bundt pans to facilitate more even cooking. This is because the center area in a round or oval dish generally cooks more slowly than the outside. Round cookware with a small glass inserted open end up in the center works just as well to eliminate undercooked centers. When a particular size or shape of container is specified in a recipe, it should be used. Varying the container size or shape may change cooking time. A 2-quart casserole called for in a recipe refers to a bowl-shaped cooking utensil. A 12×8-inch or a 9-inch round baking dish refers to a shallow cooking dish. In the case of puddings, sauces, and candies, large containers are specified to prevent the liquids, especially milk-based ones, from boiling over. For best results, try to use the dish cited in the recipe.

Materials Checklist

☐CHINA, POTTERY: Ideal for microwave use if no metallic trim or glaze. Fine for micro/convection and convection if heatproof.

☐GLASS: Excellent cooking material for microwave, micro/convection, and convection cooking. Since oven-proof glass is always safe, "microproof" is not mentioned when a glass or ceramic item is specified.

☐PAPER: Approved for short-term microwave cooking. Must not be foil-lined. Paper towels and waxed paper are acceptable microwave coverings. No micro/convection or convection uses approved.

☐PLASTICS: Plastics designed for microwave cooking may be used and a growing number of plastic products are available. Follow manufacturer's instructions and carefully observe maximum temperature recommendations. Plastic wraps recommended by the manufacturers make a fine cover for microwave cooking but cannot be used for micro/convection or convection cooking. (Be sure to remove the plastic wrap if a recipe calls for a shift from microwave to micro/convection or convection cooking.)

☐PLASTIC COOKING BAGS, POUCHES: Can be used for microwave cooking but slit pouches so steam can escape. Cooking bags generally approved for micro/convection and convection use. Check package or manufacturer's instructions for heatproof qualities on cooking pouches.

☐METALS: Excellent for convection. Limited use *on the ceramic tray only* for micro/convection cooking. Not suitable for microwave cooking, except as follows:

Small amounts of aluminum foil may be used to cover areas on large pieces of meat or poultry that defrost or cook more rapidly than the remainder. In microwave cooking or defrosting, this method is known as shielding.

Aluminum frozen TV dinner trays with foil covers removed can be heated microwave if the trays do not exceed ¾-inch depth. However, convection works better. Just follow the package directions for conventional ovens.

Frozen poultry containing metal clamps may be defrosted by the microwave method without removing the clamps.

Any aluminum foil or metal item must be at least 1 inch from oven walls when microwave or micro/convection cooking is in process.

□THERMOMETERS: The temperature probe provided with the oven is used to determine internal food temperature for all cooking methods. Conventional meat thermometers may be used with convection cooking if desired. For microwave cooking, use special microwave food thermometers. Some of these have temperatures in ranges needed for making candy. Because all candy is made by the microwave method,you will find these thermometers especially useful.

□STRAW AND WOOD: If no metal fasteners are present, these can be used with the microwave method only for quick warming (rolls, chips, etc.)

A Micro/Convection Note

As we've said earlier, metal acts as a barrier to microwaves, preventing them from cooking the food. For that reason, the use of metal pans with the micro/convection method is usually not advised. However, occasionally metal pans can be used in micro/convection cooking if they are placed on the ceramic tray. In this case, foods cook only from the top, because of the metal barrier. For best results, use a metal pan on the ceramic tray for micro/convection cooking only when specified in a recipe.

Ceramic Tray

Because the ceramic tray is used for all microwave-method cooking, you will probably find it to be your most frequently used cooking surface. It may also be used for micro/convection method cooking. However, the ceramic tray must be removed from the oven whenever cooking by the convection method is planned as a part of a recipe sequence. It is not necessary to remove it from the oven when preheating, unless cooking by the convection method follows.

The ceramic tray should always be in the oven when either the microwave or micro/convection method is used. This is recommended even when you are planning to place the food on the wire rack in either the lower or upper position. Microwaves pass through the tray and are reflected by the oven bottom back up to the underside of the food. As a result, the food (in microproof or microproof/heatproof cookware) receives microwave energy on the bottom, top, and sides all at the same time.

Wire Rack

The removable wire rack has three positions: upper, lower, and oven bottom. To change rack from upper to lower position, simply turn it over. For bottom position, rack rests directly on the oven bottom.

A GUIDE TO COOKWARE

ITEM	GOOD USE	MICRO	MICRO/ CONVEC	CONVEC
Aluminum foil products	Shielding, broiling, many cooking functions	ltd.	ltd.	ok
Boilable pouches	Heating frozen food	ok	no	no
Candy thermometers	Making candy	*	*	*
Cast aluminum, stainless steel, cast iron	Most cooking functions	no	ltd.	ok
China plates, cups	Heating	ok	no	no
Corelle®	Heating, cooking vegetables	ok	*	*
Corning Ware®	Most cooking functions	ok	ok	ok
Metal pans	Most cooking functions	no	ltd.	ok
Metal-trimmed or glazed pottery	Cooking casseroles, soup, many cooking functions	no	no	ok
Oven cooking bags	Cooking roasts, poultry	ok	ok	ok
Paper towels, plates, liners, cups, etc.	Covering, heating, or cooking (as specified)	ok	no	no
Plastic wrap	Covering	ok	no	no
Plastic cookware, dishes, roasting racks	Heating, cooking, elevating food	ok	*	*
Pottery, earthenware, clay cookers	Most cooking functions	ok	ok	ok
Pyrex®, and heat-proof glass	Most cooking functions	ok	ok	ok
Soft plastics, sherbet cartons	Reheating for very short periods	ok	no	no
Microproof meat thermometers	Determining internal temperature of food	ok	ok	ok
Waxed paper	Covering	ok	no	no
Wood products	Spoons for stirring, skewers for kabobs	ok	no	no
Straw baskets (no metal trim)	Warming bread	ok	no	no

* Check manufacturers' recommendations. Must be microproof for microwave or micro/convection use and heatproof for convection use.

ltd.= limited use approved. See "About Utensils" and "Materials Checklist"

ABOUT METHODS

The speed and effectiveness of microwave and micro/convection cooking are not only determined by the characteristics of the food, but also by certain techniques. You have used many of these techniques before in conventional cooking, but they do have particular applications with this oven due to the special qualities of microwave energy. Those that are used regularly in conventional cooking will continue to be important when cooking with the convection method. Becoming familiar with these terms and methods will make your cooking easier and will help assure success.

Arrangement

The way food is arranged in the oven and in the dish helps assure evenness in cooking and facilitates defrosting, heating, and cooking when the microwave and micro/convection methods are used. The microwaves always penetrate the outer portion of food first, so food should be arranged with the thicker areas near the edge of the dish and the thinner portions near the center. For example, when cooking Oven-Fried Chicken (page 117 and above), the thick, meaty portions of the breasts and thighs are placed at the edge of the dish with the thin sides

Oven-Fried Chicken (page 117) is shown properly arranged for micro/convection cooking. Note oven mitt, needed for hot air micro/convection and convection environment (above). Lamb chops should be arranged with thickest portion toward outside of dish (top left). Arrange tomatoes in a circle for even cooking (middle left). Place potatoes in a circle end to end on a paper towel or microproof roasting rack (bottom left).

toward the center. The thinner, bony ends of the drumsticks are also placed toward the center. Food such as tomatoes, potatoes, and corn should be arranged in a circle, rather than in rows. Such arrangement techniques can also provide attractive cook-and-serve opportunities. Check the garden vegetable medley (page 13) and cauliflower-broccoli-carrot dish (page 149) and let your own imagination go!

Rearranging

Sometimes food that cannot be stirred must be repositioned in the dish during cooking. Be sure to use tongs and pot holders when cooking with the micro/convection or convection method because the dishes and oven will be hot. Checking food during cooking is the best way to judge whether or not rearranging is necessary.

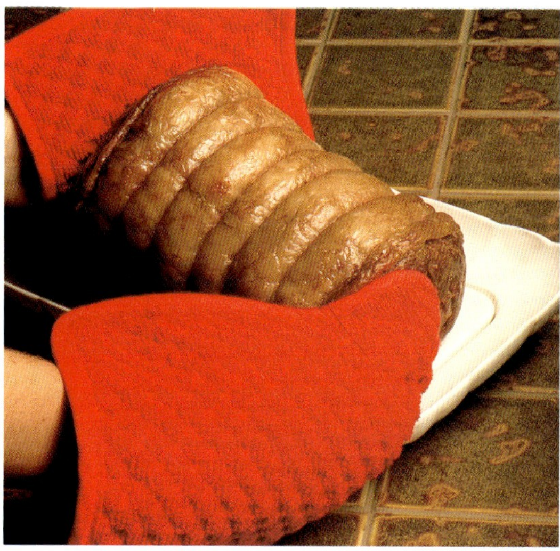

Use mitts to turn large food (above). Some recipes recommend rearranging food in the dish (top right). In microwave cooking, stir from the outside to the center (right).

Turning Over

As in conventional cooking, some food, such as steaks, large roasts, whole poultry, ham, hamburgers, or chops, may require turning over to brown or crisp each side and to promote even cooking. Use mitts to turn large food; they provide a secure grip and juices are not lost by piercing meat with a fork. You can always wash the mitts if soiled.

Stirring

Little stirring is required when cooking in this oven. If necessary, stir from the outside to the center because the outside area heats faster than the center when microwaves are in use. Stirring blends the flavors and promotes even heating. Stir only as directed in the recipes: constant stirring is never required, frequent stirring is rare.

Some muffins and cakes need to be rotated (above left). Paper towels and plastic wrap are good microwave-method covers (above). Dishes with lids are best for micro/convection and convection methods (left).

Rotating

At times, recipes for some baked items, such as pies, cakes, or quiches that cannot be stirred, turned over, or rearranged, call for adjusting the position of the dish for more even cooking. Rotate one-quarter or one-half turn only if the baked food is not cooking or rising evenly. Most food does not need to be rotated.

Covering

Covers are used to trap steam, prevent dehydration, speed cooking time, and help food retain its natural moisture. Suitable covers for microwave cooking may differ from micro/convection and convection methods. Heat in the oven cavity will melt plastic wrap or cause paper to burn. When covering with paper towels or waxed paper, a good microwave cooking practice, be sure to use a double width that will enable you to tuck the paper under the bottom of the cooking dish. Otherwise, it will tend to rise off the dish due to the air movement. Plastic wrap generally adheres to the dish, of course. Paper towels are especially useful for cooking bacon because they absorb fat, yet allow the bacon to cook crisply because the paper does not trap steam. Waxed paper is best for covering poultry, fish, and any food where the retention of heat is important for even cooking but where there is no need to trap steam. Remember: paper towels and waxed paper may only be used when cooking by the microwave method. Casseroles which usually have their own lids are the best choice when covers are needed in micro/convection and convection cooking. A handy idea to keep in mind: a heatproof plate is a good substitute for a lid.

Standing Time

During standing time, heat continues to be conducted from the outside of the food to the center. After the oven is turned off, food may remain in the oven for standing time or may be placed on a heatproof surface. This procedure has long been used by professional chefs and knowledgeable cooks to retain the natural juices in turkeys, roasts, chickens, and all food that requires time to "firm up," such as custards, pies, and quiches. In roasts and poultry, juices are close to the surface after cooking. If sliced immediately, all the juice will run out. A standing time of 15 to 20 minutes gives the juices time to redistribute and the last slice can be as full of natural juice as the first. That's true with all cooking. If you are using the microwave method, standing time is even more essential. That's because there is more internal cooking activity in process with food cooked by the microwave method.

Piercing

Certain foods, such as egg yolks, potatoes, liver, chicken giblets, eggplant, and whole squash, have skins or membranes that retain moisture. These skins or membranes should be pierced so that the moisture can escape as steam. Use a toothpick to pierce egg yolks, a fork to pierce potatoes, and a knife to pierce or slit plastic pouches. Pierce sausage casings in several places. Pierce squash deeply 6 or 7 times with a long-tined meat fork.

Piercing (above right). Standing time completes cooking and redistributes juices (right). Place food on a flat, heatproof surface during standing time (above).

Browning

Many foods do not brown as much in microwave cooking as they do in conventional cooking. In convection cooking, however, browning is usually superior to conventional methods, since the constantly moving hot air promotes more even browning. That's why this oven was designed: to combine the two systems, creating a unique new environment for food to cook better than ever. But don't be fooled: some browning does occur with the microwave method alone. Usually, food does not crisp, although the high fat content in bacon enables it to crisp and brown in minutes. However, when browning or crispness is the goal, the micro/convection or convection method is the best choice.

You've probably heard of a "browning dish" and may have one if you are a second-generation microwave cook. Although it may be used in microwave cooking on the ceramic tray, according to the browning dish manufacturer's instructions, it's not a necessary item for this oven. All browning dish functions are accomplished with the convection cooking ability of the oven.

Adjusting for High Altitudes

As in conventional cooking, microwave cooking at high altitudes requires adjustments in cooking time for leavened products like breads and cakes. Other foods may require a slightly longer cooking time to become tender, since water boils at a lower temperature. Usually, for every 3 minutes of microwave cooking time you add 1 minute for the higher altitude. Therefore, a recipe calling for 3 minutes needs 4 minutes and a recipe requiring 6 minutes needs 8 minutes. The wisest procedure is to start with the time given in the recipe and then check for doneness. Adding time is easy, but overcooking can be a real problem. Here again your judgment is vital.

The wire rack is used primarily for convection and micro/convection cooking. It can be placed in three positions: upper, lower, and oven bottom. The desired distance of the food from the upper and lower heat sources determines which position is selected. For crisp bottom crusts on your pies, for example, the wire rack in the oven bottom position is often the best choice. For heat-seared burgers and steaks, the upper position is best. Poultry, roasts, and many other foods use the lower position. The wire rack is also used for cooking more than one dish at a time, as in whole-meal microwave cooking. Always remove the wire rack when not in use.

Getting to Know Your Oven

Your micro/convection oven gives you the ability to select from many power settings with the microwave method and from a range of temperatures with the convection method. These settings give you flexibility and control, just as in conventional cooking. Selection of the appropriate power settings and temperatures is automatic, as is the timing, for the 300 preset recipes. For your own recipes and for items identified in the *Cooking Guides* (see recipe chapters), you set the power and/or temperature. For the microwave method, in addition to HI, there are 99 settings. The control panel lists the main settings and gives them familiar cooking terms. You may find, however, that other settings work better for you. You may want to warm certain foods on 13 or 15, for example.

The oven automatically pairs microwave power with a convection temperature of 350°F for micro/convection cooking. The microwave power can't be altered with this method but you can change the oven temperature, if a higher or lower temperature is better for the food being cooked.

Oven temperature is adjustable in ten-degree increments from 200°F to 450°F. In convection cooking, you select the oven temperature, preheating when necessary, just as you do in conventional cooking. 350°F is set by the oven automatically. Temperatures other than 350°F must be set manually.

The Guide below will help you select the cooking method for most food. The most satisfactory results will be achieved when you use the cooking method listed as "Best." Equal and alternate methods are listed as "Good." If a method is not recommended, "No" is indicated.

Touch Pad

The touch pads on the oven control panel need only to be touched to be

GUIDE TO COOKING METHODS

FOOD	MICRO	MICRO/ CONVEC	CONVEC
Appetizers	Good	Good	Good
Bread, baking	No	Good	Best
rising	Best	No	No
Cakes, batter	Good	Good	Best
angel food	No	No	Best
Candies	Best	No	No
Casseroles	Good	Best	Good
Cookies, drop	No	Good	Best
bar	Good	Best	Good
Defrosting	Best	No	No
Eggs	Best	Good	Good
Fruit	Best	Good	Good
Hot drinks	Best	No	No

FOOD	MICRO	MICRO/ CONVEC	CONVEC
Meat, searing	No	Good	Best
roasting	Good	Best	Good
Pies, 1-crust	Good	Best	Good
2-crust	No	Best	Good
Poultry	Good	Best	Good
Quiches	Good	Best	Good
Reheating	Best	Good	Good
Sauces	Best	No	No
Seafood, poaching	Best	Good	No
broiling	No	Good	Best
Soufflés	No	No	Best
Soup	Best	Good	No
Vegetables	Best	Good	No

activated. A beep tone assures that the setting is being entered.

Temperature Probe

When inserted into the food, the temperature probe enables you to cook food to a preselected internal temperature. When the desired temperature is reached, the oven automatically holds food warm up to 1½ hours. Instead of setting the oven to a certain number of minutes, you set the probe at the exact temperature you want the food to reach prior to standing time to attain desired doneness. The oven must also be set at the power level and/or oven temperature at which the food is to be cooked. Probe temperature, power setting and oven temperature are automatically determined for the preset recipes that use the probe. The probe provides accuracy in cooking almost any food, from instant coffee and sauces to beef casseroles and roast chicken. You can even watch the display window as the food

Insert temperature probe into the meatiest part of poultry, avoiding fat and bone. Note placement of probe in breast of the duckling (top). The horizontal position is preferred in roasts (top right). No more guessing for meatloaf or hot drinks (middle right and right). In microwave cooking, plastic wrap covering is not pierced by the probe (above).

A beef tenderloin is cooked, using the temperature probe, by convection for heat-seared flavor. Be sure to remove the ceramic tray and place wire rack in upper position.

reaches the selected temperature.

The probe must be carefully and properly inserted in the food for the best results. The probe tip should be in the center of the dish, cup, or casserole or in the thickest portion of the meat. Do not allow the probe to touch bone, fat, or any metal foil being used as a shield. After using the probe, remove it from the oven. Use warm, soapy water to wash the part that contacted the food. Rinse and dry. Do not immerse the probe in water or wash it in a dishwasher.

The "Guide to the Temperature Probe" provides a range from 120°F to 180°F. Follow the directions in the recipes for placement of the probe and covering of the dish, if specified, and consult the "Tips for Probe Use" for step-by-step directions.

Standing time is essential for most food to reach its optimum serving temperature. Because of the nature of microwave energy, during standing time the temperature of most food rises about 5°F to 15°F. For example, after 10 minutes of standing time, the temperature of rare beef will reach 135°F; well done lamb will reach its proper serving temperature of 170°F to 180°F. The temperature of beverages, however, drops in 10 minutes from 150°F to 136°F.

Guide to the Temperature Probe*

Suggested Temperature Probe Settings

120°	Rare Beef, Fully Cooked Ham
130°	Medium Beef
140°	Fish Steaks and Fillets, Well Done Beef
150°	Vegetables, Hot Drinks, Soups, Casseroles
155°	Veal
165°	Well Done Lamb, Well Done Pork
170°	Poultry Parts
180°	Well Done Whole Poultry

**Refer to individual Cooking Guides (see Index) for specific instructions.*

Tips for Probe Use

1. Place food in container, as recipe directs.
2. Place temperature probe in the food with the first inch of probe secured in the center of the food. Probe should not touch bone or a fat pocket. Probe should be inserted from the side or the front, not from the top of the food, except when inserting into casseroles, a cup of soup, etc. Try to insert probe as close to a horizontal position as possible.
3. Place dish in oven on wire rack or ceramic tray, as the recipe directs. (Be sure to remove the ceramic tray if you plan to cook by the convection method.)
4. Plug probe into receptacle on side wall of oven cavity.

5. Make sure the end of the temperature probe, inserted in the food, does not touch the cooking container, or sides of oven.
6. Touch "Clear."
7. Touch "Oven Temp/Preheat." Or, touch "Micro Control" if cooking by the microwave method.
8. Touch "4-0-0" for 400°F (or the correct numbers for oven temperature desired). If the temperature is 350°F, this step is eliminated because that temperature is set automatically.

   If cooking by the microwave method, touch "8-0" for 80 or correct number for power setting desired. HI is automatically set unless changed.
9. Touch "Convec Temp," or "Micro/Temp" to select the cooking method.
10. Touch "1-2-0" for 120°F (or correct numbers for internal food temperature desired).
11. Touch "Start."
12. Steps 5 through 10 are not necessary for any of the 300 preset recipes that use the probe.
13. Never operate the oven with the temperature probe in the cavity unless the probe is plugged in and inserted into food.

Reheating

One of the major assets of the microwave oven is its efficiency in reheating cooked food. Not only does most food reheat quickly, but it also retains moisture and its just-cooked flavor when properly arranged and covered. Reheat food in serving dishes or on paper plates and save extra clean-up time. Follow these tips to help get excellent results:

- ☐ Use 80 except when otherwise specified. You can use the temperature probe for reheating casseroles, beverages, and other food. Set "Micro Temp" control at 150°F to 160°F.
- ☐ To arrange a combination of food on a plate, place dense food, like meat, at the edges and more porous food, like bread, toward the center.
- ☐ Dense food, such as mashed potatoes and casseroles, reheats better if a depression is made in the center, or if the food is shaped in a ring.
- ☐ To retain moisture during reheating, cover food with plastic wrap or a microproof lid.
- ☐ As a general guide to reheating a plate of food, start with 1½ to 2 minutes, then check for doneness. If the plate on which the food is cooked feels warm, the food is probably heated through. Its warmth has heated the plate.

Food Drying

Your micro/convection oven includes a special dehydration feature that enables you to dry apples, mushrooms, flowers, and other items expertly. Chapter 20, "Food Preservation for Today," provides instructions and suggestions. You may also want to consult your Use & Care Manual.

Let's Use the Oven

Now it's time for some practical experience using your Kenmore Auto Recipe 300 Micro/Convection Oven. First, a quick hot drink, then we will bake some Hot Dog Wrap-Ups without using the preset method to familiarize you with convection cooking. A micro/convection Baked Apple is next and, finally, you'll experience the special convenience of the automatic, preset recipes with a first course soup. Ready? Let's go!

Lesson One

Uses the microwave method because it's best to heat liquids.

Take your favorite mug or cup, making sure it has no gold or silver trim. (If you are not certain your mug is microproof, test it as directed on page 15.) Follow these step-by-step directions:

1. Fill mug with water and place on the ceramic tray, in the center of the oven. Close the oven door.

CLEAR

2. Touch the "Clear" pad to clear any previous programming.

MICRO TIME

2 0 0

3. Touch the "Micro Time" pad, then touch pads 2-0-0. Your oven is now programmed to cook (micro) on HI for 2 minutes. It was not necessary to touch "Micro Control" because your oven is automatically on HI when the microwave method is used unless programmed to another setting.

START

4. Now touch the "Start" pad.
5. The timer will beep when 2 minutes are up. The oven turns off automatically. Open the door.
6. Remove the mug. The handle will be cool enough to hold and the cup warm from the heated water.
7. Stir in instant coffee, tea, or soup . . . enjoy!

Lesson Two

Convection provides the hot, dry environment for Hot Dog Wrap-Ups.

1. Remove ceramic tray.

2. Place wire rack in lower position.

3. Touch "Clear" pad; touch "Oven Temp/Preheat" pad; touch 3-8-0. The oven is programmed to preheat to 380°F.

START

4. Touch "Start".

5. Prepare recipe for Hot Dog Wrap-Ups, arranging 8 on a cookie sheet and 8 on a plate. Cover plate well with plastic wrap and refrigerate for later use.

6. When beep tone begins, oven has reached 380°F. Place cookie sheet on wire rack and close the oven door.

7. Touch "Oven Temp/Preheat" pad; touch "Convec Time" pad; touch 1-5-0-0. Oven is programmed to cook by the convection method at 380°F for 15 minutes.

START

8. Touch "Start".

9. When the programmed time ends, the beep tone is heard and the oven turns off automatically.

Hot Dog Wrap-Ups is also one of your preset automatic recipes. See page 47 and go automatic the next time.

Lesson Three

A micro/convection treat, a Baked Apple. Microwaves cook the fruit and the hot air helps caramelize the topping.

1 large apple
3 tablespoons water
2 teaspoons brown sugar
1 teaspoon chopped walnuts
¼ teaspoon cinnamon

1. Remove stem from apple and cut small circle around top in criss-cross fashion. Carefully remove small portion of pulp. Place apple in microproof and heatproof small dish. Add water. Place sugar and walnuts in center of apple and sprinkle with cinnamon.

2. Touch "Clear" pad; touch "Micro/Convec Time" pad; touch 6-0-0. Touch "Start." Oven is programmed to cook by the micro/convection method at 350°F for 6 minutes. Because the 350°F oven temperature is automatic with micro/convection cooking unless a different temperature is entered, we did not have to program the oven temperature for this recipe.

3. When the 6 minutes are up, the beep tone is heard, and the oven shuts off automatically. Such a nice after-school treat.

Surprise! Don't your Hot Dog Wrap-Ups, Baked Apple, and Hot Tea with Lemon make a nice "just you" lunch?

Lesson Four

First Course Soup

Why not surprise the family with a first course of homemade soup as your first microwave recipe tonight? It's really easy, thanks to the convenience of the preset feature with your Kenmore Auto Recipe 300 oven. We've selected Cream of Corn Soup, Recipe No. 22 (page 56).

Cream of Corn Soup

1 can (17 ounces) cream-style corn
1 can (13¾ ounces) chicken broth
⅔ cup water
¼ cup thinly sliced zucchini
2 tablespoons water
1 tablespoon cornstarch
2 large eggs, lightly beaten
1 green onion, finely chopped

1. Combine corn, broth, ⅔ cup water, and zucchini in 2-quart microproof casserole or soup tureen. Cover with casserole lid and place in oven.

2. Touch "Clear" pad; touch "Recipe #" pad; then touch pads 2 and 2. Oven is ready to cook.

START

3. Touch "Start". (Oven will cook on HI for 13 minutes.)

PAUS

4. At the end of first cooking sequence, timer will beep and "Pause" will appear in display window. Combine 2 tablespoons water and cornstarch; stir until cornstarch is dissolved. Open door and add cornstarch to soup; blend well. Do not cover.

START

5. Close door. Touch "Start" pad. (Oven will cook on HI for 5 minutes.)
6. Pour eggs into hot soup in thin stream, stirring briskly. Garnish with green onion — voila! — serve to smiles all around.

On Your Own

There is so much more that you can do in this oven than ever before possible in a single-cavity unit. Because you have such flexibility, you may be concerned about proper selection of the cooking method to use — microwave, micro/convection, or convection — when you are cooking on your own. It's truly not difficult. When you are ready to convert one of your own favorite recipes to this oven, look through the cookbook for a similar one — you should get some ideas on how to proceed. Also, the beginning of each chapter has hints on recipe converting to help you along. Here are a few guidelines.

- ☐ Candies, always difficult to prepare by conventional cooking because of the need for double boilers, the mess of scorched pans, constant stirring, and other time-consuming techniques, are now easy to make. Ingredient adjustments are not needed and the microwave method is best.

- ☐ Chicken recipes will benefit from micro/convection cooking when converted. If the exterior must be very crisp, preheating the oven will enable micro/convection cooking to provide superior results over any other method.

- ☐ Prepare most casseroles and stews exactly as you would conventionally and use the micro/convection method. Cheese toppings for casseroles should usually be added just before the end of the cooking time.

- ☐ As a general rule, you can assume that most microwave recipes are cooked in about one-quarter to one-third of the conventional recipe time. Check for doneness after one-quarter of the time before continuing to cook.

Now let's try converting a conventional recipe to the micro/convection method. Suppose you have a favorite recipe for Chicken Cacciatore that you would like to prepare in this oven. The closest recipe in this book turns out to be Chicken Marengo, Recipe No. 129 on page 118. Let's see how to go about converting.

Chicken Cacciatore

Conventional Style
4 to 6 servings

¼ cup butter or margarine
1 medium onion, chopped
1 medium green pepper, thinly sliced
1 can (28 ounces) whole tomatoes
¼ cup all-purpose flour
1 bay leaf
1 tablespoon parsley flakes
½ teaspoon salt
1 clove garlic, minced
½ teaspoon oregano
1 teaspoon paprika
¼ teaspoon basil
1 cup dry red wine
1 frying chicken (about 3 pounds), cut up

Preheat oven to 350°F. Melt butter in medium skillet over medium heat. Add onion and green pepper and cook, stirring occasionally, until onion is transparent. Add tomatoes and flour and stir until smooth. Add all remaining ingredients, except chicken. Cover and cook until sauce is slightly thickened, about 5 minutes, stirring every minute. Arrange chicken in a baking dish and pour sauce over top. Cover and bake about 45 minutes or until chicken is tender.

Reviewing the Chicken Cacciatore recipe will help point out some of the differences between conventional cooking and this unit. Notice that the amount of butter needed in the traditional skillet is much greater than that needed when cooking by the microwave method. The skillet needs to be well lubricated so the food does not stick and burn from the direct heat essential in stove-top cooking. More wine is needed in the conventional version to prevent evaporation during the longer cooking time. Here's the converted recipe:

Chicken Cacciatore

Micro/convection Style
4 to 6 servings

1 medium onion, chopped
1 medium green pepper, thinly sliced
1 tablespoon butter or margarine
1 can (28 ounces) whole tomatoes
¼ cup all-purpose flour
1 bay leaf
1 clove garlic, minced
1 tablespoon parsley flakes
1 teaspoon paprika
½ teaspoon salt
½ teaspoon oregano
¼ teaspoon basil
½ cup dry red wine
1 frying chicken (about 3 pounds), cut up

Combine onion, green pepper, and butter in 3-quart microproof and heatproof casserole. Cover and cook (micro) on HI 4 to 5 minutes, or until onion is transparent. Add tomatoes and flour and stir until smooth. Blend in all remaining ingredients except chicken. Cover with casserole lid and cook (micro) on HI 5 minutes. Add chicken, covering pieces completely with sauce. Cover dish, set on ceramic tray and cook (micro/convec) at 350°F 25 to 30 minutes, or until chicken is tender.

Cooking Casseroles

Micro/convection cooking is particularly good for preparing casseroles. Vegetables keep their bright fresh color and crisp texture and meat is tender and flavorful. Generally economical, too, the casserole is growing in popularity for family meals and is perfectly in order for entertaining. Here are some hints:

☐ Most casseroles can be made ahead of time, refrigerated or frozen, then reheated later by the microwave method.

☐ Store leftover casserole portions in disposable single-serving containers for easy reheating and quick lunches when needed.

☐ Casseroles usually are cooked covered. Uncover to melt cheese topping or to provide top browning during the final minutes of cooking.

☐ Sauté any vegetables in the casserole dish first with microwave energy, then add other ingredients and change to micro/convection.

About Lower Calories

You can use less fat when cooking with the microwave or micro/convection methods. And, of course, cooking the convection way is the naturally low-calorie way to heat-seared steaks and chops. In general, you can reduce calories in many recipes by:

Using bouillon or water instead of butter when sautéing or softening vegetables.

Substituting fresh vegetables for pasta or other starchy food.

Removing the skin from chicken or turkey before cooking.

Using milk instead of cream or half-and-half for quiches.

Substituting skim milk for whole milk.

Substituting skim milk cheeses like low-fat cottage, ricotta, or mozzarella for creamy, high-butterfat cheeses.

Substituting herbs mixed with natural juices from food for cream or butter-based sauces.

Substituting fruit cooked in its natural juices for fruit cooked with added sugar.

Using Preset Recipes

The flexibility of this oven is truly amazing. There's just no end to what it can do for you and you can be creative in your approach to it. For example, there's no reason why you cannot use a preset recipe's functions for a totally new recipe of your own creation! That's why you'll find the oven's functions included in italics within each recipe. You can use that information to decide which preset recipe might cook your new dish best.

You can also combine preset recipes by setting two, or more, recipe numbers in sequence to cook your new recipe. In fact, some of the preset recipes employ that technique to extend the usefulness of your oven. *(See Recipe Number 4, Sausage Rolls, for an example of this technique.)*

Preheating

Convection and micro/convection cooking sometimes call for preheating the oven, just as you do a conventional oven. When the desired temperature is reached, a beep tone is heard intermittently to remind you that the oven is ready. The tone stops when the oven door is opened or when the "Stop" pad is touched. ("Pause" appears in the display window if you touch the "Stop" pad or open the door when one of the 300 preset recipes is being used.)

If you are planning to cook by the convection method, remove the ceramic tray prior to preheating. This is because, in convection cooking, both the top and bottom heat coils are in operation. However, only the top heat coil operates during preheating and during micro/convection cooking. By removing the ceramic tray prior to preheating, you avoid needing to handle the tray when it is hot.

By the Way . . .

To get the greatest pleasure out of your oven, keep in mind that certain food is best prepared by cooking methods that do not use the closed environment of the oven. We don't advise using the oven for:

☐ Eggs cooked in the shell, because the light membrane surrounding the yolk collects energy, which then causes a steam build-up that could explode the egg. Don't experiment. It's a mess to clean up!

☐ Deep-fat frying, because the confined environment of the oven is not suited to the handling of the food or oil and is not safe.

☐ Pancakes, because no crust forms. (But the oven is great for reheating pancakes, waffles, and similar items.)

☐ Home canning, because it is impossible to judge exact boiling temperatures inside jars and you cannot be sure that the temperature and length of cooking are sufficient to prevent contamination of the food.

☐ Heating bottles with small necks, like those for syrups and toppings, because they are apt to break from the pressure build-up.

☐ Large items, such as a 25-pound turkey, are also not recommended for preparation in this unit.

Finally, about popcorn:

Do not attempt to pop corn in a paper bag, since the corn may dehydrate and overheat, causing the paper bag to catch on fire. Due to the many variables, such as the age of the corn and its moisture content, popping corn in the microwave oven is not recommended. Microwave popping devices are available. While safe to use, they usually do not give results equal to those of conventional popping methods. If the microwave device is used, *carefully follow the instructions provided with the product.*

From Freezer To Table — Fast!

One of the most appreciated features of any microwave oven is its ability to defrost food in a fraction of the time required by conventional methods. With today's "everybody-on-the-go" lifestyles, it's not hard to see microwave defrosting as a nearly essential part of our lives. Your Kenmore Auto Recipe 300 oven makes microwave defrosting more convenient than ever through an automatic defrosting capability called Auto Defrost. With the Auto Defrost feature, you tell the oven the type and weight of the food you want to defrost. The oven does the rest, even pausing automatically for you to remove thawed portions or to turn and reposition an item to promote more uniform defrosting. What's more, if you wish, you can set the oven to start cooking automatically after the defrosting sequence has ended.

In addition to the Auto Defrost feature described in detail in this chapter, you may also choose to use manual or "attended" defrosting techniques. Guides for manual defrosting are in the meat, poultry, and seafood chapters. Manual defrosting techniques are helpful when you want to give more attention to the food, perhaps to speed the defrosting process by use of a cold water bath during the standing time, or when you want to use the oven immediately for other cooking or defrosting needs. (Standing time is

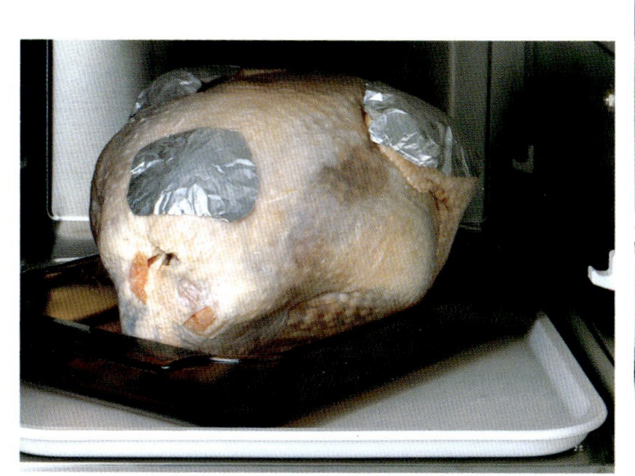

Large items, such as turkey, are turned over and shielded to promote even defrosting (above left). Thawed portions of ground beef (above) are removed from the oven so cooking does not start. Fish fillets (far left) are separated as soon as possible. Vegetables wrapped in microproof packages may be defrosted without unwrapping.

calculated as a part of the Auto Defrost sequences in the oven.)

Whatever method you choose, Auto Defrost or manual, many of the same principles and techniques that apply to microwave cooking also apply to microwave defrosting. Microwaves are attracted to water or moisture molecules. As soon as the microwaves have thawed a portion of an item, they tend to be more attracted to the increased moisture in the thawed portion. The frozen portion continues to thaw, due in part to the warmth produced in the thawed portion. Special techniques, such as shielding, turning, and rotating, are frequently helpful in preventing the thawed portion from starting to cook before the rest is defrosted. Because of the unknown differences in fat content, density, percentage of bone, etc. in food that the oven can't judge, the defrosting times provided by the Auto Defrost feature and in the manual defrosting method guides are conservative. Food should be "workable" though it may still be cold or even icy when removed from the oven. Additional standing time may be required to thoroughly defrost some foods. Here are some tips.

- ☐ Poultry, seafood, and meat should be removed from their original packages and placed on a microproof plate. Steam can develop within closed packages and cause cooking to begin before an item is defrosted.
- ☐ You may leave metal clips in poultry during defrosting but be sure to position the poultry item with the metal at least 1 inch from the oven wall. Remove any metal clips before cooking.
- ☐ Poultry wings, legs, breastbone, and the small or bony ends of meat may need to be shielded with small pieces of foil for part of the thawing time to prevent cooking.
- ☐ Food textures influence thawing time. Relatively porous foods like cake and bread defrost very quickly and must be checked frequently. As a result, the Auto Defrost method is not recommended.
- ☐ Remove portions of ground meat as soon as thawed (at "PAUS" in Auto Defrost sequence), returning solidly-frozen portions to the oven.
- ☐ Thin or sliced items, such as fish fillets, shrimp, meat patties, etc. should be separated as soon as possible (at "PAUS" in Auto Defrost sequences). Remove nearly-thawed pieces and allow others to continue thawing.
- ☐ Casseroles, saucy foods, vegetables, and soups usually require stirring two or three times during defrosting to redistribute heat. Manual defrosting methods are best. For broth-based soups: start at HI and reduce power to 50 halfway through defrosting time. Stir twice. For stirrable casseroles and thick or cream-based soups: start at 70 and reduce power to 30 halfway through defrosting time. Stir three times.

VOLUME	TIME
1 pint	10 - 15 min.
1 quart	25 - 35 min.
2 quarts	35 - 40 min.
3 quarts	40 - 45 min.
4 quarts	45 - 55 min.

- ☐ Large items should be turned and rotated approximately halfway through the defrosting time (at "PAUS" in Auto Defrost sequences) to provide more even thawing.
- ☐ Freezing ground meat in a doughnut shape will provide speedier and more even thawing later. When preparing patties, form them at least ½ inch thick.

Auto Defrost

To help you be thoroughly familiar with the convenient Auto Defrost method and its use, we have provided step-by-step instructions for you. Choose an item from your freezer that you would like to prepare today. You will soon see how microwave defrosting can transform defrosting from a time-consuming nuisance to a simple preparation step.

1. Unwrap food and place in a microproof dish or tray (to catch drippings). Set dish in the oven on the ceramic tray.
2. Touch CLEAR.
3. Touch DEF 1, DEF 2, or DEF 3 to select the appropriate defrosting sequence. The AUTO DEFROST indicator light will be illuminated on the display window and the sequence selected (dEF1, dEF2, or dEF3) will be displayed.
4. Enter the weight of your food in decimal increments from .1 pound to 9.9 pounds. Remember to convert ounces to tenths of a pound. For example, to defrost 2 pounds 8 ounces, touch number pads "2" and "5" for 2.5 pounds. The display window will show "2.5."
5. Touch START. The oven will begin the defrosting sequence you selected and the display window will show the time of the first segment as it "counts down." The oven will stop automatically at the end of the first time segment and "PAUS" will appear in the display window.
6. At the pause, follow the Guide instructions for separating, covering, turning over, and/or rotating.

NOTE: If the oven door is not opened during the pause time segment, the oven will restart automatically after 5 minutes. Because turning, rotating, and separating are usually necessary for proper defrosting, follow steps 1 through 7 for best results.

7. After performing Guide instructions, touch START. The oven resumes defrosting and the display window shows the time remaining.

   At the end of the required time, a tone will sound and "End" will appear in the display window for 2 seconds. The oven shuts off automatically.

NOTE: You can set your oven to begin cooking automatically following the AUTO DEFROST cycle. After entering AUTO DEFROST information as described above, touch MEMORY/RECALL. Then set the time, power levels, and paues as necessary for up to 4 cooking cycles.

AUTO DEFROST GUIDE — DEFROST 1

Meat up to 2 inches thick, Chicken, Cornish Hen

Food	Special Notes
Beef	Meat of irregular shape and large, fatty cuts of meat should have the narrow or fatty areas shielded at the beginning of a defrost sequence.
Ground Beef	Remove thawed portions with fork. Turn over. Return remainder to oven. We do not recommend defrosting less than 1/4 pound ground beef.
Round steak Flank steak Tenderloin steak Chuck Roast	Use a microproof roasting rack. Turn over. Cover warm areas with aluminum foil.
Stew beef	Remove thawed portions with fork. Separate remainder. Return remainder to oven.
Lamb Cubed for stew	Remove thawed portons with fork. Separate remainder. Return remainder to oven.
Ground lamb	Remove thawed portions with fork. Turn over. Return remainder to oven.
Chops (1-inch thick)	Use a microproof rack. Separate and rearrange.
Pork Chops (1/2-inch thick)	Use a microproof roasting rack. Separate and rearrange.
Spareribs Country-style ribs	Use a microproof roasting rack. Turn over. Cover warm areas with aluminum foil.
Sausage, bulk	Remove thawed portions with fork. Turn over. Return remainder to oven.
Sausage, links	Separate and rearrange.
Veal Chops (1/2-inch thick)	Use a microproof roasting rack. Separate and rearrange.
Variety Meat Liver, sliced	Separate pieces and rearrange.
Chicken Whole (4 pounds & under)	Place chicken breast-side up in microproof roasting rack. Turn over (end defrost breast-side down). Cover warm areas with aluminum foil. Remove giblets when chicken is only partially defrosted. Finish defrosting by immersing in cold water.
Cut up	Use a microproof roasting rack. Separate pieces and rearrange. Turn over. Cover warm areas with aluminum foil.
Cornish Hens Whole	Place hens breast-side up in microproof roasting rack. Turn over. Cover warm areas with aluminum foil.

Frozen foods come in an increasingly wide variety of microproof packages.

AUTO DEFROST GUIDE — DEFROST 2

Meat over 2 inches thick, Turkey

Food	Special Notes
Beef Pot roast, Chuck roast, Rib roast, rolled Rump roast	Use a microproof roasting rack. Turn over. Cover warm areas with aluminum foil
Lamb Leg	Use a microproof roasting rack. Turn over. Cover warm areas with aluminum foil.
Pork Roast	Use a microproof roasting rack. Turn over. Cover warm areas with aluminum foil.
Veal Roast	Use a microproof roasting rack. Turn over. Cover warm areas with aluminum foil.
Variety Meat Tongue, whole	Use a microproof roasting rack. Turn over. Cover warm areas with aluminum foil.
Turkey Whole	Place turkey breast side up in microproof roasting rack. Turn over (end defrost breast-side down.) Cover warm areas with aluminum foil.
Breast	Use a microproof roasting rack. Turn over. Cover warm areas with aluminum foil.
Drumsticks	Use a microproof roasting rack. Turn over. Separate pieces and rearrange.
Roast, boneless	Use a microproof roasting rack. Remove from foil pan. Cover with waxed paper.

AUTO DEFROST GUIDE — DEFROST 3

Fish and Seafood

Food	Special Notes
Fish Fish Fillets	Use a microproof roasting rack. Turn over. Separate fillets when partially thawed. Carefully separate fillets under cold water.
Fish steak	Use a microproof roasting rack. Separate and rearrange.
Whole fish	Use a microproof roasting rack. Cover head and tail with aluminum foil. Turn over.
Seafood Lobster tails	Use a baking dish. Turn over and rearrange.
Crabmeat	Use a baking dish. Break apart. Turn over.
Shrimp	Use a baking dish. Break up and stir to rearrange.

A Good Beginning

Appetizers can be the most creative food of today's entertaining. They can be hot or cold, simple or fancy, light or hearty depending upon the occasion. There are no rules, so you can let your imagination soar. Until now *hot* appetizers were the most troublesome and time-consuming for the host or hostess. But that's no longer true with the microwave oven. Parties are much easier and more enjoyable because the microwave eliminates all that last-minute hassle and lengthy cooking over a hot stove. You can assemble most appetizers and nibbles in advance, and at the right moment, just coolly "heat 'n serve!" This chapter presents many recipes for entertaining your guests, but you'll also be tempted to prepare delicious snacks and munchies just for the family. There's no doubt about it — appetizers cooked in the microwave oven are fun to make, fun to serve, and fun to eat.

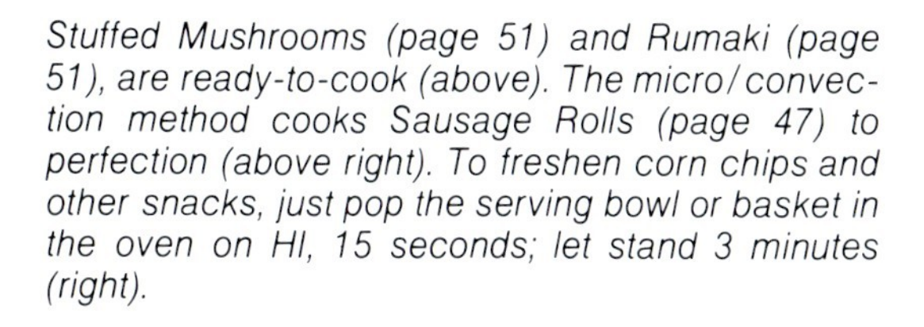

Stuffed Mushrooms (page 51) and Rumaki (page 51), are ready-to-cook (above). The micro/convection method cooks Sausage Rolls (page 47) to perfection (above right). To freshen corn chips and other snacks, just pop the serving bowl or basket in the oven on HI, 15 seconds; let stand 3 minutes (right).

Converting Your Own Recipes

For most appetizers, the cool convenience of the microwave method will probably be your first choice. You can use your prettiest platters (microproof) or paper plates for informal times. Use micro/convection for items that require a browned outside or top and will also profit from speedier cooking of the inside. The convection method is best for appetizers that are pastry-based and need a flaky crust. Appetizers generally don't need any ingredient changes to fit either of this oven's cooking methods. Do be sure to match the cooking dish to the method you plan to use. Find a similar recipe in this chapter or refer to pages 15 through 19 for a review of recommended cookware. Here are some helpful tips:

- ☐ For a crisper bottom crust on items cooked on the wire rack by the micro/convection method, line the bottom of a glass baking dish with aluminum foil. The technique is illustrated with Sausage Rolls in the photo on page 43.
- ☐ Because of its very delicate nature, a sour cream dip should be covered and heated with the temperature probe to 90°F on 50.
- ☐ Toppings for canapés can be made ahead, but to assure a crisp base, do not place on bread or crackers until just before heating.
- ☐ Cover appetizers or dips only when the recipe specifies doing so. Use fitted glass lids, waxed paper, plastic wrap, or paper toweling.
- ☐ You can heat two batches of the same or similar appetizers at one time with the microwave method by using both oven levels, the wire rack in the upper position and the bottom ceramic tray. Watch closely; those on top may cook more quickly than those on bottom.
- ☐ The temperature probe set at 130°F on 70 provides an excellent alternative for heating hot dips containing seafood, cheese, or food to be served in a chafing dish or fondue pot.

COOKING GUIDE — CONVENIENCE APPETIZERS*

Food	Programming Method	Programming Setting	First Cook Time	Second Cook Time	Probe Method	Special Notes
Dips, cream, ½ cup	micro	10	1½-2½ min.		130°	Cover with plastic wrap.
Eggrolls, 6 oz. (12)	convec		follow package directions			Remove ceramic tray. Upper position. Preheat.
Meat spread, 4 oz. can	micro	80	30-45 sec.			Use microproof bowl.
Sausages, 5 oz. can	micro	80	1½-2 min.			Use microproof casserole. Cover.
Tacos, mini, 5½ oz.	convec	400°	follow package directions			Remove ceramic tray. Upper position. Preheat. Use cookie sheet or foil tray.
Swiss fondue, 10 oz.	micro	80	5-6 min.		150°	Slit pouch. Set on microproof plate.

* Due to the tremendous variety in convenience food products available, times given here should be used only as guidelines. We suggest you cook food for the shortest recommended time and then check for doneness. Be sure to check the package for microwave and oven (convec) instructions.

Recipe No. 01

Sombrero Dip

Cooking Time: 24 minutes

- 1 pound lean ground beef
- 1 large onion, chopped
- ½ cup catsup
- 1 tablespoon chili powder
- 1 teaspoon garlic salt
- 1 teaspoon cumin
- 1 teaspoon oregano
- 3 drops hot pepper sauce
- 1 can (24 ounces) kidney beans, undrained
- ½ cup shredded Cheddar cheese
- Green pepper slices

Combine beef and onion in 2-quart microproof bowl. Cover with plastic wrap. Place in oven. Set recipe number 01. Touch START. *(Oven cooks: micro, HI, 5 minutes.)*

At Pause, stir through several times. Cover. Touch START. *(Oven cooks: micro, HI, 3 minutes.)*

At Pause, pour off any fat. Add catsup, chili powder, garlic salt, cumin, oregano, and hot pepper sauce and blend well. Purée beans in food processor or blender. Stir into beef. Cover. Place in oven. Touch START. *(Oven cooks: micro, HI, 8 minutes.)*

At Pause, stir. Cover. Touch START. *(Oven cooks: micro, HI, 8 minutes.)* Stir through several times. Turn into serving dish. Sprinkle with cheese and garnish with green pepper. Serve hot with crackers or chips.

about 5 cups

Recipe No. 02 ⊞

Fresh Vegetable Dip

Cooking Time: 5 minutes

- 1 package (10 ounces) frozen chopped spinach
- 1 cup dairy sour cream
- ½ cup chopped fresh parsley
- ½ cup chopped green onions
- ½ cup mayonnaise
- 1 teaspoon fines herbes seasoning
- ½ teaspoon dillweed

Set unopened spinach on microproof plate. Place in oven. Set recipe number 02. Touch START. *(Oven cooks: micro, HI, 5 minutes.)* Drain well; squeeze dry. Transfer to bowl. Add all remaining ingredients and blend thoroughly. Season with salt and pepper. Cover and refrigerate overnight. Serve with fresh vegetables, crackers, or chips.

about 3½ cups

Recipe No. 03

Miniature Hot Dog Treats

Cooking Time: 15 minutes

- 2 frankfurters
- 1 package (8 ounces) butterflake roll dough
- 1 egg yolk, beaten

Remove ceramic tray. Place wire rack in lower position. Set recipe number 03. Touch START. *(Oven preheats: convec, 380°F.)* Cut each frankfurter into 6 equal pieces. Separate dough into 12 equal pieces. Arrange dough on baking sheet. Push frankfurter slices firmly into center of each piece of dough. Brush with egg glaze.

At 380°F, place baking sheet in oven on wire rack. Touch START. *(Oven cooks: convec, 380°F, 15 minutes.)* Serve hot.

12 canapés

⊞ *Recipe can be increased. See "Quantity", page 12.*

Recipe No. 04

Sausage Rolls

Cooking Time: 17 minutes

1 medium onion, chopped
1 tablespoon vegetable oil
½ pound lean bulk sausage, crumbled
1 tablespoon tomato sauce or catsup
1 teaspoon fresh lemon juice
1 package (8 ounces) crescent roll dough
1 egg yolk, beaten

Combine onion and oil in 1-quart glass measure or microproof bowl. Place in oven. Set recipe number 13. Touch START. *(Oven cooks: micro, HI, 4 minutes.)*

At Pause, stir. Add sausage to bowl. Place in oven. Touch START. *(Oven cooks: micro, HI, 3 minutes.)* Drain off fat. Stir in tomato sauce and lemon juice. Set aside.

Place wire rack in upper position. Set recipe number 04. Touch START. *(Oven preheats: convec, 400°F.)* Meanwhile, line bottom of 9×13-inch glass baking dish with aluminum foil; grease foil. Cut pastry into 4 rectangles. Divide sausage mixture into fourths. Spread sausage mixture down center of dough. Brush edge of pastry with beaten egg. Fold pastry over, enclosing sausage completely. Brush with egg yolk. Cut each length into 1-inch pieces. Arrange in prepared dish.

At 400°F, place dish in oven on wire rack. Touch START. *(Oven cooks: micro/convec, 400°F, 10 minutes.)* Serve hot.

16 appetizers

This is one of several recipes that use the preset functions of another recipe for part of the cooking sequence. Set recipe number 13 first. At the end of that sequence, set recipe number 04.

← *Sombrero Dip (page 45), Sausage Rolls, Hot Dog Wrap-Ups*

Recipe No. 05

Crab Meat Puffs

Cooking Time: 10 minutes

2 egg whites
½ cup mayonnaise
1 can (6½ ounces) crabmeat, rinsed, drained, and flaked
½ teaspoon salt
¼ teaspoon paprika
¼ teaspoon dried tarragon
50 cheese or rye crackers

Remove ceramic tray. Place wire rack in upper position. Set recipe number 05. Touch START. *(Oven preheats: convec, 380°F.)* Meanwhile, beat egg whites until stiff. Fold in all remaining ingredients except crackers. Spread crab mixture over crackers. Arrange half of canapés on baking sheet.

At 380°F, place baking sheet in oven on wire rack. Touch START. *(Oven cooks: convec, 380°F, 5 minutes.)*

At Pause, remove from oven. Arrange remaining canapés on baking sheet. Place in oven. Touch START. *(Oven cooks: convec, 380°F, 5 minutes.)* Serve immediately.

about 50 appetizers

Recipe No. 06

Hot Dog Wrap-Ups

Cooking Time: 15 minutes

1 package (8 ounces) crescent roll dough
16 cocktail-size frankfurters
1 egg yolk, beaten

Remove ceramic tray. Place wire rack in upper position. Set recipe number 06. Touch START. *(Oven preheats: convec, 380°F.)* Meanwhile, divide dough into 8 wedges. Cut each wedge lengthwise through tip, making 16 equal triangles. Place frankfurter at widest part of dough and roll up, ending with point at top. Repeat with remaining dough and frankfurters. Brush with egg glaze. Transfer to baking sheet. At 380°F, place baking sheet in oven on wire rack. Touch START. *(Oven cooks: convec, 380°F, 15 minutes.)* Serve hot with mustard.

16 canapés

Recipe No. 07

Cheddar Cheese Canapés

Cooking Time: 30 seconds

- ½ cup (2 ounces) grated Cheddar cheese
- 2 tablespoons light cream
- 1 tablespoon grated Parmesan cheese
- 1 tablespoon sesame seed
- ⅛ teaspoon Worcestershire sauce
- ⅛ teaspoon hot pepper sauce
- 12 crisp crackers or toast rounds
- Chopped parsley

Combine Cheddar cheese, cream, Parmesan cheese, sesame seed, Worcestershire, and hot pepper sauce; blend until smooth. Spread about 1 teaspoon mixture on each cracker. Arrange canapés on microproof plate. Place in oven. Set recipe number 07. Touch START. *(Oven cooks: micro,* 70, 30 *seconds.)*

Garnish with parsley and serve warm.

12 canapés

Recipe No. 08

Crab Suprême

Cooking Time: 1½ minutes

- 1 can (6½ to 7 ounces) crab meat, drained
- ½ cup finely minced celery
- ½ cup mayonnaise
- 4 teaspoons sweet pickle relish
- 2 teaspoons prepared mustard
- 2 green onions, thinly sliced
- 24 crisp crackers or toast rounds

Place crab meat in bowl; pick over and remove cartilage. Flake with fork. Add celery, mayonnaise, relish, mustard, and onions; blend well. Spoon about 1 tablespoon mixture onto each cracker. Arrange 12 canapés on microproof plate. Place in oven. Cover with waxed paper. Set recipe number 08. Touch START. *(Oven cooks: micro,* 70, 45 *seconds.)*

At Pause, remove from oven. Arrange remaining 12 canapés on microproof plate. Place in oven. Cover. Touch START. *(Oven cooks: micro,* 70, 45 *seconds.)*

Serve warm.

24 canapés

Recipe No. 09

Curry Dipper

Cooking Time: 2 minutes

- 1 can (10¾ ounces) cream of mushroom soup, undiluted
- 1½ tablespoons curry powder
- 1 teaspoon lemon juice
- 1 clove garlic, minced

Combine all ingredients in 4-cup glass measure; blend well. Place in oven. Set recipe number 09. Touch START. *(Oven cooks: micro, HI, 2 minutes.)*

Serve hot with Tiny Meatballs (page 50), cubed sirloin, shrimp, or scallops.

1¼ cups

Shrimp (Guide, page 129) makes an especially attractive appetizer when combined with marinated artichokes and fresh dill. Tiny Meatballs (page 50), and Nachos (page 50) complete this party table that also includes a bowl of toasted pecans, freshened before serving by cooking, micro, HI, 45 seconds. →

Recipe No. 10

Tiny Meatballs

Cooking Time: 12 minutes

- 1 pound lean ground beef
- ½ pound ground pork
- 1 cup dry bread crumbs
- 1 cup milk
- 1 small onion, finely minced
- 1 large egg, lightly beaten
- 2 teaspoons soy sauce
- 1 teaspoon salt
- ¼ teaspoon pepper
- ¼ teaspoon allspice

Combine all ingredients; blend well. Shape into 1-inch balls. Arrange half of the meatballs in single layer on microwave roasting rack. Place in oven. Set recipe number 10. Touch START. *(Oven cooks: micro,* 90, 6 *minutes.)*

At Pause, remove meatballs from oven and place in chafing dish to keep warm. Arrange remaining meatballs on rack as above. Place in oven. Touch START. *(Oven cooks: micro,* 90, 6 *minutes.)*

Add to chafing dish. Use toothpicks to spear meatballs. Serve hot with Curry Dipper (page 48.)

60 meatballs

Meatballs can be prepared in advance and reheated on HI 2 *to* 3 *minutes.*

Recipe No. 11

Nachos

Cooking Time: 2 minutes

- 1 can (3⅛ ounces) jalapeno bean dip
- 1 bag (8 ounces) tortilla chips
- 1½ cups (6 ounces) grated Cheddar cheese
- 1 can (2¼ ounces) sliced jalapeno peppers

Spread bean dip lightly on chips. Top with cheese and peppers. Arrange 10 chips on microproof plate. Place in oven. Set recipe number 11. Touch START. *(Oven cooks: micro,* 70, 40 *seconds.)*

At Pause, remove from oven. Arrange 10 more chips on microproof plate. Place in oven. Touch START. *(Oven cooks: micro,* 70, 40 *seconds.)*

At Pause, repeat with remaining 10 chips. Touch START. *(Oven cooks: micro,* 70, 40 *seconds.)*

Serve warm.

30 canapés

Recipe No. 12

Cold Eggplant Appetizer

Cooking Time: 9 minutes

- 1 eggplant (1 pound)
- 1 small onion, minced
- ½ medium green pepper, seeded and minced
- 1 clove garlic, minced
- 1 teaspoon lemon juice
- ½ teaspoon salt
- ⅛ teaspoon pepper
- 1 cup plain yogurt

Wash eggplant and pierce skin in several places. Place on microwave roasting rack. Place in oven. Set recipe number 12. Touch START. *(Oven cooks: micro, HI,* 7 *minutes.)*

At Pause, remove from oven; set aside. Combine onion, green pepper, garlic, and lemon juice in small microproof bowl. Place in oven. Touch START. *(Oven cooks: micro, HI,* 2 *minutes.)*

Cut eggplant in half lengthwise. Scoop pulp into serving bowl. Add onion mixture, salt, and pepper; blend well. Stir in yogurt. Cover and chill thoroughly before serving. Serve with pumpernickel bread, party rye, or crackers.

2 cups

Cold Eggplant Appetizer is a wonderful low-calorie topping for cut-up raw vegetables.

Recipe No. 13

Rumaki

Cooking Time: 7 minutes
(repeat twice)

- ½ pound chicken livers, rinsed and drained
- ¼ cup soy sauce
- ¼ teaspoon garlic powder
- 12 thin slices bacon, cut into thirds
- 1 can (8 ounces) sliced water chestnuts, drained

Cut chicken livers into thirty-six 1-inch pieces; discard membranes; set aside. Combine soy sauce and garlic powder; blend well. Dip 1 piece liver in soy sauce mixture. Place on 1 piece bacon. Top with 1 slice water chestnut. Roll up and fasten with toothpick; repeat with remaining liver pieces. Place 12 rumaki in circle on microwave roasting rack. Place in oven. Cover with paper towel. Set recipe number 13. Touch START. *(Oven cooks: micro, HI, 4 minutes.)*

At Pause, turn over. Cover. Touch START. *(Oven cooks: micro, HI, 3 minutes.)*

Repeat procedure for remaining rumaki, cooking 12 at a time. Set recipe number for each batch.

36 appetizers

Recipe No. 14

Cheese Fondue

Cooking Time: 8 minutes

- 4 cups (16 ounces) shredded Swiss cheese
- ¼ cup all-purpose flour
- ¼ teaspoon salt
- ¼ teaspoon nutmeg
- Pinch pepper
- 2 cups dry white wine
- 2 tablespoons kirsch
- 1 loaf French bread, cut into cubes

Combine cheese, flour, salt, nutmeg, and pepper in 1½-quart microproof casserole and stir gently to coat cheese with flour. Blend in wine. Cover with casserole lid. Place in oven. Set recipe number 14. Touch START. *(Oven cooks: micro, 50, 2 minutes.)*

At Pause, stir. Cover. Touch START. *(Oven cooks: micro, 50, 2 minutes.)*

At Pause, stir. Cover. Touch START. *(Oven cooks: micro, 50, 2 minutes.)*

At Pause, stir. Cover. Touch START. *(Oven cooks: micro, 50, 2 minutes.)* Stir through several times to finish melting cheese. Mix in kirsch. Serve immediately with cubes of French bread for dipping. If fondue cools, cook (micro) on 50, 1 to 2 minutes.

6 to 8 servings

Recipe No. 15

Stuffed Mushrooms

Cooking Time: 4 minutes

- 24 medium mushrooms, stems removed
- 2 green onions, finely chopped
- ½ cup (2 ounces) shredded Cheddar cheese
- ⅓ cup dry bread crumbs
- ¼ cup butter or margarine, melted
- ½ teaspoon salt
- ½ teaspoon Italian seasoning
- ¼ teaspoon garlic powder
- ⅛ teaspoon pepper
- ½ teaspoon Worcestershire sauce

Chop mushroom stems finely; set caps aside. Combine chopped stems, onions, and cheese; blend well. Add bread crumbs, butter, seasonings, and Worcestershire; blend well. Spoon mixture into caps, mounding slightly in center. Arrange on 10-inch round microproof plate. Place in oven. Set recipe number 15. Touch START. *(Oven cooks: micro, HI, 4 minutes.)*

24 appetizers

The Lunch Counter

Soups, sandwiches, some surprises, and salads will make the family happy at lunchtime or anytime. And, for the cook, there's more preparation ease than ever before. Microwave, micro/convection, and convection methods all contribute special and soon-to-be-favorite recipes. You'll especially like soups! Try Country Vegetable Soup (page 57) with a splendid assortment of vegetables or our approach to the traditional favorite, Chicken in the Pot (page 56). Japanese Cauliflower Soup (page 57) will please fans of that vegetable and just might convert those who "wouldn't touch it." Perhaps the nicest contribution of the oven is its ability to reheat single portions of soup by the microwave method right in the serving cup, mug, or bowl.

Ahhh, sandwiches! Why stick with the same old thing when you can liven-up appetites so easily? Meal-in-One Sandwich (page 65) is enough for a small crowd while Bacon-Tomato-Cheese Grill (page 65) is just-for-you. Deep Dish Pizza (page 66), something like a big open-faced sandwich, also finds a home in this chapter along with other surprises. Try them all with a nice hot beverage!

If you are a fan of French onion soup with a baked cheese topping, the convection method is the easy answer. Place wire rack in the upper position and preheat to 450°F. Place soup bowls in oven as shown (above left) and cook, convec, at 450°F 5 minutes, or until cheese is melted and brown. The temperature probe can be used when heating 1 to 4 cups of soup. Arrange cups in a circle and insert probe in one cup. Cook, micro, 80 to 150°F (above right).

← *Japanese Cauliflower Soup (page 57), Tuna Turnovers (page 64)*

Converting Your Own Soup and Hot Beverage Recipes

Up to now, you've probably looked solely to the stove top in order to cook soup or heat a beverage. Well, soup adapts so well to this oven and hot beverage preparation is so easy that you might not look to the stove for them ever again! To convert soup, find a recipe in this book similar in density and volume to the conventional soup you want to try. Most soup is cooked by the microwave method but you will want to use micro/convection as well for navy bean, split pea, and others (Old World Lentil Soup, below, is a good guide for those). Here are some tips to remember.

- ☐ Be careful with milk-based liquids or quantities larger than 2 quarts. They can boil over quickly. Always select a large enough microproof or microproof *and* heatproof container. Fill individual cups no more than two-thirds full.
- ☐ Soup is cooked covered. Use microproof and heatproof lids or a plate for micro/convection; use those or plastic wrap for microwave.
- ☐ Cooking time varies with the volume of liquid and density of food in soup. Remember that the shorter cooking times mean less evaporation of liquid. You may want to reduce liquid just a bit when converting.

Recipe No. 16

Old World Lentil Soup

Cooking Time: 1 hour

- ¾ cup dried lentils, rinsed and drained
- 5 cups water
- ½ pound Polish sausage, cut into ½-inch slices
- 1 cup chopped onions
- ½ cup chopped celery
- 1 medium tomato, peeled, seeded, and chopped
- 1 clove garlic, minced
- ¼ teaspoon pepper
- ¼ teaspoon salt
- 1 bay leaf

Combine lentils and water in 3-quart microproof and heatproof casserole, and let soak 45 minutes. Add remaining ingredients and mix well. Cover. Place in oven on ceramic tray. Set recipe number 16. Touch START. *(Oven cooks: micro/convec, 320°F, 60 minutes.)* Discard bay leaf. Serve hot.

4 to 6 servings

Recipe No. 17

Chili Con Queso Soup

Cooking Time: 18 minutes

- 3 tablespoons butter or margarine
- 1 large onion, minced
- 1 can (28 ounces) peeled tomatoes, drained and cut into pieces, liquid reserved
- 1 can (4 ounces) diced green chilies
- 1 jar (2 ounces) pimientos, diced
- Salt and pepper to taste
- ½ pound Cheddar cheese, shredded
- ¼ pound Monterey Jack Cheese, shredded

Combine butter and onion in 2-quart microproof bowl or soup tureen. Cover with plastic wrap. Place in oven. Set recipe number 17. Touch START. *(Oven cooks: micro, HI, 4 minutes.)*

At Pause, stir through once. Touch START. *(Oven cooks: micro, HI, 3 minutes.)*

At Pause, add tomatoes and liquid, chilies, pimientos, salt, and pepper and blend well. Cover. Touch START. *(Oven cooks: micro, HI, 10 minutes.)*

At Pause, stir in cheeses. Touch START. *(Oven cooks: micro, HI, 1 minute.)* Serve hot.

4 to 6 servings

Recipe No. 18

Canadian Pea Soup

Cooking Time: 1 hour 10 minutes

- 5 cups water
- 1 package (6 ounces) split pea soup mix
- 1 potato, peeled and finely chopped
- 1 carrot, finely chopped
- 1 large onion, chopped
- 1½ cups chopped celery
- 2 parsley sprigs
- 1 clove garlic, minced
- 1 bay leaf
- 2 teaspoons chicken bouillon granules

Combine all ingredients in 3-quart microproof casserole or bowl and blend well. Cover with casserole lid. Place in oven. Set recipe number 18. Touch START. *(Oven cooks: micro, HI,* 10 *minutes.)*

At Pause, stir. Touch START. *(Oven cooks: micro, HI,* 10 *minutes.)*

At Pause, stir through several times. Cover. Touch START. *(Oven cooks: micro,* 50, 25 *minutes.)*

At Pause, stir through several times. Cover. Touch START. *(Oven cooks: micro,* 50, 25 *minutes.)* Let stand 15 minutes. Discard bay leaf. Add hot water to thin, if desired.

4 to 6 servings

Recipe No. 19

English Beef Rib Broth

Cooking Time: 1 hour 45 minutes

- 1 pound beef short ribs
- 1 package (6 ounces) dry vegetable soup mix with mushrooms
- 1 teaspoon salt
- 1 teaspoon basil, crumbled
- 3 small potatoes, peeled and diced
- 2 large carrots, peeled and diced
- 1 medium parsnip, peeled and diced
- 1 large celery stalk, diced, leaves reserved
- 1 bay leaf
- 7 cups boiling water

Rinse ribs well under hot running water and drain. Arrange in 5-quart glass or ceramic casserole. Add all remaining ingredients, setting celery leaves on top. Cover with casserole lid. Place in oven on ceramic tray. Set recipe number 19. Touch START. *(Oven cooks: micro, HI,* 30, *minutes.)*

At Pause, stir through several times. Cover. Touch START. *(Oven cooks: micro,* 50, 60 *minutes;* 20, 15 *minutes.)* Discard bay leaf. Reheat briefly before serving, if necessary.

6 servings

Recipe No. 20

Canned Soup

Approximate Cooking Time: 5 minutes

- 1 can (10¾ ounces) soup, undiluted

Pour soup into 1½- to 2-quart microproof casserole. Add milk or water as directed on can; blend well. Place in oven. Insert temperature probe. Set recipe number 20. Touch START. *(Oven cooks: micro,* 80, 1 *to* 2½ *minutes to* 120°*F.)*

At Pause, stir. Touch START. *(Oven cooks: micro,* 80, *to* 150°*F; holds warm:* 1.)

2 servings

Recipe No. 21

Chicken in the Pot

Cooking Time: 1 hour 15 minutes

Boiling water
1 chicken (4 pounds), cut up, giblets except liver and kidney reserved
5 to 6 cups hot water
4 large carrots, cut into chunks
3 medium stalks celery, cut into chunks, tops reserved
1 medium onion, cut into quarters
1 small parsnip, peeled and cut into chunks
1 tablespoon chicken bouillon granules
⅛ teaspoon pepper
Minced parsley

Pour boiling water over chicken to rinse; drain well. Arrange chicken and giblets in 4-quart microproof casserole. Add remaining ingredients except parsley; add more hot water to cover chicken if necessary. Cover with casserole lid and place in oven. Set recipe number 21. Touch START. *(Oven cooks: micro, HI,* 1 *hour; stands:* 0, 15 *minutes.)*

Discard celery tops. Divide parsley among individual soup bowls. Ladle soup over parsley.

4 to 6 servings

The boiling water rinse reduces fat and helps eliminate foam. If desired, soup can be strained after cooking and broth served separately. Arrange chicken and vegetables on serving platter, and sprinkle with parsley.

Recipe No. 22 ⊞

Cream of Corn Soup

Cooking Time: 18 minutes

1 can (17 ounces) cream-style corn
1 can (13¾ ounces) chicken broth
⅔ cup water
¼ cup thinly sliced zucchini
2 tablespoons water
1 tablespoon cornstarch
2 large eggs, lightly beaten
1 green onion, finely chopped

Combine corn, broth, ⅔ cup water, and zucchini in 2-quart microproof casserole or soup tureen. Cover with casserole lid and place in oven. Set recipe number 22. Touch START. *(Oven cooks: micro, HI,* 13 *minutes.)*

At Pause, combine 2 tablespoons water and cornstarch; stir until cornstarch is dissolved. Add to soup; blend well. Do not cover. Touch START. *(Oven cooks: micro, HI,* 5 *minutes.)*

Pour eggs into soup in thin stream, stirring briskly. Garnish with onion and serve immediately.

4 servings

⊞ *Recipe can be increased.* *See "Quantity", page 12.*

Recipe No. 23

Country Vegetable Soup

Cooking Time: 50 minutes

- 4 cups beef broth
- 2 medium potatoes, peeled and cut into ½-inch cubes
- 2 medium carrots, thinly sliced
- 2 small onions, chopped
- 1 can (12 ounces) whole-kernel corn, drained, or 1½ cups fresh corn
- 1 cup shredded cabbage
- 1 can (16 ounces) stewed tomatoes
- 1 teaspoon salt
- ½ teaspoon thyme
- ⅛ teaspoon pepper
- 1 bay leaf
- ⅓ cup chopped parsley

Combine all ingredients except parsley in 4-quart microproof casserole. Cover with casserole lid and place in oven. Set recipe number 23. Touch START. *(Oven cooks: micro, HI,* 20 *minutes.)*

At Pause, stir. Cover. Touch START. *(Oven cooks: micro,* 50, 25 *minutes; stands:* 0, 5 *minutes.)*

Discard bay leaf. Divide parsley among 6 individual soup bowls, and ladle soup over parsley. Serve with crackers or hard rolls.

6 servings

Recipe No. 24

Japanese Cauliflower Soup

Cooking Time: 28 minutes

- 3 tablespoons butter or margarine
- ¼ cup all-purpose flour
- ⅛ teaspoon ground nutmeg
- 4 cups chicken broth
- 1 head cauliflower (2½ pounds), broken into florets
- ¼ cup heavy cream or undiluted evaporated milk
- 1 egg yolk
- Minced parsley

Place butter in 3-quart microproof casserole or soup tureen. Place in oven. Set recipe number 24. Touch START. *(Oven cooks: micro, HI, 2 minutes.)*

At Pause, add flour and nutmeg; stir until smooth. Blend in broth. Cover with casserole lid. Touch START. *(Oven cooks: micro, HI, 7 minutes.)*

At Pause, add cauliflower; blend well. Cover. Touch START. *(Oven cooks: micro, HI,* 15 *minutes.)*

At Pause, remove soup from oven; let stand 10 minutes. Transfer soup in batches to blender or food processor container; cover and purée. Return to casserole. Cover and place in oven. Touch START. *(Oven cooks: micro, HI,* 4 *minutes.)*

Combine cream and egg yolk; blend well. Add small amount warm soup to egg yolk mixture; blend well; gradually blend into soup. Sprinkle with parsley and serve immediately.

4 servings

You can make a lower-calorie soup by substituting whole or undiluted evaporated skim milk for the heavy cream.

If desired, 4 cups water and 4 teaspoons chicken bouillon granules can be substituted for the chicken broth.

Recipe No. 25

Hearty Cheese and Frank Soup

Cooking Time: 23 minutes

- ½ cup sliced celery
- 1 medium carrot, thinly sliced
- ¼ cup chopped onion
- ¼ cup butter or margarine
- 2 tablespoons all-purpose flour
- 2 cans (13¾ ounces each) chicken broth
- ½ pound frankfurters, sliced
- 2 cups (8 ounces) shredded Cheddar cheese
- 1½ cups milk or half-and-half

Combine celery, carrot, onion, and butter in 3-quart microproof casserole or soup tureen. Cover with casserole lid and place in oven. Set recipe number 25. Touch START. *(Oven cooks: micro, HI,* 4 *minutes.)*

At Pause, stir. Cover. Touch START. *(Oven cooks: micro, HI,* 4 *minutes.)*

At Pause, add flour; stir until smooth. Stir in broth and frankfurters. Cover. Touch START. *(Oven cooks: micro, HI,* 10 *minutes.)*

At Pause, add cheese; stir until melted. Stir in milk. Cover. Touch START. *(Oven cooks: micro,* 50, 5 *minutes.)*

6 servings

Recipe No. 26

Instant Soups, Soup Mixes

Approximate Cooking Time: 2 minutes

- 1 envelope (1¼ ounces) instant soup mix
- ⅔ cup water

Combine soup mix and water in 8-ounce microproof mug or cup; blend well. Place in oven. Insert temperature probe. Cover with waxed paper. Set recipe number 26. Touch START. *(Oven cooks: micro, HI, to* 150°F; *holds warm:* 1.)

1 serving

Recipe No. 27

Quick Green Pea Soup

Cooking Time: 11 minutes

- 1 can (2 ounces) mushroom stems and pieces
- 1 tablespoon butter or margarine
- 2 cans (11½ ounces each) green pea soup, undiluted
- 1 cup grated carrots
- ½ teaspoon salt

Drain mushroom liquid into 2-cup measure. Add water to equal 2 cups liquid; set aside. Place butter in 2-quart microproof casserole or soup tureen. Place in oven. Set recipe number 27. Touch START. *(Oven cooks: micro,* 60, 1 *minute.)*

At Pause, add mushrooms, soup, and mushroom-water mixture; stir with fork until blended. Add carrots and salt; blend well. Cover with waxed paper. Touch START. *(Oven cooks: micro,* 80, 10 *minutes.)*

Serve hot with croutons or crackers.

4 to 6 servings

Recipe No. 28

New England Clam Chowder

Cooking Time: 19 minutes

- 1/4 cup butter, melted
- 1/4 cup all-purpose flour
- 2 cans (7 1/2 ounces each) minced clams
- 2 slices bacon, diced
- 2 medium potatoes, peeled and cut into 1/2-inch cubes
- 1 medium onion, chopped
- 3 cups milk
- 1/2 teaspoon salt
- 1/8 teaspoon white pepper

Combine butter and flour; blend well; set aside. Drain clam liquid into 2-cup measure; add water to equal 2 cups liquid; set aside. Place bacon in 3-quart microproof casserole or soup tureen. Place in oven. Set recipe number 28. Touch START. *(Oven cooks: micro, HI, 3 minutes.)*

At Pause, add potatoes and onion. Cover with casserole lid. Touch START. *(Oven cooks: micro, 90, 10 minutes.)*

At Pause, add flour mixture; blend well. Stir in clam-water mixture, clams, milk, salt, and pepper. Cover. Touch START. *(Oven cooks: micro, HI, 1 minute.)*

At Pause, stir. Cover. Touch START. *(Oven cooks: micro, HI, 5 minutes.)*

4 to 6 servings

⊞ *Recipe can be increased. See "Quantity", page 12.*

Recipe No. 29 ⊞

Cream of Mushroom Soup

Cooking Time: 7 minutes

- 3 cups chopped mushrooms
- 2 1/2 cups chicken broth
- 1/2 teaspoon onion powder
- 1/4 teaspoon salt
- 1/8 teaspoon garlic powder
- 1/8 teaspoon white pepper
- 1 cup heavy cream

Combine mushrooms, broth, and seasonings in 2-quart microproof casserole or soup tureen. Place in oven. Set recipe number 29. Touch START. *(Oven cooks: micro, HI, 5 minutes.)*

At Pause, blend in cream. Touch START. *(Oven cooks: micro, 60, 2 minutes.)*

6 servings

Recipe No. 30

Tomato Soup Piquante

Cooking Time: 20 minutes

- 1/2 cup finely chopped celery
- 1 tablespoon butter or margarine
- 1 quart tomato juice
- 1 can (10 1/2 ounces) beef consommé, undiluted
- 1 tablespoon dry sherry
- 1 teaspoon sugar
- 1/2 teaspoon thyme
- 1/2 teaspoon celery salt
- 1/8 teaspoon hot pepper sauce
- 4 to 6 slices lemon

Combine celery and butter in 2-quart microproof casserole or soup tureen. Place in oven. Set recipe number 30. Touch START. *(Oven cooks: micro, HI, 5 minutes.)*

At Pause, add remaining ingredients except lemon. Cover with casserole lid. Touch START. *(Oven cooks: micro, 80, 12 minutes; stands: 0, 3 minutes.)*

Garnish with lemon slices before serving.

4 to 6 servings

Recipe No. 31

Cappuccino

Cooking Time: 3½ minutes

- 2 cups milk
- ¼ cup semisweet chocolate pieces
- 2 teaspoons sugar
- 2 teaspoons instant coffee powder
- ½ cup brandy
- Whipped cream

Combine milk, chocolate, sugar, and coffee in 4-cup glass measure. Place in oven. Set recipe number 31. Touch START. *(Oven cooks: micro, HI, 2 minutes.)*

At Pause, stir. Touch START. *(Oven cooks: micro, HI, 1½ minutes.)*

Stir until sugar is dissolved. Divide among 4 mugs. Stir 2 tablespoons brandy into each mug. Top each with dollop of whipped cream before serving. Sprinkle with cinnamon or nutmeg, if desired.

4 servings

Recipe No. 32 ⊞

Irish Coffee

Cooking Time: 2 minutes

- 3 tablespoons Irish whiskey
- 1 tablespoon instant coffee powder
- 2 teaspoons sugar
- Whipped cream

Pour whiskey into 8-ounce microproof mug or cup. Add coffee and sugar. Add water to fill three-fourths full; blend well. Place in oven. Set recipe number 32. Touch START. *(Oven cooks: micro, HI, 2 minutes.)*

Stir until sugar is dissolved. Top with dollop of whipped cream. Do not stir. Coffee should be sipped through the layer of cream.

1 serving

Recipe No. 33 ⊞

Spicy Apple Drink

Cooking Time: 10 minutes

- 1 quart apple cider
- ¼ cup firmly-packed brown sugar
- 2 sticks cinnamon
- 8 whole cloves
- ½ medium lemon, thinly sliced
- Pinch mace
- Pinch nutmeg
- 1 medium orange, thinly sliced

Combine cider, brown sugar, cinnamon, cloves, lemon, mace, and nutmeg in 2-quart glass measure; stir until brown sugar is dissolved. Place in oven. Set recipe number 33. Touch START. *(Oven cooks: micro, HI, 10 minutes.)*

Strain into 4 mugs. Garnish with orange slices before serving.

4 servings

Recipe No. 34 ⊞

Hot Buttered Rum

Cooking Time: 1½ minutes

- ¼ cup rum
- 2 teaspoons brown sugar
- 1½ teaspoons unsalted butter
- Dash nutmeg
- 1 stick cinnamon

Combine rum and brown sugar in tall microproof mug or cup. Add water to fill two-thirds full. Place in oven. Set recipe number 34. Touch START. *(Oven cooks: micro, HI, 1½ minutes.)*

Add butter and stir until melted. Sprinkle with nutmeg. Insert cinnamon stick as stirrer.

1 serving

⊞ *Recipe can be increased. See "Quantity", page 12.*

Recipe No. 35 ⊞

Hot Cranberry Punch

Cooking Time: 11 minutes

3 cups cranberry juice
1 cup apple juice
½ cup orange juice
3 tablespoons lemon juice
3 tablespoons sugar
Whole cloves
1 stick cinnamon
1 orange, sliced

Combine juices, sugar, 4 cloves, and cinnamon in 2-quart microproof casserole. Cover with casserole lid and place in oven. Set recipe number 35. Touch START. *(Oven cooks: micro, HI, 11 minutes.)*

Stir until sugar is dissolved. Strain into warmed punch bowl. Stick cloves into orange slices and float slices on punch as garnish.

8 servings

Recipe No. 36

Hot Devilish Daiquiri

Cooking Time: 6½ minutes

½ cup light rum
1½ cups hot water
1 can (6 ounces) frozen lemonade concentrate
1 can (6 ounces) frozen limeade concentrate
¼ cup sugar
2 sticks cinnamon
8 whole cloves

Pour rum into 1-cup glass measure; set aside. Combine remaining ingredients in 2-quart microproof casserole; blend well. Place in oven. Set recipe number 36. Touch START. *(Oven cooks: micro, HI, 6 minutes.)*

At Pause, remove from oven; set aside. Place rum in oven. Touch START. *(Oven cooks: micro, HI, 30 seconds.)*

Remove rum from oven. Ignite and pour flaming rum over hot juice mixture. Ladle into punch cups and serve. Garnish with lemon slice and whole clove, if desired.

8 to 10 servings

Recipe No. 37 ⊞

Russian Tea Mix

Cooking Time: 2 minutes

1 jar (9 ounces) powdered orange breakfast drink
1 package (3 ounces) lemonade mix
1½ cups instant unsweetened tea
⅓ cup sugar
1 teaspoon cinnamon
1 teaspoon ground cloves
¾ teaspoon ginger
¼ teaspoon nutmeg
1 cup water or cider

Combine all ingredients. Store in covered jar or container until ready to use. To make 1 serving, place 1 to 2 teaspoons mix in 8-ounce microproof mug or cup. Add water or cider; blend well. Place in oven. Set recipe number 37. Touch START. *(Oven cooks: micro, HI, 2 minutes.)* Stir before serving.

64 servings (about 3 cups mix)

For a lower-calorie drink, omit the sugar. If you'd like to serve your guests the regular drink but fix a low-calorie one for yourself, place 1 cup water, 1½ teaspoons instant unsweetened tea, ½ teaspoon grated orange peel, and 1 whole clove in microproof mug. Cook on HI 1½ minutes. If desired, artificial sweetener equal to 2 teaspoons sugar, or to taste, can be added after mixture is heated. Stir with cinnamon stick.

⊞ *Recipe can be increased. See "Quantity", page 12.*

Recipe No. 38 ⊞

Tomato Warmer

Cooking Time: 6 minutes

2½ cups tomato juice
1 can (10½ ounces) beef broth
¼ cup lemon juice
1 teaspoon prepared horseradish
1 teaspoon parsley flakes
½ teaspoon celery salt
¼ cup dry sherry (optional)

Combine all ingredients except sherry in 4-cup glass measure. Place in oven. Set recipe number 38. Touch START. *(Oven cooks: micro, HI, 6 minutes.)*

Pour into 6 mugs. Stir 2 teaspoons sherry into each mug before serving.

6 servings

Recipe No. 39 ⊞

West Coast Cocoa

Cooking Time: 7 minutes

⅓ cup unsweetened cocoa powder
¼ cup sugar
3 cups milk
2 teaspoons grated orange peel
¼ teaspoon almond extract
4 sticks cinnamon

Combine cocoa and sugar in 4-cup glass measure. Add ½ cup milk; blend to make smooth paste. Stir in remaining 2½ cups milk, orange peel, and almond extract; stir until sugar is dissolved. Place in oven. Set recipe number 39. Touch START. *(Oven cooks: micro, 70, 7 minutes.)*

Pour into 4 mugs. Insert cinnamon sticks as stirrers.

4 servings

← *West Coast Cocoa, Cappuccino (page 60), Hot Devilish Daiquiri (page 61)*

Recipe No. 40

Hot Milk

Approximate Cooking Time: 3 minutes

1 cup (8 ounces) milk

Pour milk into microproof mug or cup. Place in oven. Insert temperature probe. Set recipe number 40. Touch START. *(Oven cooks: micro, 70, to 140°F; holds warm: 1.)*

1 serving

This is an ideal way to heat milk for hot chocolate or any milk-based beverage.

Recipe No. 41

Wassail Punch

Cooking Time: 6 minutes

2 cups apple cider
2 cups cranberry juice
1 cup dry red wine
½ cup orange juice
½ cup lime juice
10 red hot candies
2 sticks cinnamon
4 whole cloves

Mix all ingredients in 2-quart glass measure. Place in oven. Set recipe number 41. Touch START. *(Oven cooks: micro, 80, 6 minutes.)*

10 to 12 servings (1½ quarts)

Recipe No. 42 ⊞

Hot Water for Instant Beverages

Cooking Time: 1½ minutes

1 cup (8 ounces) water

Pour water into microproof mug or cup. Place in oven. Set recipe number 42. Touch START. *(Oven cooks: micro, HI, 1½ minutes.)*

1 serving

⊞ *Recipe can be increased.* *See "Quantity", page 12.*

Converting Your Own Sandwich Recipes

With the renewed interest in bread baking, as well as the whole grain and wonderful French and Italian breads available commercially, the enormous variety of sandwich combinations you can create will tickle your imagination. They are easy to heat in your oven and will leave you well nourished. Unless you want a very crisp bread texture or a grilled effect, you will enjoy doing most sandwiches by the microwave method. Use micro/convection and be sure to preheat the oven if you want a crunch in the bread. It is also helpful to place the sandwich directly on the wire rack whenever you can. Use the convection method with the wire rack in the upper position for all kinds of grilled sandwiches. You can warm meat sandwiches, filled only with several thin slices of meat per sandwich. Cook, micro, on HI as follows:

1 sandwich: 45 to 50 seconds
2 sandwiches: 1 to 1½ minutes
4 sandwiches: 2 to 2½ minutes

- ☐ The best breads to use for warmed sandwiches are day-old, full-bodied breads such as rye and whole wheat, and breads rich in eggs and shortening.
- ☐ When using the microwave method, heat sandwiches on paper napkins, paper towels, or paper plates to absorb the steam and prevent sogginess. Wrap with a paper towel to prevent splattering. Remove wrapping immediately after warming.
- ☐ Several thin slices of meat heat more quickly and taste better than one thick slice. The slower-cooking thick slice often causes bread to overcook before meat is hot.
- ☐ Moist fillings, such as that in a Sloppy Joe or a barbecued beef sandwich, should generally be heated separately from the rolls, to prevent sogginess.
- ☐ For frozen pizza, remove ceramic tray, place wire rack in lower position, and preheat to 350°F. Cook, convec, at 350°F 15 to 17 minutes or until brown and crisp.

Recipe No. 43

Tuna Turnovers

Cooking Time: 20 minutes

2 hard-cooked eggs
1 can (6½ ounces) tuna, drained
¼ cup chopped celery
¼ cup thinly sliced green onion
½ cup mayonnaise
Salt and pepper to taste
1 package (8 ounces) crescent roll dough
1 cup shredded Cheddar cheese
1 egg, beaten

Remove ceramic tray. Place wire rack in lower position. Set recipe number 43. Touch START. *(Oven preheats: convec, 350°F.)* Mash eggs coarsely in mixing bowl. Add tuna, celery, onion, mayonnaise, salt, and pepper and blend well. Unroll dough and separate into 4 rectangles, smoothing perforated lines together. Sprinkle ¼ cup cheese over half of each rectangle. Divide tuna mixture evenly over cheese. Fold dough over tuna mixture, crimping edges to seal. Transfer to heatproof baking pan. Brush turnovers with beaten egg.

At 350°F, place dish in oven. *(Oven cooks: convec, 350°F, 20 minutes.)*

4 servings

If additional browning is desired, cook, convec, at 350°F, 1 to 3 minutes.

Recipe No. 44

Meal-in-One Sandwich

Cooking Time: 4 minutes

1 loaf (1 pound) French bread
1 to 2 tablespoons mustard
2 to 4 tablespoons mayonnaise
2 jars (6 ounces each) marinated artichoke hearts, drained, liquid reserved
1 small onion, thinly sliced into rings
1 large tomato, thinly sliced
1 pound sliced meat
½ pound sliced Monterey Jack or mozzarella cheese

Place wire rack in lower position. Set recipe number 44. Touch START. *(Oven preheats: convec, 450°F.)* Slice bread in half lengthwise. Spread one half with mustard and the other half with mayonnaise. Break up artichoke hearts and arrange on both halves. Overlap onion rings on bottom half; top with tomato slices. Alternate half of meat on both sides of bread. Spoon some of the artichoke liquid over meat. Top with half of cheese. Add another layer of meat and cheese to both halves.

At 450°F, place halves in oven directly on wire rack. Touch START. *(Oven cooks: micro/convec, 450°F, 4 minutes.)* Remove from oven and close into sandwich. Slice and serve.

6 to 8 servings

Salami, corned beef, ham, turkey, roast beef, or bologna. Choose your favorite or combine them all for this king-size sandwich.

Recipe No. 45

Bacon-Tomato-Cheese Grill

Cooking Time: 8 minutes

1 tablespoon butter or margarine
2 slices bread
2 slices Cheddar cheese
2 slices bacon, cooked
1 slice tomato, ½-inch thick

Remove ceramic tray. Place wire rack in upper position. Set recipe number 45. Touch START. *(Oven preheats: convec, 450°F.)* Butter both slices of bread on one side only. Place 1 slice of bread, buttered side down, on baking sheet or aluminum foil tray. Top with 1 slice cheese, then bacon, tomato, and remaining cheese. Top with remaining bread, buttered side up.

At 450°F, place in oven. Touch START. *(Oven cooks: convec, 450°F, 4 minutes.)*

At Pause, turn sandwich over. Touch START. *(Oven cooks: convec, 450°F, 4 minutes.)* Serve immediately.

1 serving

Recipe No. 46

Hamburgers (medium)

Cooking Time: 15 minutes

1 pound lean ground beef
2 tablespoons minced onion
1 large clove garlic, minced
¼ teaspoon salt
⅛ teaspoon pepper

Remove ceramic tray. Place wire rack in upper position. Set recipe number 46. Touch START. *(Oven preheats: convec, 450°F.)* Combine all ingredients in medium bowl and mix lightly. Shape into 4 patties. Place on aluminum broiling pan or on sizzle platter.

At 450°F, place in oven. Touch START. *(Oven cooks: convec, 450°F, 10 minutes.)*

At Pause, turn hamburgers over. Touch START. *(Oven cooks: convec, 450°F, 5 minutes.)* Serve immediately.

4 servings

Recipe No. 47

Deep Dish Pizza

Cooking Time: 35½ minutes

- 1 loaf (1 pound) frozen white bread dough, thawed
- 1 can (8 ounces) tomato sauce
- 1 large clove garlic, minced
- ½ teaspoon sugar
- ½ teaspoon oregano
- ¼ teaspoon salt
- ⅛ teaspoon pepper
- ¾ cup shredded Monterey Jack cheese
- ¾ cup shredded mozzarella cheese
- ¼ cup grated Parmesan cheese

Roll dough out into 12-inch circle. Transfer to 10- to 12-inch deep-dish pizza pan. Cover with towel. Let stand in warm draft-free area. Combine tomato sauce, garlic, sugar, oregano, salt, and pepper in 1-quart glass measure. Cover with plastic wrap. Place in oven. Set recipe number 31. Touch START. *(Oven cooks: micro, HI, 2 minutes.)*

At Pause, stir. Touch START. *(Oven cooks: micro, HI, 1½ minutes.)*

Set sauce aside. Remove ceramic tray. Place wire rack in lower position. Set recipe number 47. Touch START. *(Oven preheats: convec, 350°F.)*

At 350°F, set crust on wire rack. Touch START. *(Oven cooks: convec, 350°F, 20 minutes.)*

At Pause, cover with sauce, spreading evenly. Top with cheeses and your choice of other toppings. Place in oven. Touch START. *(Oven cooks: convec, 350°F, 12 minutes.)* Cut into wedges and serve immediately.

6 to 8 servings

This is one of several recipes that use the preset functions of another recipe for part of the cooking sequence. Set recipe number 31 first. At the end of that sequence, set recipe number 47.

Recipe No. 48

Pita Pizza

Cooking Time: 7½ minutes

- 6 pita (pocket) breads
- 3 cups Italian-style tomato sauce
- 1 cup shredded Cheddar cheese
- Minced parsley

Split pitas in half, as for English muffins. Set 4 halves, split side up, on large microproof plate. Spoon ¼ cup sauce over each half and sprinkle with cheese. Repeat with remaining halves on separate microproof plates. Place in oven. Set recipe number 48. Touch START. *(Oven cooks: micro, HI, 2½ minutes.)*

At Pause, place second plate in oven. Touch START. *(Oven cooks: micro, HI, 2½ minutes.)*

At Pause, place third plate in oven. Touch START. *(Oven cooks: micro, HI, 2½ minutes.)* Sprinkle with parsley before serving.

12 servings

Reben Sandwich (page 69) →

Recipe No. 49

Beef Tacos

Cooking Time: 7 minutes

1 pound lean ground beef
1 small onion, chopped
1 envelope (1¼ ounces) taco seasoning mix
10 taco shells
1½ cups (6 ounces) shredded Cheddar cheese, divided
2 cups shredded lettuce
2 medium tomatoes, chopped
1 avocado, peeled and diced
Dairy sour cream (optional)
Hot pepper sauce (optional)

Crumble beef into 2-quart microproof casserole. Add onion. Place in oven. Set recipe number 49. Touch START. *(Oven cooks: micro, HI, 2 minutes.)*

At Pause, stir to break up beef. Touch START. *(Oven cooks: micro, HI, 3 minutes.)*

At Pause, remove from oven. Stir beef; drain. Stir in seasoning mix. Stand taco shells in large, shallow, microproof baking dish. Divide beef mixture among shells. Top each with about 1 tablespoon cheese. Place in oven. Touch START. *(Oven cooks: micro, HI, 2 minutes.)*

Remove tacos from oven. Top each with lettuce, tomatoes, remaining cheese, and avocado. Pass sour cream and hot pepper sauce separately.

10 tacos

Diced radishes, cucumber, or green onions also make delicious toppings.

Recipe No. 50

Italian Meatball Sandwich

Cooking Time: 9 minutes

1 pound lean ground beef
1 cup cooked rice
1 small onion, finely chopped
2 large eggs, lightly beaten
1 tablespoon Italian seasoning
1 jar (15 ounces) spaghetti sauce
1 loaf (1 pound) French or Italian bread, cut in half lengthwise
Grated Parmesan cheese

Combine beef, rice, onion, eggs, and seasoning; blend well. Shape into 8 balls. Arrange meatballs in circle on microwave roasting rack. Place in oven. Set recipe number 50. Touch START. *(Oven cooks: micro, HI, 3 minutes.)*

At Pause, turn over. Touch START. *(Oven cooks: micro, HI, 2 minutes.)*

At Pause, remove meatballs from oven. Place in microproof casserole. Top with sauce. Cover and place in oven. Touch START. *(Oven cooks: micro, HI, 4 minutes.)*

Spoon meatballs and sauce onto bottom half of loaf. Sprinkle generously with cheese. Cover with top of loaf, slice in half, and serve hot.

2 sandwiches

Recipe No. 51 ⊞

Coney Island Hot Dog

Cooking Time: 1¼ minutes

1 jumbo (3-ounce) hot dog
1 hot dog bun, split
Prepared mustard
2 tablespoons drained sauerkraut
Pickle relish, chili, grated cheese, chopped onion (optional)

Score opposite sides of hot dog in several places. Place on microproof plate. Place in oven. Set recipe number 51. Touch START. *(Oven cooks: micro, HI, 1 minute.)*

At Pause, remove from oven. Place hot dog in bun. Place in oven. Touch START. *(Oven cooks: micro, HI, 15 seconds.)*

Top with mustard, sauerkraut, and selected garnish.

1 serving

Recipe No. 52

Reuben Sandwich

Cooking Time: 6 minutes

4 slices rye or pumpernickel bread
Butter or margarine
6 ounces corned beef, thinly sliced
½ cup drained sauerkraut
2 heaping tablespoons Thousand Island dressing
2 slices Swiss cheese

Remove ceramic tray. Place wire rack in lower position. Set recipe number 52. Touch START. *(Oven preheats: convec, 450°F.)* Lightly butter one side of each slice of bread. Place 2 slices bread, buttered side down, on baking sheet or aluminum foil tray. Layer remaining ingredients evenly over tops. Cover with remaining slices of bread, buttered side up.

At 450°F, place in oven. Touch START. *(Oven cooks: convec, 450°F, 3 minutes.)*

At Pause, turn sandwiches over. Touch START. *(Oven cooks: convec, 450°F, 3 minutes.)* Serve immediately.

2 servings

Recipe No. 53

Hot Tuna Buns

Cooking Time: 2 minutes

1 can (6½ to 7 ounces) tuna, drained and flaked
1 cup chopped celery
¼ cup mayonnaise
2 tablespoons catsup
1 teaspoon lemon juice
Salt and pepper to taste
4 hamburger buns, split

Combine tuna, celery, mayonnaise, catsup, and lemon juice. Season with salt and pepper. Spoon mixture onto bottom halves of buns; cover with tops of buns. Place 2 sandwiches on microwave roasting rack. Place in oven. Set recipe number 53. Touch START. *(Oven cooks: micro, 80, 1 minute.)*

At Pause, remove sandwiches from oven. Place remaining 2 sandwiches on rack in oven. Touch START. *(Oven cooks: micro, 80, 1 minute.)*

4 sandwiches

Recipe No. 54

Hot Ham and Swiss

Approximate Cooking Time: 3 minutes

2 slices rye bread
Butter or margarine
Mayonnaise
2 thin slices boiled ham
1 slice Swiss cheese

Spread bread with butter and mayonnaise. Place ham and cheese between bread slices. Place on microwave roasting rack. Place in oven. Insert temperature probe at least 1 inch into center of sandwich. Set recipe number 54. Touch START. *(Oven cooks: micro, HI, to 110°F; stands: 0, 2 minutes.)*

1 sandwich

⊞ *Recipe can be increased. See "Quantity", page 12.*

Recipe No. 55

Bacon Cheesewiches

Cooking Time: 4 minutes

- ½ cup (2 ounces) grated Cheddar cheese
- 1 tablespoon mayonnaise
- 2 teaspoons catsup
- 1 large egg, hard-cooked and chopped
- 2 slices bacon
- 2 hamburger buns, split

Combine cheese, mayonnaise, catsup, and egg; blend well; set aside. Place bacon on paper towel-lined microproof plate. Place in oven. Cover with paper towel. Set recipe number 55. Touch START. *(Oven cooks: micro, HI, 2½ minutes.)*

At Pause, remove from oven. Break each slice in half; set aside. Spread half of the cheese mixture on bottom half of each bun. Place on microwave roasting rack. Place in oven. Touch START. *(Oven cooks: micro,* 50, 1 *minute.)*

At Pause, place 2 halves bacon on each sandwich. Cover with tops of buns. Touch START. *(Oven cooks: micro,* 50, 30 *seconds.)*

2 sandwiches

Recipe No. 56

Barbecued Beef-on-a-Bun

Cooking Time: 19 minutes

- 1 pound top round steak
- ¼ cup butter or margarine
- 1½ tablespoons cornstarch
- ¼ cup beef broth
- ¼ cup lemon juice
- ½ cup chili sauce
- 1 tablespoon brown sugar
- 1 tablespoon instant minced onion
- 1 tablespoon Worcestershire sauce
- 1 teaspoon prepared horseradish
- ½ teaspoon salt
- ¼ teaspoon paprika
- ¼ teaspoon hot pepper sauce
- 1 small clove garlic, minced
- 6 heated buns

Cut steak across grain into very thin strips; set aside. Place butter in 2½-quart microproof casserole. Place in oven. Set recipe number 56. Touch START. *(Oven cooks: micro, HI,* 1 *minute .)*

At Pause, add steak; stir to coat. Cover with casserole lid. Touch START. *(Oven cooks: micro,* 50, 5 *minutes.)*

At Pause, stir. Cover with casserole lid. Touch START. *(Oven cooks: micro,* 50, 3 *minutes.)*

At Pause, combine broth and lemon juice. Add cornstarch and stir until dissolved. Pour over steak. Add remaining ingredients except buns; blend well. Cover. Touch START. *(Oven cooks: micro,* 50, 10 *minutes.)*

Let stand 2 minutes before serving on buns.

6 sandwiches

It's hard to imagine a sandwich that is not improved by warming the buns first. Cook 6 buns on 20 for 2 to 3 minutes; 4 buns take 1 to 1½ minutes.

Recipe No. 57

Sausage and Pepper Heroes

Cooking Time: 6½ minutes

- 4 Italian sausages
- ½ cup barbecue sauce
- 1 medium green pepper, seeded and cut into strips
- 4 hero rolls

Score sausages on opposite sides in several places. Place on microwave roasting rack. Place in oven. Cover with paper towel. Set recipe number 57. Touch START. *(Oven cooks: micro, HI, 3 minutes.)*

At Pause, remove from oven; set aside. Combine barbecue sauce and green pepper in 2-cup glass measure. Place in oven. Touch START. *(Oven cooks: micro, HI,* 2 *minutes.)*

At Pause, remove from oven. Split rolls in half without cutting all the way through. Place 1 sausage in each roll. Top each with sauce. Wipe rack clean with paper towel. Arrange rolls on rack. Place in oven. Touch START. *(Oven cooks: micro,* 50, 1½ *minutes.)*

4 sandwiches

The Baker's Secret

Press your face against the "window" of this scrumptious array of breads, sweet rolls, muffins, and coffee cakes. Imagine the aroma of yesterday that they can bring to your kitchen! The baker's secret? Convection ovens were first employed by commercial bread bakers to circulate the heated air and provide even browning. How natural it is, then, that the convection method performs at its best with baked goods in your new oven. If you are new to baking, so much the better — you're lucky to begin now with the advantage of commercial baking technology. You will find, of course, that the microwave and micro/convection methods make their own contributions to your success, too.

There are many breads and rolls here, including a fancy Braided Bread (page 73), the basic Homemade White Bread (page 76), and Cinnamon Loaf (page 74). Shortcut baking is also provided with rising and baking instructions for Bread-from-the-Freezer (page 73). Next comes an array of muffins and quick-breads to delight even the fussiest family. Buttermilk fans have their choice of Buttermilk Bran Muffins (page 73) or Buttermilk Corn Bread (page 74). If you want smiles all-around the table, why not wake the gang up to a piping-hot Sour Cream Coffeecake (page 80). Go ahead! Your oven knows the way.

One of the aids to fine baking that the microwave method provides is a shortcut approach to the dough-rising process. Nearly-fill a 1-cup glass measure with water and place in the oven. Cook, micro, HI, 3 minutes. Place loaf pan in oven with glass measure as illustrated (above left). Cook, micro 10, 5 minutes. Turn dough over and continue to cook, micro, 10, for another 5 minutes. The procedure is preset for you in the Bread-from-the-Freezer recipe (page 73). Don't forget your conventional cooking knowledge! Test as usual for doneness (above).

Converting Your Recipes

The convection method is the starting point for conversion of your own bread, coffeecake or muffin recipes. Remember that except for the increased efficiency of the fan-circulated hot air, this method is identical to your conventional oven.

There are, however, several times when the micro/convection method is appropriate, Oatmeal Muffins (page 79) is an example. The microwaves assist the cooking process. But the best clue, again, will be a recipe here that is similar to the one you want to try. Tips:

- ☐ Frozen bread dough is remarkably versatile. Don't hesitate to substitute it for homemade dough, and vice versa.
- ☐ When baking with the microwave or micro/convection method, fill cake pans and muffin pans only one-half full to allow for the increased rising those methods produce.
- ☐ Heat bread slices on paper napkins or paper towels to absorb excess moisture. Cook, micro, 80, 10 seconds for 1 to 3 slices.

GUIDE TO CONVENIENCE BREADS*

Food	Programming		First Cook Time	Second Cook Time	Special Notes
	Method	Setting			
Buttermilk biscuits, refrigerated, 8 oz.	convec	follow package directions			Remove ceramic tray. Preheat. Oven bottom position. Cookie sheet or foil tray.
Caramel rolls, refrigerated, 11 oz.	convec	follow package directions			Remove ceramic tray. Preheat. Oven bottom position. Cookie sheet or foil tray.
Cinnamon rolls, refrigerated, 9½ oz.	convec	follow package directions			Remove ceramic tray. Preheat. Oven bottom position. Cookie sheet or foil tray.
Cornbread mix, 15 oz.	convec	follow package directions			Remove ceramic tray. Preheat. Lower position. 8-inch square baking dish.
English muffins, waffles, frozen, (2)	micro	HI	30 - 45 sec.		Place on paper towels.
Hamburger buns, hot dog rolls, frozen, 1 lb.	micro	30	1 - 2 min.	1 - 2 min.	Place on paper plate or towels. On microproof rack.
Muffin mix	micro or convec	follow package directions			Remove ceramic tray for convec. Lower position. Preheat.
Refrigerated crescent, butter-flake, other rolls, 8 oz.	convec	380°	10 - 13 min.		Remove ceramic tray. Preheat. Oven bottom position. Cookie sheet or foil tray.
Sweet rolls, muffins, (4)	micro	80	35 - 45 seconds		Place on paper plate or towels. Add 15 seconds if frozen.

* Due to the tremendous variety in convenience food products available, times given here should be used only as guidelines. We suggest you cook food for the shortest recommended time and then check for doneness. Be sure to check the package for microwave and oven (convec) instructions.

Recipe No. 58

Braided Bread

Cooking Time: 35 minutes

Dough for Homemade White Bread (page 76)
1 egg yolk, beaten
Poppy seeds, sesame seeds, or uncooked oatmeal flakes

Prepare dough and let rise as directed. Generously grease baking dish. Set aside. Divide dough into thirds. Stretch each into cylinder about 9 inches long. Attach strips at one end and braid. Transfer to prepared baking dish. Cover with towel. Let stand in warm, draft-free area until doubled.

Remove ceramic tray. Place wire rack in bottom position. Set recipe number 58. Touch START. *(Oven preheats: convec, 350°F.)* Brush top of loaf with egg yolk and sprinkle with topping.

At 350°F, place in oven on wire rack. Touch START. *(Oven cooks: convec, 350°F, 35 minutes.)* Turn loaf out onto wire rack and let cool before slicing.

1 loaf

Recipe No. 59

Bread-from-the Freezer

Cooking Time: 48 minutes

1 loaf (1 pound) frozen bread dough
1 cup water
1 egg, beaten
Poppy seeds, sesame seeds, uncooked oatmeal flakes dehydrated onion flakes (optional)

Place frozen dough in 8×5-inch microproof loaf pan or in microproof dish. Nearly fill 1-cup glass measure with water. Place in oven. Set recipe number 59. Touch START. *(Oven cooks: micro HI, 3 minutes.)*

At Pause, place loaf pan in oven (leave water in oven). Touch START. *(Oven cooks: micro, 10, 5 minutes.)*

At Pause, turn dough over in pan. Touch START. *(Oven cooks: micro, 10, 5 minutes.)*

Let dough stand in pan until at least doubled, 45 to 60 minutes. Dough may now be worked, if desired, and shaped into rolls or fitted into pizza pan. To bake loaf: generously grease 8×5-inch metal loaf pan. Turn dough into pan. Cover with towel. Let stand in warm, draft-free area until at least doubled.

Remove ceramic tray. Place wire rack in oven bottom position. Set recipe number 62. Touch START. *(Oven preheats: convec, 350°F.)* Brush top of loaf with egg. Sprinkle with topping, if desired.

At 350°F, place in oven. Touch START. *(Oven cooks: convec, 350°F, 35 minutes.)* Turn loaf out onto wire rack and let cool before slicing.

1 loaf

Recipe No. 60

Buttermilk Bran Muffins

Cooking Time: 8 minutes

2 cups whole wheat flour
1½ cups whole unprocessed bran or bran bud cereal
2 tablespoons sugar
1½ teaspoons baking soda
¼ teaspoon salt
2 cups buttermilk
½ cup molasses
1 egg, beaten
3 tablespoons butter or margarine, melted
1 cup chopped nuts

Place wire rack in lower position. Set recipe number 60. Touch START. *(Oven preheats: convec, 370°F.)* Meanwhile, prepare microproof and heatproof muffin pan with paper liners. Mix flour, cereal, sugar, baking soda, and salt in medium bowl. Blend buttermilk, molasses, egg, and butter in large bowl. Add dry ingredients and mix thoroughly. Fold in nuts. Fill liners three-quarters full.

At 370°F, place in oven. Touch START. *(Oven cooks: micro/convec, 370°F, 4 minutes.)*

At Pause, remove from oven. Prepare second batch with remaining batter. Place pan in oven. Touch START. *(Oven cooks: micro/convec, 370°F, 4 minutes.)*

16 to 20 muffins

Recipe No. 61

Buttermilk Corn Bread

Cooking Time: 35 minutes

- 1½ cups cornmeal
- 1½ cups all-purpose flour
- ½ cup sugar
- 1 tablespoon baking powder
- ⅛ teaspoon salt
- 1 cup buttermilk
- 2 eggs, lightly beaten
- ½ cup vegetable oil
- 1 can (7 ounces) corn kernels with green peppers and pimiento, drained

Remove ceramic tray. Place wire rack in lower position. Set recipe number 61. Touch START. *(Oven preheats: convec, 350°F.)* Lightly grease a 9-inch square metal baking pan. Set aside. Stir together cornmeal, flour, sugar, baking powder, and salt. Mix buttermilk, eggs, and oil in separate bowl until well blended. Gradually add dry ingredients, stirring just until moistened. Stir in corn. Pour into prepared pan.

At 350°F, place in oven. Touch START. *(Oven cooks: convec, 350°F, 35 minutes.)* Remove from oven and cool in pan 5 minutes. Cut into 3-inch squares, and serve warm or at room temperature.

9 squares

Recipe No. 62

Cinnamon Loaf

Cooking Time: 35 minutes

- Dough for Homemade White Bread (page 76)
- ¼ cup butter or margarine, melted, divided
- ½ cup firmly-packed light brown sugar
- ¼ cup cinnamon

Prepare dough as directed. Grease 8×5-inch metal loaf pan; set aside. Roll dough out into 8×12-inch rectangle. Brush with all but 2 teaspoons melted butter. Sprinkle brown sugar and cinnamon evenly over top. Carefully roll up into cylinder; shape into loaf. Transfer to prepared pan. Cover with towel and let stand in warm, draft-free area until doubled.

Remove ceramic tray. Place wire rack in oven bottom position. Set recipe number 62. Touch START. *(Oven preheats: convec, 350°F.)* Brush top of loaf with remaining melted butter.

At 350°F, place in oven. Touch START. *(Oven cooks: convec, 350°F, 35 minutes.)* Transfer to wire rack. Serve warm.

1 loaf

Recipe No. 63

Garlic Bread

Cooking Time: 6 minutes

- 1 loaf (1 pound) French or sourdough bread
- ½ cup mayonnaise
- ¼ cup grated Parmesan cheese
- 3 cloves garlic, minced or 1 teaspoon garlic powder
- Paprika

Remove ceramic tray. Place wire rack in lower position. Set recipe number 63. Touch START. *(Oven preheats: convec, 450°F.)* Set foil or aluminum pan underneath rack to catch drippings. Slice bread in half lengthwise. Set halves, cut side up, on work surface. Combine mayonnaise, cheese, and garlic in small bowl and blend well. Spread mixture generously over each half of loaf. Sprinkle lightly with paprika.

At 450°F, place bread in oven directly on wire rack. Touch START. *(Oven cooks: convec, 450°F, 6 minutes.)* Serve immediately.

8 servings

Yes, that's right, this delicious garlic bread uses mayonnaise! The more traditional way is to substitute ¼ cup butter or margarine for the mayonnaise.

Onion Board (page 76), Quick Crescent Rolls (page 78), Buttermilk Corn Bread →

Recipe No. 64

Homemade White Bread

Cooking Time: 35 minutes
(repeat once)

- 4 to 5 cups all-purpose flour, divided
- 2 tablespoons sugar
- 1 package active dry yeast
- 1 teaspoon salt
- 3/4 cup water
- 3/4 cup milk
- 2 tablespoons butter or margarine
- 1 egg, at room temperature

Combine 2 cups flour, sugar, yeast, and salt in large mixing bowl; set aside. Place water, milk, and butter in 1-quart glass measure. Place in oven. Set recipe number 167. Touch START. *(Oven cooks: micro, HI, 2 minutes.)* Add to dry ingredients and beat with electric mixer on low speed 30 seconds. Add egg and beat on high 3 minutes.

Stir in enough of remaining flour to make a soft dough. Turn out onto lightly floured board and knead 7 minutes or until smooth and elastic. Cover dough and let rest 20 minutes.

Grease four 3¼×5½×2¼-inch pans. Divide dough into 4 pieces, shape into small loaves, and place in pans. Cover with greased waxed paper. Let rise in warm, draft-free area 30 to 45 minutes, or until doubled in bulk.

Remove ceramic tray. Place wire rack in oven bottom position. Set recipe number 64. Touch START. *(Oven preheats: convec, 350°F.)*

At Pause, place 2 loaves in oven. Touch START. *(Oven cooks: convec, 35 minutes.)* Repeat with remaining loaves.

4 loaves

You may make two 9×5-inch loaves with this recipe. Bake one loaf at a time, increasing cooking time to 40 minutes per loaf.

Recipe No. 65

Onion Board

Cooking Time: 40 minutes

- 3/4 cup dehydrated onion flakes
- 3/4 cup water
- 1 loaf (1 pound) frozen white bread dough
- 1 egg yolk, lightly beaten
- 1 teaspoon poppy seeds (optional)

Combine onions and water in small bowl. Set aside. Thaw dough and let rise according to directions for Bread-from-the-Freezer (page 73). Roll dough into 12-inch circle. Transfer to aluminum deep-dish pizza pan. Cover with towel and let stand in warm, draft-free area 1 hour.

Remove ceramic tray. Place wire rack in oven bottom position. Set recipe number 65. Touch START. *(Oven preheats: convec, 370°F.)* Meanwhile, drain onions well. Spread evenly over dough, leaving 1-inch border around edge. Brush border and any other exposed dough with egg yolk. Sprinkle with poppy seeds.

At 370°F, place pan in oven on wire rack. Touch START. *(Oven cooks: convec, 370°F, 30 minutes; stands: 0, 10 minutes.)* Cut into wedges and serve. For additional crisping, let stand on rack in cool area several hours.

6 to 8 servings

For real New York bakery Onion Board, spread onion mixture over dough before letting dough rise. Let rise just slightly; flatten, then bake as directed above.

---

*Chocolate Soufflé (page 190), →
Braided Bread (page 73),
Homemade White Bread*

Recipe No. 66

Onion-Cheese Loaf

Cooking Time: 35 minutes

Dough for Homemade White Bread (page 76)
½ cup dehydrated onion flakes, divided
½ cup warm water
1 cup (4 ounces) shredded Cheddar cheese
2 tablespoons poppy seeds, divided
1 tablespoon butter or margarine, melted

Prepare dough as directed. Generously grease 8×5-inch metal loaf pan. Combine onions and warm water in 1-cup measure. Let stand 5 minutes to soften; drain well. Set aside 1½ tablespoons onion. Transfer remainder to small bowl. Add cheese and 1 tablespoon poppy seeds and mix well. Roll dough into 6×12-inch rectangle. Sprinkle with cheese mixture. Roll up into cylinder. Shape into loaf and seal edges. Transfer to prepared metal loaf pan. Cover with towel. Let stand in warm, draft-free area until doubled.

Remove ceramic tray. Place wire rack in oven bottom position. Set recipe number 66. Touch START. *(Oven preheats: convec, 350°F.)* Brush top of loaf with melted butter. Sprinkle with remaining onion and poppy seeds.

At 350°F, place in oven. Touch START. *(Oven cooks: convec, 350°F, 35 minutes.)* Turn out onto rack and let cool before slicing.

1 loaf

Recipe No. 67

Pumpkin Nut Ring

Cooking Time: 16 minutes

1 cup canned pumpkin
1 cup sugar
½ cup buttermilk
⅓ cup vegetable oil
2 eggs, well beaten
1⅔ cups all-purpose flour
1 cup chopped walnuts
2 teaspoons pumpkin pie spice
1 teaspoon baking soda
½ teaspoon salt

Set recipe number 67. Touch START. *(Oven preheats: convec, 350°F.)* Generously grease 6-cup microproof and heatproof ring mold. Combine pumpkin, sugar, buttermilk, oil, and eggs in large bowl and mix thoroughly. Blend flour, nuts, spice, baking soda, and salt in another bowl. Add to pumpkin mixture and blend well. Pour into prepared mold.

At 350°F, place in oven on ceramic tray. Touch START. *(Oven cooks: micro/convec, 350°F, 8 minutes.)*

At Pause, rotate dish one-half turn. Touch START. *(Oven cooks: micro/convec, 350°F, 8 minutes.)* Let cool slightly before removing from mold.

8 to 10 servings

Recipe No. 68

Quick Crescent Rolls

Cooking Time: 15 minutes

1 loaf (1 pound) frozen bread dough
1 egg yolk

Thaw dough and let rise as directed for Bread-from-the-Freezer (page 73). Roll dough into 8×12-inch rectangle. Cut into 6 equal pieces. Cut each piece into 2 triangles. Beginning with wide end, roll each triangle, ending with point on top. Transfer to baking sheet. Cover with towel. Let stand in warm, draft-free area until doubled. Gently brush tops with egg yolk.

Remove ceramic tray. Place wire rack in lower position. Set recipe number 68. Touch START. *(Oven preheats: convec, 350°F.)*

At 350°F, place rolls in oven. Touch START. *(Oven cooks: convec, 350°F, 15 minutes.)* Serve warm.

12 rolls

For cloverleaf rolls: Divide dough into 36 pieces and form each piece into ball. Place 3 in each cup of muffin pan. Cover with towel. Let stand in warm, draft-free area until doubled. Gently brush tops with egg yolk. Sprinkle with poppy seeds, if desired. Set recipe number 68 and continue as above.

For cinnamon rolls: Roll dough into 8×12-*inch rectangle. Brush with 2 tablespoons melted butter. Combine 2 teaspoons cinnamon, ½ cup sugar, and ¼ cup raisins. Sprinkle over dough, reserving 2 tablespoons. Beginning with long side, roll dough up tightly jelly-roll fashion. Cut into 12 slices. Place in lightly buttered 9-inch pie plate. Brush with 1 tablespoon melted butter and sprinkle with remaining cinnamon mixture. Cover with towel. Let stand in warm, draft-free area until doubled. Set recipe number 68 and continue as above.*

Recipe No. 69

Quick Date Nut Bread

Cooking Time: 55 minutes

- 2½ cups all-purpose flour
- 1 cup firmly-packed brown sugar
- 1 tablespoon baking powder
- 1 teaspoon cinnamon, divided
- ½ teaspoon salt
- 1¼ cups milk
- 3 tablespoons butter or margarine, melted
- 1 egg, beaten
- ¾ cup chopped dates
- ¾ cup chopped walnuts
- 2 teaspoons granulated sugar

Remove ceramic tray. Place wire rack in oven bottom position. Set recipe number 69. Touch START. *(Oven preheats: convec, 350°F.)* Grease a 9×5-inch metal loaf pan. Set aside.

Stir together flour, brown sugar, baking powder, ½ teaspoon cinnamon, and salt in 2-quart bowl until well mixed. Add milk, butter, and egg and stir until blended. Fold in dates and walnuts. Pour batter into prepared pan and sprinkle with granulated sugar and remaining cinnamon.

At 350°F, place in oven on wire rack. Touch START. *(Oven cooks: convec, 350°F, 55 minutes.)* Turn out onto wire rack and let cool completely before slicing.

1 loaf

Recipe No. 70

Oatmeal Muffins

Cooking Time: 12 minutes

- 3 tablespoons chopped nuts
- 2 tablespoons brown sugar
- Dash nutmeg
- ⅔ cup firmly-packed brown sugar
- ½ cup vegetable oil
- ½ cup buttermilk or sour milk
- 2 large eggs, beaten
- 1 cup all-purpose flour
- ⅔ cup rolled oats
- 1 teaspoon baking powder
- ½ teaspoon baking soda
- ½ teaspoon salt

Combine nuts, 2 tablespoons brown sugar, and nutmeg; set aside. Combine ⅔ cup brown sugar, oil, buttermilk, and egg and blend well. Add remaining ingredients except nut mixture and stir just until moistened.

Place wire rack in lower position. Set recipe number 70. Touch START. *(Oven preheats: convec, 370°F.)* Spoon one-third of batter into 6 paper-lined microproof and heatproof muffin cups, filling cups half full. Sprinkle with one-third of nut mixture.

At 370°F, place in oven on wire rack. Touch START. *(Oven cooks: micro/convec, 370°F, 4 minutes.)*

At Pause, remove from oven. Turn out of molds and cool on rack. Prepare 6 additional muffin cups. Place in oven on wire rack. Touch START. *(Oven cooks: micro/convec, 370°F, 4 minutes.)*

At Pause, remove from oven. Turn out of molds and cool on rack. Prepare final 6 muffin cups. Place in oven on wire rack. Touch START. *(Oven cooks: micro/convec, 370°F, 4 minutes.)*

18 muffins

Recipe No. 71

Sour Cream Coffeecake

Cooking Time: 23 minutes

- ½ cup chopped nuts
- ⅓ cup firmly-packed brown sugar
- 2 tablespoons all-purpose flour
- 2 tablespoons butter or margarine
- 1 teaspoon cinnamon
- ¼ teaspoon salt
- ½ cup butter or margarine, softened
- ½ cup sugar
- 2 large eggs
- 1 teaspoon vanilla
- 1½ cups all-purpose flour
- 1 teaspoon baking soda
- ½ cup dairy sour cream
- ¼ cup buttermilk

Remove ceramic tray. Place wire rack in lower position. Set recipe number 71. Touch START. *(Oven preheats: convec, 350°F.)* Grease an 8-inch round microproof and heatproof baking dish. Set aside.

Combine nuts, brown sugar, 2 tablespoons flour, 2 tablespoons butter, cinnamon, and salt, and mix until crumbly. Set aside. Cream ½ cup butter and sugar with electric mixer until light and fluffy. Add eggs and vanilla and blend well. Stir together 1½ cups flour and baking soda. Add flour mixture to creamed mixture alternately with sour cream and buttermilk, beating until well blended. Spread half of the batter in prepared baking dish. Sprinkle with half of the nut mixture. Carefully spread remaining batter on top. Sprinkle with remaining nut mixture.

At 350°F, place in oven on wire rack. Touch START. *(Oven cooks: micro/convec, 350°F, 8 minutes; convec, 350°F, 15 minutes.)* Serve warm.

9 servings

Recipe No. 72

Zucchini Carrot Bread

Cooking Time: 30 minutes

- 1½ cups all-purpose flour
- ½ cup brown sugar
- ½ cup granulated sugar
- 1½ teaspoons baking powder
- 1½ teaspoons baking soda
- 1 teaspoon cinnamon
- ½ teaspoon nutmeg
- ¼ teaspoon cloves
- ½ teaspoon salt
- ½ cup vegetable oil
- ½ cup buttermilk
- 2 eggs
- 1 teaspoon vanilla
- ½ cup grated carrot
- ½ cup grated peeled zucchini

Remove ceramic tray. Place wire rack in lower position. Set recipe number 72. Touch START. *(Oven preheats: convec, 350°F.)* Grease an 8½×4-inch microproof and heatproof loaf pan; set aside.

Combine flour, sugars, baking powder, baking soda, spices, and salt. Set aside. Stir together remaining ingredients in a 2-quart mixing bowl. Add dry ingredients and stir until well mixed. Pour into prepared pan.

At 350°F, place in oven on wire rack. Touch START. *(Oven cooks: micro/convec, 350°F, 15 minutes; convec, 350°F, 15 minutes.)* Remove from oven and let stand on cooling rack 5 minutes before turning out of pan. Cool completely before slicing.

12 to 18 servings

The Butcher Shop

The perfect method for cooking meat is here: micro/convection cooking. While the outside of the roast is seared and browned by the constantly-moving hot-air (convection), the inside is being cooked quickly by the microwaves. Whether it's that elegant anniversary dinner of Prime Rib (page 90) with Yorkshire pudding or the simplicity of Chuck Roast in a Bag (page 89), you'll rate as best-cook-on-the-block with family and friends. How are you able to provide "exactly as they like it" doneness for everyone? It's simple: once you cut the rare slices you need from the roast, you can slip other slices back in the oven and cook them just a bit longer, using the microwave method. Everybody's happy and you're a genius!

The convection method will be your first choice for steaks and chops. For convection, remember to remove the ceramic tray. For steaks and chops, you'll probably want to place the oven rack in the upper position. The fan-assisted hot air movement promotes crispness of the fat without drying out the meat. You

The convection method enables the use of disposable broiling pans or other metal utensils. Steak (Guide, page 83) gets its heat-seared flavor when cooked on the wire rack in the upper position (above). The temperature probe is a true worry saver for roasting meat, such as Pork Loin Roast (page 105). Note horizontal probe position (above right). Meatloaf (page 92) has a surprise inside and uses micro/convection, lower position (right).

can expect a line-up at your door when you prepare Vegetable Stuffed Flank Steak (page 89), Lamb Chops with Mint Glaze (page 104), and other recipes. Finally, look to the microwave method for superb stews, stir-fry dishes, etc.

Converting Your Recipes

The Guides on the following pages provide detailed instructions for the defrosting and cooking of the most popular cuts of meat. If you don't find your particular favorite listed, you are sure to find a quite similar one to use as a guide. You can also refer to the individual recipes and will likely find one to use in adapting your favorite recipe.

For steaks, chops, and patties, you will have more surface browning if you preheat the oven to 450°F and cook at that temperature whenever you choose to use micro/convection or convection. Since such items vary greatly in thickness, fat content, and weight, cooking times can only be regarded as estimates. If you determine, using the Guide, that 9 minutes is recommended (ground beef patties, medium, for example), check doneness at 7 minutes.

You should be aware that a boned roast will require less cooking time than one with a bone. Be careful, too, in positioning the temperature probe, if you choose the Probe Method from the Guide. A large amount of fat running through the roast will cause an inaccurate reading of internal temperature if the probe is touching the fat. All roasts should be turned over during the cooking time to provide even browning, distribute juices, and assure even doneness.

As you cook, remember that *all meat profits from standing time of 10 to 15 minutes* after the programmed cooking time has ended. Tips:

- ☐ Special microwave roasting racks are available to elevate meat from its drippings during cooking with that method. Many are also heatproof but be sure to check manufacturer's instructions before using with micro/convection or convection methods.
- ☐ Recipe times here presume meat is at refrigerator temperature. If your meal requires lengthy preparation, during which the meat may reach room temperature, reduce cooking times.
- ☐ Baste, marinate, or season meat just as you would for conventional cooking.
- ☐ Optional method: use a tight cover and cook, micro, on 40 or 50 for the less tender cuts of meat such as chuck, bottom round, brisket, and stewing meat cooked in liquid.
- ☐ Check dishes that use relatively long cooking times to be sure liquid has not evaporated. Add liquid as necessary.
- ☐ Most ground beef recipes call for lean meat. If you are using regular ground beef, drain fat before adding sauce ingredients.
- ☐ Large cuts not usually cooked on the charcoal grill, such as ham, leg of lamb, pork roast, turkey, and whole chicken, may be partially cooked in the oven and finished on the grill for a lovely charcoal flavor. It's also a great time saver for spareribs.

Using the Defrosting Guide

1. For automatic defrosting instructions, see "From Freezer to Table — Fast," pages 37-42
2. All defrosting uses the microwave method.
3. You may *begin* defrosting meat within its original paper or plastic wrappings.
4. As soon as possible, remove wrappings and place meat in microproof dish.
5. Defrost in the oven until not quite thawed. Standing time completes thawing. Separate chops, bacon slices, and frankfurters into pieces as soon as possible. If separated pieces are not thawed, distribute evenly in oven and continue defrosting.
6. Slightly increase the time for weights larger than on the chart. Do not double.
7. If you do not plan immediate cooking, follow guide for only one-half of recommended time. Place meat in refrigerator until needed.

DEFROSTING GUIDE — MEAT

Meat	Amount	Micro Control	Time (in minutes per pound)	Standing Time (minutes)	Special Notes
Beef					
Ground beef	1 lb.	30	5-6	5	Turn over once. Remove thawed
	2 lbs.	30	5-6	5	portions with fork. Return remainder. Freeze in doughnut shape.
	1/4-lb. patty	30	1 per patty	2	Depress center when freezing. Defrost on plate.
Pot roast, chuck	under 4 lbs.	30	3-5	10	Turn over once.
	over 4 lbs.	70	3-5	10	Turn over once.
Rib roast, rolled	3 to 4 lbs.	30	6-8	30-45	Turn over once.
	6 to 8 lbs.	70	6-8	90	Turn over twice.
Rib roast, bone in		70	5-6	45-90	Turn over twice.
Rump roast	3 to 4 lbs.	30	3-5	30	Turn over once.
	6 to 7 lbs.	70	3-5	45	Turn over twice.
Round steak		30	4-5	5-10	Turn over once.
Flank steak		30	4-5	5-10	Turn over once.
Sirloin steak	1/2" thick	30	4-5	5-10	Turn over once.
Tenderloin steak	2 to 3 lbs.	30	4-5	8-10	Turn over once.
Stew beef	2 lbs.	30	3-5	8-10	Turn over once. Separate.
Lamb					
Cubed for stew		30	7-8	5	Turn over once. Separate.
Ground lamb	under 4 lbs.	30	3-5	30-45	Turn over once.
	over 4 lbs.	70	3-5	30-45	Turn over twice.
Chops	1" thick	30	5-8	15	Turn over twice.
Leg	5-8 lbs.	30	4-5	15-20	Turn over twice.
Pork					
Chops	1/2" thick	30	4-6	5-10	Separate chops halfway
	1" thick	30	5-7	10	through defrosting time.
Spareribs, country-style ribs		30	5-7	10	Turn over once.
Roast	under 4 lbs.	30	4-5	30-45	Turn over once.
	over 4 lbs.	70	4-5	30-45	Turn over twice.
Bacon	1 lb.	30	2-3	3-5	Defrost until strips separate.
Sausage, bulk	1 lb.	30	2-3	3-5	Turn over once. Remove thawed portions with fork. Return remainder.
Sausage links	1 lb.	30	3-5	4-6	Turn over once. Defrost until pieces can be separated.
Hot dogs		30	5-6	5	

DEFROSTING GUIDE — MEAT

Meat	Amount	Micro Control	Time (in minutes per pound)	Standing Time (minutes)	Special Notes
Veal					
Roast	3 to 4 lbs. 6 to 7 lbs.	30 70	5-7 5-7	30 90	Turn over once. Turn over twice.
Chops	1/2" thick	30	4-6	20	Turn over once. Separate chops and continue defrosting.
Variety Meat					
Liver		30	5-6	10	Turn over once.
Tongue		30	7-8	10	Turn over once.

Note: This chart presents manual or "attended" defrosting techniques. They require more attention from the cook. In some cases, standing time may be reduced by adding another defrosting sequence to the chart recommendations. Such additional defrosting time may be at reduced power levels (5 to 20). You can also reduce standing time by immersing the food in cold water. When using these speed-defrosting techniques, be sure to check the food for warm spots and shield with small strips of aluminum foil.

Using the Cooking Guides

1. All meat should be completely thawed before cooking.
2. Place meat fat side down on a roasting rack set in a baking dish that is safe for the cooking method planned. Rack and dish must be microproof for the microwave method; microproof and heat-proof for the micro/convection method; heatproof for convection.
3. Use the Probe Method for the most accurate cooking of larger cuts of meat. Place temperature probe as horizontally as possible in the densest area, avoiding fat pockets or bone.
4. Unless otherwise noted, times given for steaks and patties will give medium doneness.
5. Ground meat to be used in casseroles should be cooked briefly first. Crumble it into micro-proof dish and cook (micro) with a double length of paper towel covering and tucked under the dish. Drain fat and add to casserole.
6. During standing time, the internal temperature of roasts will rise to serving temperature. Allow 10 to 15 minutes standing time because it is essential to complete cooking.
7. Place wire rack in lower or upper position according to amount of browning desired and height of meat. Most roasts are cooked on the ceramic tray.
8. Cutlets and chops that are breaded are cooked at the same time and method as shown in the Guide for unbreaded.

COOKING GUIDE — MEAT

Food	Programming Method	Programming Setting	First Cook Time	Second Cook Time	Probe Method	Special Notes
Beef Ground beef, bulk	micro	HI	2 min. per lb.	3 min. per lb.		Crumble in microproof dish.
Ground beef* patties, 1 - 4 4 oz. each	convec	450°	Rare: 8 min. Med: 9 min. Well: 10 min.	3 - 4 min. 4 min. 6 min.		Remove ceramic tray. Upper position. Preheat. Use broiling pan or aluminum tray.
Meatloaf, ½ - 1¾ lbs.	micro/convec	400°	25 min.		160°	Preheat. Let stand 5 - 10 minutes.
Beef rib roast, boneless	micro/convec	330°	6 min. per lb. turn over	6 min. per lb.	Rare: 120° Med: 130°	Lower position. Microproof and heatproof dish with trivet.
Beef rib roast, bone-in, 5 lb.	micro/convec	350°	8 min. per lb. fat-side down turn over	8 min. per lb.	Rare: 120° Med: 130° Well: 140°	Lower position. Microproof and heatproof dish.
Beef pot roast boneless, 3 lbs.	micro/convec	330°	7 min. per lb. turn over	7 min. per lb.	Med: 130° Well: 140°	Lower position. Covered microproof and heatproof casserole or cooking bag.
Beef brisket, corned beef, flat cut, 2 - 3 lbs.	micro/convec	320°	15 - 20 min. per lb. check liquid add if necessary turn over	15 - 20 min. per lb.		Lower position in 4-quart covered microproof casserole. Cover with water. Let stand 15 - 20 minutes after cooking.
Top round steak, 2 - 3 lbs.	micro/convec	350°	8 - 10 min. per lb. turn over check liquid	8 - 10 min. per lb.		Microproof and heatproof casserole with tight cover or browning bag. Needs liquid.
Sirloin steak, ¾" thick	convec	450°	Rare: 7 min. Med: 7 min. Well: 8 min. turn over	6 min. 7 - 8 min. 8 - 9 min.		Remove ceramic tray. Upper position. Preheat. Metal pan or foil tray.
Minute steak, cube steak, 4 - 6 oz.	convec	450°	3 - 4 min. turn over	3 - 6 min.		Remove ceramic tray. Upper position. Preheat. Metal pan or foil tray.
Tenderloin steak, 4 - 8 oz. -inch thick	convec	450°	Rare: 5 min. Med: 5 min. Well: 6 min. turn over	3 - 6 min. 4 - 7 min. 5 - 8 min.		Remove ceramic tray. Upper position. Preheat. Metal pan or foil tray.
Rib eye or strip steak, -inch thick	convec	450°	Rare: 4 min. Med: 5 min. Well: 6 min. turn over	3 - 6 min. 4 - 7 min. 5 - 8 min.		Remove ceramic tray. Upper position. Preheat. Metal pan or foil tray.
Lamb Ground lamb* patties, 4 4 oz. each	convec	450°	Rare: 8 min. Med: 9 min Well: 10 min. turn over	3 min. 4 min. 6 min.		Remove ceramic tray. Upper position. Preheat. Metal pan or foil tray.
Lamb chops ¾" thick	convec	450°	Rare: 4 min. Med: 5 min. Well: 7 min.	3 - 5 min. 4 - 6 min. 4 - 6 min.		Remove ceramic tray. Upper position. Preheat. Metal pan or foil tray.
Lamb leg or shoulder roast, bone in. 6½ lbs.	micro/convec	330°	3 min. per lb. fat side down turn over	5 - 6 min. per lb.	Rare: 145° Med: 155° Well: 165°	Lower position in microproof and heatproof dish with trivet.
Lamb roast, boneless 3 - 4 lbs.	micro/convec	330°	4 min. per lb. fat side down turn over	4 - 5 min. per lb.	150°	Lower position in microproof and heatproof dish with trivet.
Veal Shoulder or rump roast, boneless, 3 - 3½ lbs.	micro/convec	330°	3 - 5 min per lb. turn over	4 - 5 min. per lb.	155°	Lower position in microproof and heatproof dish with trivet.
Veal chops ½" thick	convec	450°	4 min. turn over	3 - 4 min.		Remove ceramic tray. Upper position. Preheat. Metal pan or foil tray.

*For rare patties, form ¾ to 1-inch thick. For medium and well done, form thinner patties.

COOKING GUIDE — MEAT

Food	Programming Method	Programming Setting	First Cook Time	Second Cook Time	Probe Method	Special Notes
Pork Pork chops, ½ - ¾" thick	convec	450°	Med: 7 min. Well: 9 min. turn over	4 - 6 min. 5 - 7 min.		Remove ceramic tray. Upper position. Preheat. Metal pan or foil tray.
Spareribs, 3 - 4 lbs.	micro/convec	350°	15 - 20 min. per lb.	2 - 3 min. per lb. turn over 2 - 3 min. per lb.		Lower position. Begin in liquid in 3 - 4 quart casserole and transfer to baking dish to finish.
Pork loin roast, boneless, 4 - 5 lbs.	micro/convec	320°	5 - 7 min. per lb. turn over	5 - 7 min. per lb.	165°	Lower position. Microproof and heatproof baking dish.
Pork loin, center cut. 4 - 5 lbs.	micro/convec	320°	5 - 7 min. per lb. turn over	5 - 7 min. per lb.	165°	Lower position. Microproof and heatproof baking dish.
Ham, boneless precooked	micro	70	5 - 6 min. per lb. turn over	5 - 6 min. per lb.	120°	Lower position. Microproof baking dish.
Ham slice, center cut, precooked	convec	450°	4 - 5 min. turn over	5 - 6 min.		Remove ceramic tray. Upper position. Preheat. Metal pan or foil tray.
Ham, canned 3 lbs. 5 lbs.	micro	70	5 - 6 min. per lb. turn over 4 - 5 min. per lb.	5 - 6 min. per lb.	120° 120°	Lower position. Microproof and heatproof baking dish.
Sausage patties, ½ - ¾" thick	convec	450°	5 - 7 min. turn over	7 - 9 min.		Remove ceramic tray. Upper position. Preheat. Metal pan or foil tray.
Sausage, bulk 1 lb.	micro	HI	3 min. per lb. stir	1 - 2 min. per lb.		Crumble in 1½-quart microproof and heatproof dish, covered with paper towel.
Pork sausage links, ½ - 1 lb.	convec	450°	5 min. turn	7 - 9 min.		Remove ceramic tray. Upper position. Preheat. Metal pan or foil tray.
Precooked Polish sausage, knockwurst, ring bologna	micro	80	2 - 2½ min. per lb. rearrange	2 - 2½ min. per lb.		Pierce casing. Cover with paper towel.
Hot dogs - 1 2 4	micro	80	45 - 60 sec. 50 - 70 sec. 1½ - 2 min.			Shallow dish or wrapped in paper towel.
Bacon 1 slice 2 slices 4 slices 8 slices	micro	HI	45 sec. - 1 min. 2 - 2½ min. 4 - 4½ min. 5 - 6 min.			On dish or bacon rack covered with paper towel with edges tucked under rack or dish.

COOKING/DEFROSTING GUIDE — CONVENIENCE MEAT*

Food	Programming Method	Programming Setting	Time (in minutes)	Probe Method	Special Notes
Barbecued beef, chili, stews, hash etc., 16 oz. can	micro	80	3 to 5	150°	Remove from package. Place in microproof plate or casserole. Cover. Stir halfway through cooking time.
Entrées, frozen 5½-8 oz.			follow package directions		Lower position.
Man-size TV dinners, 16-20 oz.			follow package directions		Lower position.
Stuffed peppers, cabbage rolls, chow mein, etc., 16-32 oz.	micro	80	5 to 9	150°	or follow package directions.
TV dinners 11½-14 oz.			follow package directions		Lower position.
Meat pie double crust, 8 oz.	convec		follow package directions for oven (convec) cooking		Remove ceramic tray. Lower position. Preheat.

* Due to the tremendous variety in convenience food products available, times given here should be used only as guidelines. We suggest you cook food for the shortest recommended time and then check for doneness. Be sure to check the package for microwave and oven (convec) instructions.

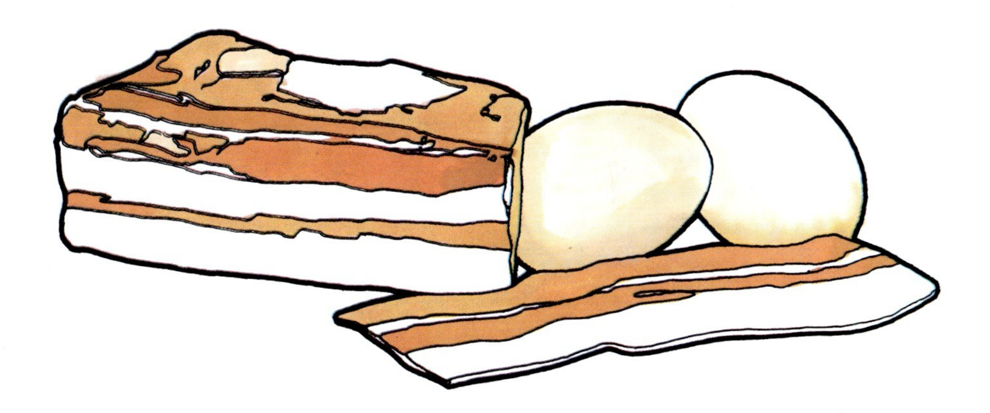

Special Tips about Bacon

- ☐ Cook bacon on a paper-lined plate, and cover with paper towels to prevent splatters and absorb drippings.
- ☐ To reserve drippings, cook bacon on a meat rack in a baking dish or on a microwave bacon rack. Bacon can also be cooked, in slices or cut up, in a casserole and removed if necessary with a slotted spoon.
- ☐ For bacon that is soft rather than crisp, cook at the minimum timing.
- ☐ Bacon varies in quality. The thickness and amount of sugar and salt used in curing will affect browning and timing. Cook thicker slices a bit longer than the chart indicates. You will also find that sweeter bacon cooks more quickly.
- ☐ Sugar in bacon causes brown spots to appear on the paper towels. If the bacon tends to stick a bit to the towel, it is due to an extra high amount of sugar.

Recipe No. 73

Filet of Beef Tenderloin (rare)

Approximate Cooking Time: 30 minutes

- **1 2- to 3-pound beef tenderloin, trimmed**
- **½ envelope onion soup mix or ½ teaspoon garlic powder**
- **½ pound mushrooms, chopped or sliced**

Remove ceramic tray. Place wire rack in upper position. Set recipe number 73. Touch START. *(Oven preheats: convec, 450°F.)* Set meat in shallow glass or ceramic baking dish and sprinkle with soup mix. Arrange mushrooms over and around roast. Insert temperature probe in thickest portion of meat.

At 450°F, place meat in oven on wire rack. Plug in probe. Touch START. *(Oven cooks: convec, 450°F, to 90°F.)*

At Pause, turn meat over and baste with mushrooms and drippings, being careful not to remove probe. Touch START. *(Oven cooks: convec, 450°F, to 120°F; stands: 0, 5 minutes.)*

4 to 6 servings

Recipe No. 74

Filet of Beef Tenderloin (medium)

Approximate Cooking Time: 35 minutes

- **1 2- to 3-pound beef tenderloin, trimmed**
- **½ envelope onion soup mix or ½ teaspoon garlic powder**
- **½ pound mushrooms, chopped or sliced**

Remove ceramic tray. Place wire rack in upper position. Set recipe number 74. Touch START. *(Oven preheats: convec, 450°F.)* Set meat in shallow glass or ceramic baking dish and sprinkle with soup mix. Arrange mushrooms over and around roast. Insert temperature probe in thickest portion of meat.

At 450°F, place meat in oven on wire rack. Plug in probe. Touch START. *(Oven cooks: convec, 450°F, to 90°F.)*

At Pause, turn meat over and baste with mushrooms and drippings, being careful not to remove probe. Touch START. *(Oven cooks: convec, 450°F, to 130°F; stands: 0, 5 minutes.)*

4 to 6 servings

Recipe No. 75

Vegetable-Stuffed Flank Steak

Cooking Time: 21½ minutes

1 1½-pound flank steak
¼ cup chopped celery
¼ cup chopped green onion
2 cloves garlic, minced
2 teaspoons chopped parsley
1 tablespoon butter or margarine
1 cup seasoned croutons, crushed
2 tablespoons dry white wine
1 tablespoon soy sauce
Pinch of pepper

Score both sides of steak using tip of sharp knife; set aside. Combine celery, onion, garlic, and parsley in small microproof bowl. Add butter. Cover with plastic wrap. Place in oven. Set recipe number 34. Touch START. *(Oven cooks: micro, HI, 1½ minutes.)* Remove vegetable mixture from oven. Stir.

Place wire rack in lower position. Set recipe number 75. Touch START. *(Oven preheats: convec, 350°F.)* Add crushed croutons to vegetable mixture and blend well. Spread stuffing over meat, leaving 1-inch border on all sides. Carefully roll meat up lengthwise; tie in 3 places. Arrange seam-side down in microproof and heatproof baking dish. Combine wine, soy sauce, and pepper and brush over meat.

At 350°F, place in oven on wire rack. Touch START. *(Oven cooks: micro/convec, 350°F, 10 minutes.)*

At Pause, brush meat with wine mixture. Turn meat over and brush again. Touch START. *(Oven cooks: micro/convec, 350°F, 10 minutes.)* Brush with remaining wine mixture. Let stand 3 to 5 minutes before serving.

4 to 6 servings

For an extra-special stuffing, place ½ pound bulk pork sausage in microproof bowl. Cook, micro, on HI 3 minutes. Add ½ cup crushed saltine crackers, ½ cup chopped tart apple, ¼ cup chopped celery, 1 tablespoon minced onion, ¼ teaspoon salt, and ¼ teaspoon paprika. Spread over flank steak. Set recipe number 75. Proceed as above.

Recipe No. 76

Chuck Roast in a Bag

Cooking Time: 1 hour 30 minutes

3 tablespoons all-purpose flour
1 tablespoon brown sugar
½ teaspoon salt
½ teaspoon dry mustard
¼ teaspoon pepper
¾ cup catsup
½ cup water
2 tablespoons Worcestershire sauce
1 tablespoon vinegar
1 4-pound chuck roast center cut
4 medium potatoes, peeled and halved
2 large carrots, peeled and cut into 2-inch chunks
1 green pepper, sliced into thin strips
1 large onion, quartered

Combine flour, sugar, salt, mustard, and pepper in small bowl. Stir in catsup, water, Worcestershire, and vinegar. Cut a 1-inch strip from open end of cooking bag. Place roast in bag. Set bag in 9×13-inch microproof and heatproof baking dish. Spoon catsup mixture over meat. Add potatoes and carrots. Close bag with strip cut from open end of bag. Place in oven on ceramic tray. Set recipe number 76. Touch START. *(Oven cooks: micro/convec, 350°F, 45 minutes.)*

At Pause, add green pepper and onion to bag. Check liquid around meat and add small amount of water if mixture seems too dry. Touch START. *(Oven cooks: micro/convec, 350°F, 30 minutes; stands: 0, 15 minutes.)*

4 to 6 servings

This is one of several recipes that use the preset functions of another recipe for part of the cooking sequence. Set recipe number 34 first. At the end of that sequence, set recipe number 75.

Recipe No. 77

Spicy Beef Short Ribs

Cooking Time: 1 hour 35 minutes

- 3 pounds beef short ribs, trimmed
- 8 to 10 cups hot water
- 1 large onion, thickly sliced into rings
- 1 teaspoon salt
- 6 celery tops with leaves
- Barbecue Sauce (page 175)

Rinse ribs with hot water and drain well. Arrange in 4-quart microproof and heat-proof baking dish. Top with onion and sprinkle with salt. Arrange celery over onions. Add enough hot water to completely cover mixture. Cover and place in oven on ceramic tray. Set recipe number 77. Touch START. *(Oven cooks: micro/convec, 350°F, 55 minutes.)*

At Pause, drain ribs, discarding onion and celery. Pour sauce over ribs, turning to coat evenly. Cover with casserole lid. Place in oven. Touch START. *(Oven cooks: micro/convec, 350°F, 15 minutes.)*

At Pause, turn ribs over; cover. Touch START. *(Oven cooks: micro/convec, 350°F, 25 minutes.)*

4 servings

Recipe No. 78

Prime Rib (rare)

Approximate Cooking Time: 45 minutes

- 1 5-pound prime rib roast of beef
- 3 cloves garlic, minced
- 1 pound sliced fresh mushrooms

Set roast in shallow microproof and heat-proof dish fat-side down. Rub entire surface with garlic. Place in oven on ceramic tray. Set recipe number 78. Touch START. *(Oven cooks: micro/convec, 330°F, 20 minutes.)*

At Pause, turn roast onto side. Touch START. *(Oven cooks: micro/convec, 330°F, 10 minutes.)*

At Pause, stand roast on bone. Arrange mushrooms in dish around roast. Insert temperature probe into thickest portion of meat without touching bone. Place roast in oven. Plug in probe. Touch START. *(Oven cooks: micro/convec, 330°F, to 120°F.)* Let stand 10 minutes before serving.

4 to 6 servings

Recipe No. 79

Prime Rib (medium)

Approximate Cooking Time: 50 minutes

- 1 5-pound prime rib roast of beef
- 3 cloves garlic, minced
- 1 pound sliced fresh mushrooms

Set roast in shallow microproof and heat-proof dish fat-side down. Rub entire surface with garlic. Place in oven on ceramic tray. Set recipe number 79. Touch START. *(Oven cooks: micro/convec, 330°F, 20 minutes.)*

At Pause, turn roast onto side. Touch START. *(Oven cooks: micro/convec, 330°F, 10 minutes.)*

At Pause, stand roast on bone. Arrange mushrooms in dish around roast. Insert temperature probe into thickest portion of meat without touching bone. Place roast in oven. Plug in probe. Touch START. *(Oven cooks: micro/convec, 330°F, to 130°F.)* Let stand 10 minutes before serving.

4 to 6 servings

Prime Rib →

Recipe No. 80

Brisket of Beef

Cooking Time: 2 hours

- 3 large onions, sliced into rings
- 1 1½- to 3-pound flat cut brisket of beef
- 1 envelope onion soup mix
- ½ cup water
- 12 large mushrooms, sliced
- 4 medium-to-large potatoes, peeled

Arrange half of onions in 4-quart microproof and heatproof casserole. Set brisket on top, cutting in half if necessary. Sprinkle with onion soup mix. Arrange remaining onions on top. Cover with casserole lid. Place in oven on ceramic tray. Set recipe number 80. Touch START. *(Oven cooks: micro/convec, 320°F, 40 minutes.)*

At Pause, turn meat over. Add mushrooms and potatoes. Spoon onions and accumulated liquid over top, adding water if necessary. Cover. Place in oven. Touch START. *(Oven cooks: micro/convec, 320°F, 20 minutes.)*

At Pause, turn meat and potatoes over. Cover. Touch START. *(Oven cooks: micro/convec, 320°F, 40 minutes.)*

At Pause, transfer meat to cutting board. Keep potatoes and sauce covered. Slice meat thinly across grain. Return to dish. Place in oven. Touch START. *(Oven cooks: micro/convec, 320°F, 20 minutes.)* Serve immediately.

4 to 6 servings

Recipe No. 81 ⊞

Baked Beefy Macaroni

Cooking Time: 21 minutes

- 1 pound lean ground beef
- 1 jar (15 ounces) spaghetti sauce or 2 cups Homemade Spaghetti Sauce (page 176)
- 10 ounces elbow macaroni, cooked
- 1½ cups shredded Cheddar cheese

Crumble beef into 8-inch round microproof and heatproof baking dish. Place in oven. Set recipe number 38. Touch START. *(Oven cooks: micro, HI, 6 minutes.)* Remove from oven. Stir through meat once. Drain well.

Place wire rack in lower position. Set recipe number 81. Touch START. *(Oven preheats: convec, 350°F.)* Add spaghetti sauce and macaroni to meat and mix well.

At 350°F, place in oven on wire rack. Touch START. *(Oven cooks: micro/convec, 350°F, 10 minutes.)*

At Pause, sprinkle cheese over top. Place in oven. Touch START. *(Oven cooks: micro/convec, 350°F, 5 minutes.)* Serve immediately.

4 to 6 servings

Recipe No. 82

Meatloaf

Approximate Cooking Time: 25 minutes

- 1½ pounds lean ground beef
- 2 eggs, beaten
- 1 medium onion, finely chopped
- 1 can (8 ounces) tomato sauce, divided
- 2 slices bread, rinsed with warm water, squeezed dry and torn into pieces
- 1 teaspoon Worcestershire sauce
- ½ teaspoon salt
- ¼ teaspoon pepper
- 1 clove garlic, crushed
- 3 hard-cooked eggs

Place wire rack in lower position. Set recipe number 82. Touch START. *(Oven preheats: convec, 400°F.)* Combine beef, beaten eggs, onion, ⅓ cup tomato sauce, bread, Worcestershire, salt, pepper, and garlic in large bowl and mix lightly to blend well. Turn half of mixture into 9×5-inch microproof and heatproof loaf dish, spreading evenly. Arrange hard-cooked eggs down center. Cover with remaining meat mixture, smoothing top. Brush remaining tomato sauce over meat. Insert temperature probe into center of loaf.

At 400°F, place in oven on wire rack. Touch START. *(Oven cooks: micro/convec, 400°F, to 160°F.)* Pour off accumulated liquid. Serve meatloaf immediately.

6 to 8 servings

What a surprise! Each slice of this special loaf contains a cross-section of egg.

⊞ *Recipe can be increased. See "Quantity", page 12.*

Recipe No. 83

Beef Stew

Cooking Time: 1 hour 45 minutes

- 2 pounds beef stew meat, cut into 1½-inch cubes
- ½ teaspoon salt
- 1 package (1½ ounces) brown gravy mix with mushrooms
- 1½ cups water
- 3 celery stalks, cut into 1-inch slices
- 4 medium carrots, peeled and cut into chunks
- 4 medium potatoes, peeled and halved
- 1 large onion, cut into rings

Arrange meat in 3-quart microproof casserole and sprinkle with salt. Blend gravy mix with water in small bowl. Pour over meat. Cover with casserole lid. Place in oven. Set recipe number 83. Touch START. *(Oven cooks: micro,* 70, 30 *minutes.)*

At Pause, stir in vegetables, coating evenly with sauce. Cover. Place in oven. Touch START. *(Oven cooks: micro,* 50, 30 *minutes.)*

At Pause, stir. Touch START. *(Oven cooks: micro,* 50, 30 *minutes; stands:* 0, 15 *minutes.)* Serve immediately.

4 to 6 servings

Recipe No. 84

Beef Stroganoff

Cooking Time: 27 minutes

- 2 tablespoons butter
- 1 medium onion, sliced
- 1 round steak, boneless (1 pound), cut into thin strips
- 2 cloves garlic, minced
- ¼ teaspoon salt
- ¼ teaspoon pepper
- ⅓ cup red wine
- 1 cup sliced mushrooms
- 2 tablespoons chopped parsley
- 1 cup dairy sour cream

Combine butter, onion, meat, garlic, salt, and pepper in 2-quart microproof casserole. Cover with casserole lid. Place in oven on ceramic tray. Set recipe number 84. Touch START. *(Oven cooks: micro, HI,* 5 *minutes.)*

At Pause, add wine and stir. Cover with casserole lid. Touch START. *(Oven cooks: micro,* 50, 10 *minutes.)*

At Pause, add mushrooms and stir. Cover. Touch START. *(Oven cooks: micro,* 50, 10 *minutes.)*

At Pause, add parsley and stir in sour cream. Leave uncovered. Touch START. *(Oven cooks: micro,* 50, 2 *minutes.)*

Serve hot over freshly cooked rice or noodles.

4 servings

Recipe No. 85

Rolled Vegetable Meatloaf

Cooking Time: 28 minutes

- 1¾ pounds lean ground beef
- 2 eggs, lightly beaten
- 2 tablespoons catsup
- ¼ cup dry breadcrumbs
- 1 teaspoon salt
- ¼ teaspoon pepper

Filling:

- ¾ cup chopped onions
- ½ cup chopped green pepper
- ½ cup chopped celery
- 1 jar (2 ounces) pimiento, drained
- ½ teaspoon garlic powder

Place wire rack in lower position. Set recipe number 85. Touch START. *(Oven preheats: convec,* 400°*F.)* Meanwhile, combine beef, eggs, catsup, breadcrumbs, salt, and pepper and mix lightly. Turn mixture out onto waxed paper and shape into 8×10-inch rectangle. Mix remaining ingredients in medium bowl. Spread evenly over meat, leaving 1-inch border on all sides. Carefully roll meat up from short end, pressing edges together to seal. Arrange roll seam-side down in 9×5-inch microproof and heatproof loaf dish.

At 400°F, place in oven on wire rack. Touch START. *(Oven cooks: micro/convec,* 400°*F,* 25 *minutes; stands:* 0, 3 *minutes.)* Serve immediately.

4 to 6 servings

Recipe No. 86

All-American Meatballs

Cooking Time: 20 minutes

1 pound lean ground beef
1 medium potato, peeled and coarsely grated
2 tablespoons onion soup mix
1 tablespoon parsley flakes
1 large egg, lightly beaten
2 cups beef broth
1 tablespoon Worcestershire sauce
2 tablespoons cornstarch
2 tablespoons water

Combine beef, potato, soup mix, parsley, and egg; blend well. Shape into twelve 1½-inch balls. Combine broth and Worcestershire in 2-quart microproof casserole. Add meatballs. Cover and place in oven. Set recipe number 86. Touch START. *(Oven cooks: micro,* 70, 10 *minutes.)*

At Pause, dissolve cornstarch in water. Stir into casserole. Cover. Touch START. *(Oven cooks: micro,* 70, 3 *minutes.)*

At Pause, stir. Cover. Touch START. *(Oven cooks: micro,* 70, 2 *minutes; stands:* 0, 5 *minutes.)*

4 servings

Recipe No. 87

Chili con Carne

Cooking Time: 20 minutes

1 pound lean ground beef
½ cup minced onion
½ cup chopped green pepper
1 clove garlic, minced
1 can (16 ounces) whole tomatoes, broken up
1 can (16 ounces) kidney beans
1 to 2 tablespoons chili powder, to taste
1 teaspoon salt

Crumble beef into 2-quart microproof casserole. Add onion, green pepper, and garlic. Place in oven. Set recipe number 87. Touch START. *(Oven cooks: micro, HI,* 2 *minutes.)*

At Pause, stir. Touch START. *(Oven cooks: micro, HI,* 2 *minutes.)*

At Pause, remove from oven; drain. Add remaining ingredients; blend well. Cover with casserole lid and place in oven. Touch START. *(Oven cooks: micro,* 70, 9 *minutes.)*

At Pause, stir. Cover. Touch START. *(Oven cooks: micro, 70, 7 minutes.)*

Let stand 5 minutes before serving.

4 servings

Recipe No. 88

One-Step Lasagna

Cooking Time: 37 minutes

1 pound lean ground beef
1 jar (15 ounces) spaghetti sauce
½ cup water
1 teaspoon salt
1 package (8 ounces) lasagna noodles
2 cups ricotta cheese, drained, divided
3 cups (12 ounces) shredded mozzarella cheese, divided
½ cup grated Parmesan cheese
Chopped parsley

Crumble beef into 2-quart microproof casserole. Place in oven. Set recipe number 88. Touch START. *(Oven cooks: micro, HI,* 3 *minutes.)*

At Pause, stir to break up beef. Touch START. *(Oven cooks: micro, HI,* 2 *minutes.)*

At Pause, remove from oven. Stir; drain. Stir in spaghetti sauce, water, and salt. Spread one third of the beef mixture in 11×7-inch microproof baking dish. Arrange half of the noodles over sauce. Spread with 1 cup ricotta cheese. Sprinkle with 1 cup mozzarella cheese. Repeat layers once. Top with remaining beef mixture. Sprinkle with Parmesan cheese. Double wrap with plastic wrap, and place in oven. Touch START. *(Oven cooks: micro,* 50, 30 *minutes.)*

At Pause, sprinkle with remaining 1 cup mozzarella cheese. Do not cover. Touch START. *(Oven cooks: micro,* 50, 2 *minutes.)*

Sprinkle with parsley, and serve with additional Parmesan cheese, if desired.

6 servings

← *One-Step Lasagna*

Recipe No. 89

Stuffed Cabbage

Cooking Time: 36 minutes

1 head (about 1½ pounds) cabbage, cored, blemished leaves discarded
¼ cup water
1 pound lean ground beef
½ pound ground pork
¾ cup cooked rice
1 large egg, lightly beaten
1 tablespoon chopped parsley
1 clove garlic, minced
1 teaspoon salt
½ teaspoon thyme
¼ teaspoon pepper
¼ cup butter or margarine
2 cans (8 ounces each) tomato sauce

Place cabbage and water in 3-quart microproof casserole. Cover with casserole lid and place in oven. Set recipe number 89. Touch START. *(Oven cooks: micro, HI,* 6 *minutes.)*

At Pause, remove from oven; drain. Let stand to cool slightly. Separate 6 to 8 large outside leaves, discarding tough centers; set aside. Combine beef, pork, rice, egg, parsley, garlic, salt, thyme, and pepper; blend well. Divide mixture evenly among large outside cabbage leaves, wrapping leaves tightly around mixture. Line bottom of 13×9-inch microproof baking dish with some of the remaining cabbage leaves. Top with stuffed cabbage rolls. Cover with remaining leaves. Dot with butter. Cover with tomato sauce. Cover with plastic wrap and place in oven. Touch START. *(Oven cooks: micro,* 80, 15 *minutes.)*

At Pause, baste with pan juices. Touch START. *(Oven cooks: micro,* 80, 10 *minutes;* 10, 5 *minutes.)*

Discard top leaves before serving.

4 servings

Recipe No. 90

Beef Shanghai

Cooking Time: 9 minutes

2 tablespoons vegetable oil
1 top round or sirloin steak, boneless (1 pound), cut into thin strips
1 can (16 ounces) whole tomatoes, broken up
1 medium onion, finely chopped
1 clove garlic, minced
1 teaspoon salt
⅛ teaspoon pepper
2 large green peppers, seeded and cut into thin strips
2 teaspoons cornstarch
2 tablespoons soy sauce

Pour oil into 3-quart microproof casserole. Add beef; stir to coat. Add tomatoes, onion, garlic, salt, and pepper. Cover and place in oven. Set recipe number 90. Touch START. *(Oven cooks: micro, HI,* 2 *minutes.)*

At Pause, stir. Cover with casserole lid. Touch START. *(Oven cooks: micro, HI,* 2 *minutes.)*

At Pause, add green peppers. Dissolve cornstarch in soy sauce; stir into beef mixture. Cover. Touch START. *(Oven cooks: micro, HI,* 5 *minutes.)*

Serve over hot rice and sprinkle with chow mein noodles.

4 servings

Recipe No. 91

Barbecued Beef, Chili, Stew, Hash, Meatballs

Approximate Cooking Time: 4 minutes

1 can (16 ounces) barbecued beef, chili, stew, hash, or meatballs

Pour beef mixture into microproof casserole. Place in oven. Insert temperature probe into beef mixture, and cover with plastic wrap. Set recipe number 91. Touch START. *(Oven cooks: micro,* 80, *to* 110°*F.)*

At Pause, stir. Cover. Touch START. *(Oven cooks: micro,* 80, *to* 150°*F; holds warm:* 1.)

1 to 2 servings

Recipe No. 92

Green Peppers and Steak

Cooking Time: 14 minutes

- ½ cup soy sauce
- ½ cup dry sherry
- ½ cup water
- 1 tablespoon sugar
- 1 clove garlic, minced
- 2 thin slices fresh ginger, minced
- 1 sirloin steak, boneless (1½ to 2 pounds), cut into thin strips
- ½ medium bunch broccoli
- ½ pound bean sprouts
- 6 green onions, cut into 2-inch pieces
- 1 can (5 ounces) sliced water chestnuts, drained

Combine soy sauce, sherry, water, sugar, garlic, and ginger in 2-quart microproof casserole. Add steak; stir to coat. Cover with casserole lid and let stand at room temperature 2 hours, stirring occasionally.

Cut broccoli stems diagonally into thin slices; break florets into individual pieces. Rinse bean sprouts in cold water, drain. Combine broccoli, bean sprouts, onions, and water chestnuts. Push marinated steak to center of casserole. Arrange vegetables around steak. Cover and place in oven. Set recipe number 92. Touch START. *(Oven cooks: micro, HI,* 11 *minutes.)*

At Pause, stir. Touch START. *(Oven cooks: micro, HI,* 3 *minutes.)* Serve with rice.

4 to 6 servings

You can substitute 1 *package (*10 *ounces) frozen broccoli spears, thawed, for fresh broccoli. If fresh bean sprouts are unavailable, substitute 2 cups drained canned bean sprouts.*

Recipe No. 93

Stuffed Green Peppers

Cooking Time: 14 minutes

- 4 large green peppers
- 1 pound lean ground beef
- 1 medium onion, finely chopped
- 1 clove garlic, minced
- 2 tablespoons minced celery
- 1 egg
- 1 cup tomato sauce, divided
- ½ cup cooked rice
- 3 tablespoons minced fresh parsley
- 1 tablespoon Worcestershire sauce
- ½ teaspoon salt
- ¼ teaspoon pepper

Wash peppers; remove tops, seeds, and membranes. Set upside down to drain. Place beef, onion, garlic, and celery in 2-quart microproof bowl. Place in oven. Set recipe number 93. Touch START. *(Oven cooks: micro, HI,* 3 *minutes.)*

At Pause, stir to crumble beef. Touch START. *(Oven cooks: micro, HI,* 2 *minutes.)*

At Pause, stir in remaining ingredients, except 4 tablespoons tomato sauce. Fill green peppers with beef mixture, mounding on top. Arrange peppers in circle in round or oval microproof baking dish or casserole just large enough to hold peppers upright. Place in oven. Touch START. *(Oven cooks: micro,* 70, 10 *minutes.)* Rotate dish one-half turn during cooking if peppers are cooking unevenly.

Spread 1 tablespoon tomato sauce on top of each pepper. Serve with crusty garlic bread, if desired.

4 servings

Recipe No. 94 ⊞

Tomato Swiss Steak

Cooking Time: 1 hour 3 minutes

- 1/4 cup all-purpose flour
- 1 teaspoon salt
- 1/4 teaspoon pepper
- 1 round steak (1 pound), 1/2 inch thick
- 1 large onion, sliced
- 1/2 green pepper, seeded and cut into strips
- 1 can (6 ounces) tomato paste
- 1 cup beef broth, or 1 cup water plus 1 beef bouillon cube

Combine flour, salt, and pepper. Place steak on cutting board; pound half of the flour mixture into both sides of steak with meat mallet. Cut steak in half; place in 8-inch round or oval microproof casserole. Sprinkle with remaining flour mixture. Spread onion, green pepper, and tomato paste over steak. Add broth to cover ingredients. Cover with casserole lid. Place in oven. Set recipe number 94. Touch START. *(Oven cooks: micro, HI,* 3 *minutes;* 30, 20 *minutes;* 30, 20 *minutes.)*

At Pause, turn meat over. Cover. Touch START. *(Oven cooks: micro,* 30, 20 *minutes.)*

2 servings

Recipe No. 95

Hungarian Goulash

Cooking Time: 1 hour 25 minutes

- 2 pounds beef for stew, cut into 1-inch cubes
- 4 large tomatoes, peeled and cut into chunks
- 1 medium onion, coarsely chopped
- 1 1/2 tablespoons paprika
- 1 teaspoon salt
- 1/2 teaspoon pepper
- 1 container (8 ounces) dairy sour cream

Combine beef, tomatoes, onion, paprika, salt, and pepper in 3-quart microproof casserole. Place in oven. Set recipe number 95. Touch START. *(Oven cooks: micro,* 50, 25 *minutes.)*

At Pause, stir. Touch START. *(Oven cooks: micro,* 50, 30 *minutes.)*

At Pause, stir. Touch START. *(Oven cooks: micro,* 50, 25 *minutes;* 20, 5 *minutes.)*

Blend in sour cream. Serve hot over freshly cooked noodles.

4 to 6 servings

Recipe No. 96

Enchilada Casserole

Cooking Time: 15 minutes

- 1 3/4 pounds lean ground beef
- 1 large onion, chopped
- 2 cloves garlic, minced
- 1 can (16 ounces) tomato purée
- 1 envelope (1 5/8 ounces) taco seasoning mix
- 6 corn tortillas
- 3 cups (12 ounces) shredded Cheddar cheese, divided

Crumble beef into 2-quart glass measure. Add onion and garlic; mix lightly. Place in oven. Set recipe number 96. Touch START. *(Oven cooks: micro, HI,* 3 *minutes.)*

At Pause, stir through several times. Touch START. *(Oven cooks: micro, HI,* 2 *minutes.)*

At Pause, stir in purée and seasoning mix. Touch START. *(Oven cooks: micro, HI,* 3 *minutes.)*

At Pause, remove from oven. Layer tortillas, beef mixture, and 2 1/2 cups cheese in 2-quart round microproof casserole. Cover with casserole lid and place in oven. Touch START. *(Oven cooks: micro, HI,* 7 *minutes.)*

Sprinkle with remaining 1/2 cup cheese. Cut into wedges and serve.

4 to 6 servings

⊞ *Recipe can be increased. See "Quantity", page 12.*

Stuffed Green Peppers (page 97) with Spaghetti Squash (Guide, page 152) →

Recipe No. 97

Veal Parmigiana

Cooking Time: 17 minutes

4 veal cutlets (1 pound)
½ cup cracker meal or dry breadcrumbs
½ cup grated Parmesan cheese
1 egg, beaten with ¼ teaspoon salt
½ cup chopped onions
1 can (8 ounces) tomato sauce
3 tablespoons tomato paste
½ teaspoon sugar
⅛ teaspoon oregano
⅛ teaspoon pepper
4 slices mozzarella cheese
2 tablespoons grated Parmesan cheese
2 tablespoons chopped fresh parsley

Pound veal slightly to even thickness. Mix cracker meal and ½ cup Parmesan cheese in shallow dish. Dip veal in egg, then roll in crumb mixture, coating completely. Sprinkle onions in bottom of microproof and heatproof baking dish. Arrange veal in single layer over onions.

Place wire rack in lower position. Set recipe number 97. Touch START. *(Oven preheats: convec, 300°F.)*

At Pause, place dish on rack. Touch START. *(Oven cooks: micro/convec, 300°F, 12 minutes.)*

Meanwhile, blend tomato sauce, tomato paste, sugar, oregano, and pepper.

At Pause, spoon tomato mixture over veal. Top with mozzarella cheese. Touch START. *(Oven cooks: micro/convec, 300°F, 5 minutes.)* Sprinkle veal with remaining Parmesan cheese, and parsley. Serve immediately.

4 servings

Recipe No. 98 ⊞

Veal Cordon Bleu

Cooking Time: 10 minutes

6 slices prosciutto ham
6 slices mozzarella cheese
6 slices veal (about 1 to 1¼ pounds), pounded thin
¼ cup seasoned breadcrumbs
¼ teaspoon salt
⅛ teaspoon pepper
1 egg, beaten
3 tablespoons vegetable oil
2 tablespoons chopped parsley

Place wire rack in lower position. Set recipe number 98. Touch START. *(Oven preheats: convec, 350°F.)* Place slice of ham and cheese on each veal slice. Roll up and secure with toothpick. Blend breadcrumbs, salt, and pepper. Coat each veal roll with breadcrumbs, dip in beaten egg, and coat again with breadcrumbs, covering completely. Pour half of oil into bottom of microproof and heatproof baking dish. Arrange veal rolls in dish and drizzle with remaining oil.

At 350°F, place in oven. Touch START. *(Oven cooks: micro/convec, 350°F, 10 minutes.)* Spoon any cheese from bottom of dish over veal. Sprinkle with parsley and serve immediately.

4 to 6 servings

⊞ *Recipe can be increased. See "Quantity", page 12.*

Ratatouille (page 162), Medallions of Veal (page 102) →

Recipe No. 99

Veal Shoulder in Pastry Dough

Approximate Cooking Time: 1 hour

- ½ cup shredded carrot
- ½ cup finely chopped onion
- 2 small celery stalks, finely chopped
- 2 tablespoons butter
- 1 2½-pound veal shoulder roast
- 2 tablespoons dry white wine
- 2 tablespoons fresh lemon juice
- ¼ teaspoon freshly ground white pepper
- 1 package (17¼ ounces) frozen puff pastry dough, thawed
- 1 egg, beaten

Combine carrot, onion, celery, and butter in 2-cup microproof bowl. Place in oven. Set recipe number 15. Touch START. *(Oven cooks: micro, HI, 4 minutes.)*

Remove vegetable mixture from oven; stir. Set aside.

Remove ceramic tray. Place wire rack in oven lower position. Set recipe number 99. Touch START. *(Oven preheats: convec, 330°F.)* Set roast in microproof and heatproof casserole. Insert probe into thickest portion of meat. Blend wine, lemon juice, and pepper and sprinkle over meat.

At 330°F, place roast in oven. Plug in probe. Touch START. *(Oven cooks: micro/convec, 330°F, to 90°F.)*

At Pause, turn roast over and baste with drippings. Touch START. *(Oven cooks: micro/convec, 330°F, to 155°F.)*

At Pause, remove roast from oven. Remove probe; let roast cool to room temperature. Spread vegetable mixture in center of puff pastry dough. Set roast on vegetables. Fold pastry over meat, enclosing completely. Brush seams with egg to seal. (Dough scraps can be used to decorate top if desired; brush decoration with egg.)

Return roast to oven. Touch START. *(Oven cooks: convec, 350°F, 30 minutes.)*

4 to 6 servings

Recipe No. 100

Medallions of Veal

Cooking Time: 10 minutes

- ¼ cup all-purpose flour
- Salt and pepper to taste
- 8 slices veal (about ¾ pound), pounded thin
- 3 tablespoons vegetable oil
- 2 tablespoons finely minced shallots
- ½ pound fresh mushrooms, thinly sliced
- ¼ cup dry white wine

Remove ceramic tray. Place wire rack in upper position. Set recipe number 100. Touch START. *(Oven preheats: convec, 450°F.)* Meanwhile, combine flour, salt, and pepper in shallow dish. Coat veal on both sides with flour mixture, covering completely. Mix oil and shallots in shallow glass or ceramic baking dish.

At 450°F, place shallot mixture in oven. Touch START. *(Oven cooks: convec, 450°F, 2 minutes.)*

At Pause, add veal to dish. Place in oven. Touch START. *(Oven cooks: convec, 450°F, 4 minutes.)*

At Pause, turn veal over. Add mushrooms and wine. Touch START. *(Oven cooks: convec, 450°F, 4 minutes.)* Serve immediately.

2 to 3 servings

Recipe No. 101

Leg of Lamb

Approximate Cooking Time: 55 minutes

1 5- to 7-pound leg of lamb
2 medium cloves garlic, finely minced
1 teaspoon freshly ground pepper
Juice of ½ lemon

Set recipe number 101. Touch START. *(Oven preheats: convec, 380°F.)* Meanwhile, rub lamb with garlic, pepper, and lemon juice. Place in microproof and heatproof casserole.

At 380°F, place roast in oven. Touch START. *(Oven cooks: micro/convec, 380°F, 45 minutes.)*

At Pause, baste lamb with pan juices. Turn meat over and baste again. Insert probe into thickest portion of meat without touching bone. Touch START. *(Oven cooks: micro/convec, 380°F, to 155°F.)* Remove from oven. Let stand 10 minutes before carving.

6 to 8 servings

Recipe No. 102 ⊞

Lamb Shanks for Two

Cooking Time: 22 minutes

2 lamb shanks (about 1½ pounds)
1 teaspoon fresh lemon juice
1 clove garlic, finely minced or ½ teaspoon garlic powder
Pepper to taste

Place wire rack in upper position. Set recipe number 102. Touch START. *(Oven preheats: convec, 450°F.)* Sprinkle lamb with lemon juice, garlic, and pepper. Arrange in microproof and heatproof baking dish.

At 450°F, place in oven. Touch START. *(Oven cooks: micro/convec, 450°F, 15 minutes.)*

At Pause, turn shanks over. Touch START. *(Oven cooks: micro/convec, 450°F, 7 minutes.)* Serve immediately.

2 servings

Recipe No. 103

Shish Kabobs

Cooking Time: 18 minutes

1 cup prepared chili sauce
½ cup catsup
1 tablespoon honey
1 tablespoon prepared red horseradish
1 tablespoon chopped chutney
1 pound lamb, cut into 12 equal cubes
1 green pepper, cut into 12 pieces
1 large onion, cut into 12 chunks
12 small mushrooms
4 12-inch bamboo skewers

Mix chili sauce, catsup, honey, horseradish, and chutney in 1-quart glass measure. Cover with plastic wrap. Place in oven. Set recipe number 15. Touch START. *(Oven cooks: micro, HI, 4 minutes.)* Set sauce aside.

Place wire rack in upper position. Set recipe number 103. Touch START. *(Oven preheats: convec, 350°F.)* Alternate lamb, green pepper, onion, and mushrooms on wooden skewers. Set skewers in 9×13-inch microproof and heatproof baking dish. Brush generously with sauce.

At 350°F, place baking dish in oven. Touch START. *(Oven cooks: micro/convec, 350°F, 7 minutes.)*

At Pause, turn kabobs over and baste with sauce. Touch START. *(Oven cooks: micro/convec, 350°F, 7 minutes.)* Serve hot.

4 servings

This is one of several recipes that use the preset functions of another recipe for part of the cooking sequence. Set recipe number 15 first. At the end of that sequence, set recipe number 103.

⊞ *Recipe can be increased. See "Quantity", page 12.*

Recipe No. 104

Lamb Chops with Mint Glaze

Cooking Time: 19½ minutes

- ¼ cup mint jelly
- 2 tablespoons wine vinegar
- 1 tablespoon brown sugar
- 2 teaspoons fresh lemon juice
- 1 teaspoon grated lemon peel
- ¼ teaspoon dry mustard
- 4 lamb chops, ¾-inch thick
- 1 teaspoon arrowroot or cornstarch
- 1 tablespoon cold water
- Salt and pepper to taste

Combine jelly, vinegar, brown sugar, lemon juice, lemon peel, and mustard in small bowl. Whisk until smooth.

Arrange chops in 8-inch square baking dish. Pour marinade over top. Marinate 1½ to 2 hours, turning chops several times.

Drain marinade into 1-quart glass measure. Stir arrowroot and water in small cup until arrowroot is dissolved. Add to marinade. Place in oven. Set recipe number 31. Touch START *(Oven cooks: micro, HI, 2 minutes.)*

At Pause; stir. Touch START *(Oven cooks: micro, HI, 1½ minutes.)* Remove from oven; set aside.

Remove ceramic tray. Place wire rack in upper position. Set recipe number 104. Touch START. *(Oven preheats: convec, 450°F.)* Meanwhile, transfer chops to aluminum foil broiler pan and brush with marinade.

At 450°F, place in oven. Touch START. *(Oven cooks: convec, 450°F, 8 minutes.)*

At Pause, turn chops over. Touch START. *(Oven cooks: convec, 450°F, 8 minutes.)* Season with salt and pepper. Serve any remaining marinade on the side.

2 servings

Recipe No. 105

Lamb Ragout

Cooking Time: 40 minutes

- 1 pound lamb for stew, cut into 1-inch cubes
- 1 envelope (⅝ ounce) brown gravy mix
- 3 medium carrots, cut into chunks
- 2 medium stalks celery, cut into chunks
- 2 medium potatoes, peeled and cut into cubes
- 1 cup water
- ¼ cup dry red wine
- 2 tablespoons all-purpose flour
- 1 teaspoon salt
- ½ teaspoon Worcestershire sauce
- ⅛ teaspoon pepper
- 1 clove garlic, minced

Combine lamb and gravy mix in 3-quart microproof casserole. Place in oven. Set recipe number 105. Touch START. *(Oven cooks: micro,* 50, 5 *minutes.)*

At Pause, stir. Touch START. *(Oven cooks: micro,* 50, 5 *minutes.)*

At Pause, add remaining ingredients; blend well. Cover. Touch START. *(Oven cooks: micro,* 50, 15 *minutes.)*

At Pause, stir. Cover with casserole lid. Touch START. *(Oven cooks: micro,* 50, 15 *minutes.)*

Let stand 3 to 4 minutes before serving.

4 servings

Recipe No. 106

Pork Loin Roast

Approximate Cooking Time: 55 minutes

- 1 4- to 5-pound pork loin roast
- 2 tablespoons honey
- 1 tablespoon Worcestershire sauce
- 6 unpeeled, medium potatoes, halved lengthwise
- 2 medium onions, quartered

Set pork, fat side down, in 9×13-inch microproof and heatproof dish. Mix honey and Worcestershire in small bowl. Brush on roast. Place in oven on ceramic tray. Set recipe number 106. Touch START. *(Oven cooks: micro/convec, 320°F, 25 minutes.)*

At Pause, remove pork from dish. Arrange potatoes, cut-side down, in dish. Set roast with fat side up on top of potatoes and surround with onions. Insert probe in roast. Place in oven. Plug in probe. Touch START. *(Oven cooks: micro/convec, 320°F, to 130°F.)*

At Pause, rotate dish one-quarter turn. Touch START. *(Oven cooks: micro/convec, 320°F, to 165°F; stands: 0, 10 minutes.)*

6 to 8 servings

Recipe No. 107

Pork Ribs

Cooking Time: 50 minutes

- 4 pounds country-style pork ribs
- 7 cups water
- 1 jar (24 ounces) sauerkraut, drained and rinsed
- 1 jar (16 ounces) sweet-sour red cabbage
- 1 medium onion, chopped
- Salt and pepper to taste

Arrange ribs in 4-quart microproof and heatproof casserole. Add water. Cover with casserole lid. Place in oven. Set recipe number 275. Touch START. *(Oven cooks: micro, HI, 10 minutes.)*

At Pause, stir. Cover. Touch START. *(Oven cooks: micro, HI, 10 minutes.)* Drain ribs well and set aside.

Place wire rack in lower position. Set recipe number 107. Touch START. *(Oven preheats: convec, 300°F.)* Meanwhile, mix sauerkraut and red cabbage in 9×13-inch glass or ceramic baking dish. Arrange ribs over top. Sprinkle with onion and season with salt and pepper.

At 300°F, place in oven. Touch START. *(Oven cooks: micro/convec, 300°F, 15 minutes.)*

At Pause, rotate dish one-quarter turn. Touch START. *(Oven cooks: micro/convec, 300°F, 15 minutes.)* Serve hot.

6 servings

Recipe No. 108

Stuffed Pork Chops

Cooking Time: 20 minutes

- 1 cup coarse dry breadcrumbs
- ¾ cup chopped peeled apples
- 3 tablespoons chopped raisins
- 2 tablespoons sugar
- 2 tablespoons minced onion
- 2 tablespoons butter or margarine, melted
- ½ teaspoon salt
- ¼ teaspoon pepper
- Pinch of sage
- ¼ cup hot water
- 8 rib or loin pork chops

Place wire rack in lower position. Set recipe number 108. Touch START. *(Oven preheats: convec, 320°F.)* Combine all ingredients except pork chops in large bowl and blend well. Arrange 4 chops in 8-inch round microproof and heatproof dish. Divide stuffing evenly on top of chops and cover with 4 remaining chops, pressing together tightly.

At 320°F, place in oven. Touch START. *(Oven cooks: micro/convec, 320°F, 20 minutes.)* Serve immediately.

4 servings

Recipe No. 109

Sweet and Sour Pork

Cooking Time: 46 minutes

4 medium carrots, thinly sliced
1/4 cup vegetable oil
2 pounds lean pork, cut into 1/2-inch cubes
1 medium onion, sliced
2 green peppers, seeded and sliced
1 can (16 ounces) pineapple chunks
1/4 cup cornstarch
1/2 cup soy sauce
1/2 cup firmly-packed light brown sugar
1/4 cup vinegar
1 tablespoon Worcestershire sauce
1/4 teaspoon hot pepper sauce
1/2 teaspoon pepper

Combine carrots and oil in 3-quart microproof and heatproof casserole. Cover with casserole lid. Place in oven. Set recipe number 109. *(Oven cooks: micro, HI, 6 minutes.)*

At Pause, add pork, onion, and green peppers to casserole. Cover. Place in oven. Touch START. *(Oven cooks: micro, HI, 5 minutes.)*

At Pause, drain pineapple chunks, reserving 1/2 cup syrup. Transfer syrup to bowl. Stir in cornstarch. Blend in remaining ingredients. Add to pork with pineapple chunks, mixing thoroughly. Cover. Place in oven on ceramic tray. Touch START. *(Oven cooks: micro/convec, 350°F, 15 minutes.)*

At Pause, stir through several times. Touch START. *(Oven cooks: micro/convec, 350°F, 20 minutes.)* Serve over chow mein noodles or cooked rice.

4 to 6 servings

Recipe No. 110

Country-Style Ribs

Cooking Time: 1 hour 5 minutes

3 pounds meaty country-style pork ribs
1/2 cup barbecue sauce
3 tablespoons olive oil
1 tablespoon wine vinegar
1 tablespoon chopped onion
1 teaspoon chopped parsley
1/2 teaspoon salt
1/8 teaspoon pepper
1 clove garlic, minced

Cut a 1-inch strip from open end of cooking bag. Arrange ribs in bag in large microproof baking dish; tie bag with removed strip. Place in oven. Set recipe number 110. Touch START. *(Oven cooks: micro, 50, 35 minutes.)*

At Pause, remove from oven. Open bag; turn ribs over; drain. Combine remaining ingredients; blend well. Pour over ribs in bag. Close bag. Place in oven. Touch START. *(Oven cooks: micro, 50, 25 minutes; 20, 5 minutes.)*

4 to 6 servings

You can substitute 1/2 cup Barbecue Sauce (page 175) for ready-made sauce, if desired.

Recipe No. 111

Cranberry Pork Chops

Cooking Time: 12 minutes

2 loin pork chops, 3/4-inch thick
1/4 cup prepared cranberry-orange sauce

Place wire rack in lower position. Set recipe number 111. Touch START. *(Oven preheats: convec, 350°F.)* Place pork chops in 1-quart microproof and heatproof shallow casserole. Spoon cranberry sauce over chops. Cover with casserole lid.

At 350°F, place in oven. Touch START. *(Oven cooks: micro/convec, 350°F, 10 minutes; stands: 0, 2 minutes.)*

2 servings

Recipe No. 112

Roast Pork with Sauerkraut and Apples

Cooking Time: 44 minutes

- 2 large cooking apples, diced
- 1 large onion, chopped
- 1 cup shredded carrots
- ½ cup sliced celery
- 1 teaspoon thyme
- 1 can (32 ounces) sauerkraut
- 1 boneless pork loin roast (about 3 pounds)

Combine apples, onion, carrots, celery, and thyme in 2-quart glass measure. Cover with plastic wrap. Place in oven. Set recipe number 15. Touch START. *(Oven cooks: micro, HI, 4 minutes.)*

At Pause, remove from oven. Stir in sauerkraut; set aside. Place wire rack in lower position. Set recipe number 112. Touch START. *(Oven preheats: convec, 350°F.)* Meanwhile, set roast, fat-side down, on microproof roasting rack in 11 × 13-inch microproof and heatproof baking dish.

At 350°F, place in oven. Touch START. *(Oven cooks: micro/convec, 350°F, 20 minutes.)*

At Pause, turn roast over. Spoon sauerkraut mixture around roast. Place in oven. Touch START. *(Oven cooks: micro/convec, 350°F, 20 minutes.)*

6 to 8 servings

Recipe No. 113

Precooked Ham

Approximate Cooking Time: 35 minutes

- 1 precooked ham (3 to 5 pounds)

Place ham on microwave roasting rack in 12 × 7-inch microproof baking dish. Place in oven. Insert temperature probe horizontally into center of ham. Cover lightly with waxed paper. Set recipe number 113. Touch START. *(Oven cooks: micro, 70, to 90°F.)*

At Pause, turn over. Cover. Touch START. *(Oven cooks: micro, 70, to 120°F; stands: 0, 5 minutes.)*

6 to 10 servings

Recipe No. 114

Baked Ham with Pineapple

Approximate Cooking Time: 28 minutes

- 1 5-pound canned ham
- Whole cloves
- 1 can (8 ounces) crushed pineapple, undrained
- ½ cup firmly-packed brown sugar
- 1 tablespoon fresh lemon juice
- 1 tablespoon cornstarch
- 2 teaspoons dry mustard

Set ham, fat side up, in microproof and heatproof baking dish. Score top in checkerboard pattern and stud with cloves. Insert probe into ham. Place in oven on ceramic tray. Plug in probe. Set recipe number 114. Touch START. *(Oven cooks: micro/convec, 320°F, to 100°F.)*

At Pause, drain excess liquid and set ham aside (do not remove probe). Mix remaining ingredients in small microproof bowl. Place in oven. Touch START. *(Oven cooks: micro, HI, 2 minutes.)*

At Pause, stir. Touch START. *(Oven cooks: micro, HI, 2 minutes.)*

At Pause, spoon mixture over ham, keeping pineapple on top. Place ham in oven. Plug in probe. Touch START. *(Oven cooks: micro/convec, 320°F, to 120°F.)* Let stand 10 minutes before serving.

8 to 10 servings

Recipe No. 115

Scalloped Ham and Potatoes

Cooking Time: 31½ minutes

- 2 large onions, thinly sliced
- 2 tablespoons butter or margarine, divided
- 4 medium red potatoes (about 2 pounds), peeled and thinly sliced, divided
- 1½ to 2 cups cubed cooked ham, divided
- 3 tablespoons all-purpose flour
- ½ teaspoon salt
- ½ teaspoon pepper
- 1½ cups (6 ounces) shredded sharp Cheddar cheese, divided
- Paprika
- 1 cup milk

Combine onions and 2 tablespoons butter in 4-quart microproof casserole. Cover with casserole lid. Place in oven. Set recipe number 115. Touch START. *(Oven cooks: micro, HI, 5 minutes.)*

At Pause, stir. Touch START. *(Oven cooks: micro, HI, 5 minutes.)*

At Pause, remove onions from dish and set aside. Layer half of potatoes and half of ham in bottom of same dish. Combine flour, salt, and pepper in small bowl. Sprinkle half of mixture over ham. Top with half of onion and half of cheese. Sprinkle with paprika. Repeat layering. Pour milk into glass measure. Place in oven. Touch START. *(Oven cooks: micro, HI, 1½ minutes.)*

At Pause, pour milk over ham mixture. Cover casserole. Place in oven. Touch START. *(Oven cooks: micro, HI, 20 minutes.)* Serve immediately.

4 to 6 servings

Recipe No. 116

Ham Slice, Center Cut

Cooking Time: 12 minutes

- ¼ cup apricot nectar
- 1 teaspoon firmly-packed brown sugar
- 1 teaspoon fresh lemon juice
- ½ teaspoon cornstarch
- 1 center cut ham slice (about 1 pound)

Combine all ingredients except ham in small bowl and stir until cornstarch is completely dissolved. Place ham in glass or ceramic baking dish just large enough to contain it. Brush with some of the apricot glaze.

Remove ceramic tray. Place wire rack in lower position. Set recipe number 116. Touch START. *(Oven preheats: convec, 450°F.)*

At Pause, place dish in oven. Touch START. *(Oven cooks: convec, 450°F, 6 minutes.)*

At Pause, turn ham over. Brush with remaining apricot glaze. Touch START. *(Oven cooks: convec, 450°F, 6 minutes.)* Serve immediately.

2 to 3 servings

Recipe No. 117 ⊞

Sausage

Cooking Time: 5 minutes

- 1 package (1 pound) bulk pork sausage

Crumble sausage into 1½-quart microproof casserole. Cover with casserole lid and place in oven. Set recipe number 117. Touch START. *(Oven cooks: micro, HI, 3 minutes.)*

At Pause, stir to break up sausage. Cover. Touch START. *(Oven cooks: micro, HI, 2 minutes.)*

Drain before serving.

2 servings

⊞ *Recipe can be increased.* *See "Quantity", page 12.*

Recipe No. 118 ⊞

Bacon

Cooking Time: 4½ minutes

4 slices bacon

Place bacon on paper towel on microproof plate. Place in oven. Cover with paper towel. Set recipe number 118. Touch START. *(Oven cooks: micro, HI, 4½ minutes.)*

1 serving

Recipe No. 119

Liver, Bacon, and Onions

Cooking Time: 20 minutes

4 slices bacon
1 large onion, sliced in rings
1 pound liver, about ½- to ¾-inch thick

Arrange bacon on microproof rack set over shallow dish. Place in oven. Set recipe number 200. Touch START. *(Oven cooks: micro, HI, 5 minutes.)*

At Pause, set rack and bacon aside. Add onion slices to bacon drippings, stirring to coat. Place in oven. Touch START. *(Oven cooks: micro, HI, 5 minutes.)* Set onion mixture aside.

Place wire rack in lower position. Set recipe number 119. Touch START. *(Oven preheats: convec, 320°F.)* Set liver in shallow microproof and heatproof dish. Surround with onion.

At 320°F, place in oven on wire rack. Touch START. *(Oven cooks: micro/convec, 320°F, 5 minutes.)*

At Pause, turn liver over. Place in oven. Touch START. *(Oven cooks: micro/convec, 320°F, 5 minutes.)* Sprinkle with crumbled bacon and serve.

2 to 3 servings

This is one of several recipes that use the preset functions of another recipe for part of the cooking sequence. Set recipe number 200 first. At the end of that sequence, set recipe number 119.

Recipe No. 120 ⊞

Franks and Beans

Cooking Time: 23 minutes

½ pound bacon, chopped
½ cup chopped onion
1 can (28 ounces) baked beans
¼ cup firmly-packed brown sugar
1 teaspoon Worcestershire sauce
1 pound frankfurters

Place bacon in 2-quart microproof casserole. Place in oven. Set recipe number 120. Touch START. *(Oven cooks: micro, HI, 5 minutes.)*

At Pause, add onion. Cover with casserole lid. Place in oven. Touch START. *(Oven cooks: micro, HI, 3 minutes.)*

At Pause, stir in beans, sugar, and Worcestershire. Set aside.

Cut franks in half lengthwise; score to prevent curling. Arrange half in single layer in 8-inch square microproof and heatproof casserole. Spread half of bean mixture over top. Repeat layering. Place in oven on ceramic tray. Touch START. *(Oven cooks: micro/convec, 350°F, 15 minutes.)*

4 servings

⊞ *Recipe can be increased. See "Quantity", page 12.*

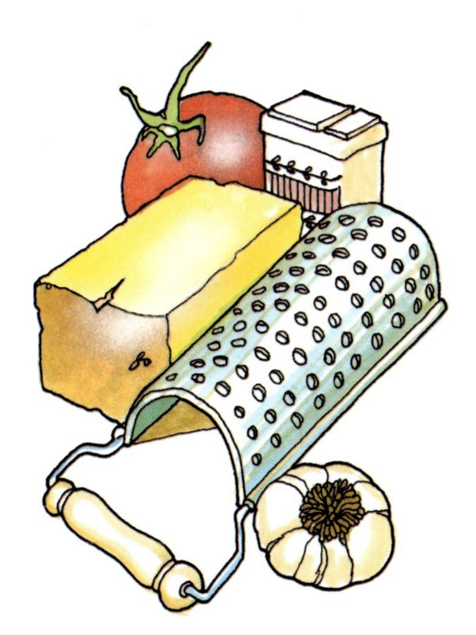

The Best from the Barnyard

Poultry turns out crisper, browner, and juicier than you ever believed possible, thanks to the micro/convection cooking method. If you've never tried your hand at a duck or goose, now's the time. Roast Duckling with Orange Sauce (page 124) is so easy to prepare in this oven that you'll want to serve it often. Don't neglect that budget-wise friend, chicken, of course. Chicken Café (page 117) is a marvel, and Oven-Fried Chicken (page 117) has that finger-lickin' quality we all love. And there are new twists for turkey, too. Breast of Turkey Jardiniere (page 123) is a microwave method treat, as are many recipes that combine poultry with sauce or vegetables, such as Chicken Sukiyaki (page 120) and Chicken Noodle Bake (page 121).

When using the microwave or micro/convection methods, keep in mind that arrangement of the food is important. Drumsticks, for example, are arranged in a circle (above left). Oven-Fried Chicken (page 117) should be turned over with tongs. Hot pads or mitts are essential (above). Breast of Turkey Jardiniere (page 123) is cooked by the microwave method and may be covered with waxed paper (left).

← *Chicken Paupiettes (page 116), Stuffed Tomatoes (page 160)*

Converting Your Recipes

Poultry recipes for which you select the micro/convection method will not need ingredient changes in preparing them for this oven. For the microwave method, compare using a similar recipe in this chapter and review the conversion explanation on page 34. However, for a heat-seared texture, cook by the convection method, removing the ceramic tray and placing the wire rack in the upper position. If you want an extra-crisp, well-browned skin (on your duckling or turkey, for example), cook for additional time using the convection method. Some additional tips:

- ☐ Placing turkey or large chickens breast-side down for the final cooking sequence may reduce crispness in that area but is suggested because it will result in juicy white meat and takes advantage of a natural basting process.
- ☐ To obtain uniform doneness and flavor, cook poultry weighing no more than 14 pounds in the oven. Poultry over 14 pounds should be cooked conventionally.
- ☐ Butter- or oil-injected turkeys often have uneven concentrations of fat and thus cook unevenly. For best results, use uninjected turkeys.
- ☐ Conventional pop-up indicators for doneness do not work correctly with the microwave or micro/convection methods.
- ☐ The temperature probe may be used in cooking whole poultry. Insert the probe in the fleshy part of the inside thigh muscle without touching the bone.
- ☐ Standing time is essential to complete cooking. Allow up to 15 minutes standing time for whole poultry depending upon size. The internal temperature will rise approximately 15°F during 15 minutes standing time. Chicken pieces and casseroles need only 5 minutes standing time.

Using the Defrosting Guide

1. For automatic defrosting instructions, see "From Freezer to Table — Fast," pages 37-42.
2. Use the microwave method.
3. Poultry can *begin* defrosting within the original paper or plastic wrapping. Remove all metal rings, wire twist ties, and any aluminum foil. Since it is difficult to remove metal clamps from legs of frozen turkey, the clamps need not be removed until after defrosting. Be careful, of course, that the metal is at least 1 inch from the oven walls.
4. Remove wrappings as soon as possible and place poultry in microproof dish while defrosting.
5. Defrost in the oven only until not quite thawed. Poultry should be cool in the center when removed from the oven.
6. To speed defrosting during standing time, poultry may be placed in a cold-water bath.
7. Separate cut-up chicken pieces as soon as partially thawed.
8. Wing and leg tips and area near breast bone may begin cooking before the center is thoroughly defrosted. As soon as these areas appear thawed, cover them with small strips of aluminum foil; this foil should be at least 1 inch from oven walls.

DEFROSTING GUIDE — POULTRY

Food	Amount	Minutes (per pound)	Micro Control	Standing Time (in minutes)	Special Notes
Capon	6 - 8 lbs.	2	70	60	Turn over once. Immerse in cold water for standing time.
Chicken, cut up	2 - 3 lbs.	5 - 6	30	10 - 15	Turn every 5 minutes. Separate pieces when partially thawed.
Chicken, whole	2 - 3 lbs.	6 - 8	30	25 - 30	Turn over once. Immerse in cold water for standing time.
Cornish hens	1, 1 - 1½ lbs. 2, 1 - 1½ lbs. ea.	12 - 13 20 - 21	30 30	20 20	Turn over once.
Duckling	4 - 5 lbs.	4	70	30 - 40	Turn over once. Immerse in cold water for standing time.
Turkey	Under 8 lbs. Over 8 lbs.	3 - 5 3 - 5	30 70	60 60	Turn over once. Immerse in cold water for standing time.
Turkey breast	Under 4 lbs. Over 4 lbs.	3 - 5 1 2	30 70 50	20 20	Turn over once. Start at 70, turn over, continue on 50.
Turkey drumsticks	1 - 1½ lbs.	5 - 6	30	15 - 20	Turn every 5 minutes. Separate pieces when partially thawed.
Turkey roast, boneless	2 - 4 lbs.	3 - 4	30	10	Remove from foil pan. Cover with waxed paper.

Note: This chart presents manual or "attended" defrosting techniques. They require more attention from the cook. In some cases, standing time may be reduced by adding another defrosting sequence to the chart recommendations. Such additional defrosting time may be at reduced power levels (5 to 20). You can also reduce standing time by immersing the food in cold water. When using these speed-defrosting techniques, be sure to check the food for warm spots and shield with small strips of aluminum foil.

Using the Cooking Guides

1. Defrost frozen poultry completely before cooking.
2. Remove the giblets, rinse poultry in cool water, and pat dry.
3. When cooking whole birds, place on a roasting rack set in a baking dish that is safe for the cooking method planned. Rack and dish must be microproof for the microwave method; microproof and heatproof for the micro/convection method; heatproof for convection.
4. Turn over, as directed in Guide, halfway through cooking time (between First and Second Cook Times).
5. Toward end of cooking time, small pieces of aluminum foil may be used for shielding to cover legs, wing tips, or breastbone area to prevent overcooking. Foil should be at least 1 inch from oven walls when microwave or micro/convection method is used.
6. Cover poultry pieces, if you wish, with waxed paper when cooking by the microwave method. Use microproof and/or heatproof lids for other methods.
7. Use the Probe Method for the most accurate cooking of whole poultry. Insert the temperature probe in the thickest part of the flesh, as near horizontal as possible, between breast and thigh muscle without touching the bone.
8. Standing time completes the cooking of poultry. Cooked whole birds may be covered with aluminum foil during standing time.

COOKING GUIDE — POULTRY

Food	Programming Method	Programming Setting	First Cook Time	Second Cook Time	Probe Method	Special Notes
Chicken, whole, 3½ - 4 lbs.	micro/convec	400°	5 - 6 min. per lb. breast up turn over	6 min. per lb.	180°	Lower position. Microproof and heatproof dish with trivet.
Chicken pieces, 3½ - 4 lbs.	micro/convec	350°	6 min. skin down turn over	4 - 5 min. per lb.	170°	Lower position. Preheat. Microproof and heatproof baking dish.
Cornish hens, 1 - 1½ lbs.	micro/convec	350°	10 min. breast up turn over	8 - 9 min.	180°	Lower position. Preheat. Microproof and heatproof baking dish.
Duckling, 4 - 5 lbs.	micro/convec	400°	5 - 6 min. breast down turn over	6 min. per lb.	170°	Lower position. For additional browning, cook (convec) at 400°.
Turkey, whole 10 - 12 lbs.	micro/convec	330°	5 - 6 min. per lb. breast up turn over	6 min. per lb.	170°	Lower position. Microproof or heatproof dish with trivet.
Turkey breast, 3 - 4 lbs.	micro/convec	350°	4 min. per lb. skin down turn over	3½ - 4½ min. per lb.	170°	Lower position. Preheat. Microproof and heatproof baking dish.
Turkey roast, boneless, 2 - 4 lbs.	micro/convec	400°	4 min. per lb. turn over	4 - 5 min. per lb.	170°	Lower position. Microproof and heatproof baking dish with trivet.
Turkey parts, 3 lbs.	micro/convec	350°	3 - 4 min. per lb.	4 - 5 min. per lb.		Lower position. Preheat. Microproof and heatproof baking dish. Start skin down.

COOKING GUIDE — CONVENIENCE POULTRY*

Food	Programming Method	Programming Setting	First Cook Time	Second Cook Time	Probe Method	Special Notes
Chicken, frozen fried, 1½ - 2 lbs.	micro/convec	350°	7 min.	7 - 8 min.		Lower position. Preheat. 13×9 microproof and heatproof baking dish.
Chicken Kiev 1 - 2 pieces	micro/convec	350°	10 min.	6 - 8 min.		Lower position. Preheat. Microproof and heatproof baking dish.
Chicken a la King, frozen, 5 oz.	micro	HI	3 - 4 min.			Place on microproof plate.
Creamed chicken, 10½ oz. can	micro	80	2 - 4 min.		150°	Stir once.
Chicken chow mein, 14 - 24 oz. can	micro	80	4 - 6 min.			Stir halfway through cooking time.
Turkey tetrazzini, frozen, 12 oz.	micro	HI	3 - 4 min.			Place on microproof plate.
Turkey, sliced in gravy, frozen, 5 oz.	micro	HI	3 - 5 min.			Slit pouch. Place in microproof dish.

* Due to the tremendous variety in convenience food products available, times given here should be used only as guidelines. We suggest you cook food for the shortest recommended time and then check for doneness. Be sure to check the package for microwave and oven (convec) instructions.

Recipe No. 121

Chicken with Old-Fashioned Dressing

Cooking Time: 38 minutes

- 1/4 cup diced onion
- 1/4 cup diced celery
- 1 tablespoon butter or margarine
- 1 cup diced fresh mushrooms
- 2/3 cup chicken stock
- 1 1/2 cups cornbread stuffing mix
- 2 tablespoons minced parsley
- 1 3- to 4-pound chicken
- 1 slice white bread
- Vegetable oil
- Garlic powder
- Paprika

Combine onion, celery, and butter in 1-quart microproof bowl. Cover with plastic wrap. Place in oven. Set recipe number 09. Touch START. *(Oven cooks: micro, HI, 2 minutes.)*

Place wire rack in lower position. Set recipe number 121. Touch START. *(Oven preheats: convec, 400°F.)* Stir in mushrooms and stock. Add stuffing mix and parsley and blend lightly. Spoon into cavity and neck of chicken. Tuck bread inside cavity to seal opening. Brush chicken with oil. Sprinkle with garlic powder and paprika. Set chicken, breast-side down, on roasting rack. Place rack in microproof and heatproof baking dish.

At 400°F, place in oven. Touch START. *(Oven cooks: micro/convec, 400°F, 17 minutes.)*

At Pause, turn chicken over. Baste with drippings and sprinkle with additional paprika. Place in oven. Touch START. *(Oven cooks: micro/convec, 400°F, 19 minutes.)*

4 to 6 servings

This is one of several recipes that use the preset functions of another recipe for part of the cooking sequence. Set recipe number 09 first. At the end of that sequence, set recipe number 121.

Recipe No. 122

Easy Baked Chicken

Cooking Time: 34 minutes

- 1 broiler-fryer chicken (3 1/2 pounds), giblets removed
- Salt and pepper
- 2 medium stalks celery, cut into 1-inch chunks
- 1 small onion, cut into quarters
- 2 tablespoons butter or margarine, softened
- 1/8 teaspoon thyme

Set recipe number 122. Touch START. *(Oven preheats: convec, 400°F.)* Meanwhile, rinse chicken in cool water and pat dry. Sprinkle cavity with salt and pepper. Place celery and onion inside cavity. Tie legs together with string; tie wings to body. Place chicken, breast-side up, on microproof and heatproof roasting rack in 12×7-inch microproof and heatproof baking dish. Spread with butter and sprinkle with thyme.

At 400°F, place in oven. Touch START. *(Oven cooks: micro/convec, 400°F, 15 minutes.)*

At Pause, turn chicken over. Baste with pan juices. Place in oven. Touch START. *(Oven cooks: micro/convec, 400°F, 19 minutes.)* Serve immediately.

4 servings

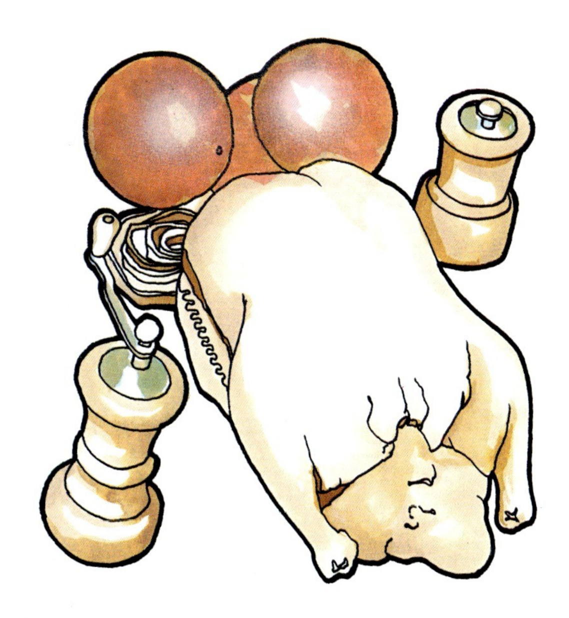

Recipe No. 123

Soy-Sherry Chicken

Approximate Cooking Time: 37 minutes

1 broiler-fryer chicken (3 pounds), giblets removed
1/4 cup soy sauce
1/4 cup dry sherry
1 small onion, sliced
3 slices fresh ginger (1/8 inch thick)

Cut off a 1-inch strip from open end of cooking bag. Rinse chicken in cool water and pat dry. Brush generously with soy sauce. Place chicken, breast-side up, in cooking bag in microproof baking dish. Add sherry, any remaining soy sauce, onion, and ginger. Place in oven. Insert temperature probe into thigh. Tie bag loosely with removed strip. Plug in probe. Set recipe number 123. Touch START. *(Oven cooks: micro, 80, to 180°F; 10, 10 minutes.)*

Turn bag over to baste chicken with juices before removing from bag. Discard ginger. Serve with cooking juices and onion.

4 servings

Recipe No. 124 ⊞

Chicken Paupiettes

Cooking Time: 25 minutes

1/4 cup butter or margarine
2 tablespoons chopped green pepper
2 tablespoons chopped celery
1 clove garlic, minced
1 tablespoon chopped green onion
1/2 teaspoon salt
1/4 teaspoon pepper
2 cups fresh bread crumbs
4 whole boneless chicken breasts, pounded thin
Paprika
Basic White Sauce (page 175)
1 tablespoon chopped parsley

Combine butter, green pepper, celery, garlic, onion, salt, and pepper in 2-quart glass measure or microproof bowl. Cover with plastic wrap. Place in oven. Set recipe number 32. Touch START. *(Oven cooks: micro, HI, 2 minutes.)* Remove from oven and stir. Set aside.

Remove ceramic tray. Place wire rack in lower position. Set recipe number 124. Touch START. *(Oven preheats: convec, 350°F.)* Meanwhile, add bread crumbs to vegetable mixture and fold in lightly. Place one-fourth of mixture in center of each chicken breast and roll up. Arrange seam side down in small microproof and heatproof baking dish. Sprinkle lightly with paprika.

At 350°F, place in oven on wire rack. Touch START. *(Oven cooks: micro/convec, 350°F, 13 minutes; convec, 350°F, 10 minutes.)* Top with hot Basic White Sauce. Sprinkle with parsley and serve.

4 servings

⊞ *Recipe can be increased. See "Quantity", page 12.*

Recipe No. 125

Chicken and Vegetables

Cooking Time: 23 minutes

2 medium carrots
2 medium stalks celery
2 small parsnips, peeled
2 small potatoes, peeled
1 medium onion
2 tablespoons butter or margarine
2 tablespoons minced parsley
1/2 teaspoon salt
1/8 teaspoon paprika
Dash pepper
2 whole chicken breasts (1 pound each), split, skinned, and boned

Cut all vegetables into 1 1/2 × 1/4-inch strips (about 4 cups total). Place in shallow round or oval microproof and heatproof baking dish. Dot with butter. Season with parsley, salt, paprika, and pepper. Cover with plastic wrap. Place in oven. Set recipe number 208. Touch START. *(Oven cooks: micro, HI, 7 minutes.)* Remove vegetables from oven and stir. Set aside.

Place wire rack in lower position. Set

recipe number 125. Touch START. *(Oven preheats: convec, 350°F.)* Arrange chicken over vegetables around outside of dish. Sprinkle with additional paprika. Cover.

At 350°F, place in oven on wire rack. Touch START. *(Oven cooks: micro/convec, 350°F, 8 minutes.)*

At Pause, rotate dish one-half turn. Touch START. *(Oven cooks: micro/convec, 350°F, 8 minutes.)* Spoon vegetables over chicken. Sprinkle with additional parsley and serve.

4 servings

This is one of several recipes that use the preset functions of another recipe for part of the cooking sequence. Set recipe number 208 first. At the end of that sequence, set recipe number 125.

Recipe No. 126

Chicken Café

Cooking Time: 33 minutes

- 1 4-pound frying chicken, cut up or 4 pounds chicken parts
- 1 teaspoon garlic salt
- ½ teaspoon ground ginger
- 1 can (8 ounces) pineapple chunks, drained, syrup reserved
- ½ cup coffee-flavored liqueur
- 1 tablespoon fresh lemon juice
- 2 tablespoons cornstarch
- 2 tablespoons coffee-flavored liqueur
- 1 can (11 ounces) mandarin orange segments, drained
- ¼ cup thinly sliced green onions

Place wire rack in lower position. Set recipe number 126. Touch START. *(Oven preheats: convec, 400°F.)* Rinse chicken and pat dry with paper towels. Arrange skin-side down in 9×13-inch microproof and heatproof baking dish. Sprinkle with garlic salt and ginger.

At 400°F, place in oven on wire rack. Touch START. *(Oven cooks: micro/convec, 400°F, 15 minutes.)*

At Pause, drain off liquid. Turn chicken skin-side up. Combine pineapple syrup, ½ cup liqueur, and lemon juice and pour over chicken. Place in oven. Touch START. *(Oven cooks: micro/convec, 400°F, 15 minutes.)*

At Pause, transfer chicken to platter. Skim off any fat from drippings in dish. Combine cornstarch with 2 tablespoons liqueur and stir until cornstarch is completely dissolved. Blend into drippings. Place in oven. Touch START. *(Oven cooks: micro, HI, 3 minutes.)*

Stir through several times. Add orange and pineapple. Return chicken to dish, spooning sauce and fruit over top. Sprinkle with onions and serve. (If chicken has cooled, reheat: micro, HI, 2 to 3 minutes.)

4 servings

Recipe No. 127

Oven-Fried Chicken

Cooking Time: 30 minutes

- 2 cups cornflake crumbs
- 1 tablespoon cornstarch
- 2 teaspoons onion powder
- ¼ teaspoon salt
- ⅛ teaspoon pepper
- 1 3-pound frying chicken, cut up, rinsed and patted dry
- 1 egg, beaten

Place wire rack in lower position. Set recipe number 127. Touch START. *(Oven preheats: convec, 350°F.)* Meanwhile, combine cornflake crumbs, cornstarch, onion powder, salt, and pepper in large plastic bag. Dip each piece of chicken into egg, then add to crumb mixture, shaking to coat well and cover completely. Arrange skin-side down in 9×13-inch microproof and heatproof baking dish.

At 350°F, place in oven. Touch START. *(Oven cooks: micro/convec, 350°F, 15 minutes.)*

At Pause, turn chicken pieces over. Touch START. *(Oven cooks: micro/convec, 350°F, 15 minutes.)* Serve immediately.

4 servings

Recipe No. 128

Barbecued Chicken

Cooking Time: 30 minutes

1 3- to 4-pound chicken, cut up
½ cup Barbecue Sauce (page 175)

Place wire rack in lower position. Set recipe number 128. Touch START. *(Oven preheats: convec, 350°F.)* Arrange chicken, skin-side down in 9×13-inch microproof and heatproof baking dish. Brush generously with sauce.

At 350°F, place in oven on wire rack. Touch START. *(Oven cooks: micro/convec, 350°F, 15 minutes.)*

At Pause, turn chicken over. Brush again with sauce. Place in oven. Touch START. *(Oven cooks: micro/convec, 350°F, 15 minutes.)* Serve immediately.

4 servings

Recipe No. 129

Chicken Marengo

Cooking Time: 50 minutes

1 broiler-fryer chicken (3½ pounds), cut up
¼ cup vegetable oil
2 cups soft bread crumbs
1 package (3 ounces) spaghetti sauce mix
2 cups sliced mushrooms
1 can (16 ounces) whole tomatoes, broken up
1 cup dry white wine

Rinse chicken and pat dry with paper towels. Brush with oil. Mix bread crumbs and sauce mix in plastic bag. Add chicken 1 piece at a time and shake to coat well. Arrange chicken in 3-quart round or oval microproof and heatproof casserole with thickest portions toward outside of casserole. Place in oven. Set recipe number 129. Touch START. *(Oven cooks: micro/convec, 350°F, 20 minutes.)*

At Pause, add remaining ingredients. Cover with casserole lid. Place in oven. Touch START. *(Oven cooks: micro/convec, 350°F, 30 minutes.)* Serve immediately.

4 to 6 servings

Recipe No. 130

Chicken Milano

Cooking Time: 20 minutes

¼ cup olive oil
1 teaspoon salt
½ teaspoon pepper
¼ teaspoon oregano
¼ teaspoon basil
4 chicken thighs (¼ pound each)
1 cup dry bread crumbs
½ teaspoon paprika
2 medium potatoes, peeled and cut into quarters

Combine oil, salt, pepper, oregano, and basil in shallow dish. Add chicken, rolling to coat all sides. Cover and refrigerate 2 hours.

Place wire rack in lower position. Set recipe number 130. Touch START. *(Oven preheats: convec, 400°F.)* Meanwhile, mix bread crumbs and paprika on plate. Remove 1 piece chicken from marinade and drain. Roll in crumb mixture to coat. Repeat with remaining chicken. Set aside remaining crumb mixture and marinade. Arrange chicken skin-side down in 9-inch round microproof and heatproof casserole with thickest portions toward outside of dish. Cut ends from potatoes to make quarters even; wipe dry. Roll potatoes in remaining marinade to coat, adding more oil to marinade if necessary. Arrange potatoes around chicken.

At 400°F, place in oven on wire rack. Touch START. *(Oven cooks: micro/convec, 400°F, 10 minutes.)*

At Pause, turn chicken and potatoes over. Sprinkle with remaining crumb mixture. Touch START. *(Oven cooks: micro/convec, 400°F, 10 minutes.)* Serve immediately.

2 servings

Recipe No. 131

Tarragon Grilled Chicken

Cooking Time: 30 minutes

- 1/4 cup olive oil
- 1/4 cup dry sherry or chicken broth
- 1 tablespoon onion flakes
- 1 clove garlic, minced
- 1 teaspoon salt
- 1/2 teaspoon tarragon
- 1/8 teaspoon white pepper
- 1 broiler-fryer chicken (3 pounds), quartered

Place wire rack in lower position. Set recipe number 131. Touch START. *(Oven preheats: convec, 350°F.)* Meanwhile, combine all ingredients except chicken. Set aside. Arrange chicken, skin-side down, in shallow oval microproof and heatproof baking dish with thickest portions toward outside of dish. Brush with half of the oil mixture.

At 350°F, place in oven on wire rack. Touch START. *(Oven cooks: micro/convec, 350°F, 15 minutes.)*

At Pause, turn chicken over. Brush generously with remaining oil mixture. Touch START. *(Oven cooks: micro/convec, 350°F, 15 minutes.)* Serve immediately.

4 servings

Recipe No. 132

Chicken Suprême

Cooking Time: 1 hour 5 minutes

- 5 slices bacon
- 1 can (10 3/4 ounces) cream of onion soup, undiluted
- 1/2 cup dry red wine or dry sherry
- 1/2 cup chopped onions
- 1 clove garlic, minced
- 1 tablespoon minced parsley
- 1 1/2 teaspoons chicken bouillon granules
- 1/2 teaspoon salt
- 1/4 teaspoon pepper
- 1/4 teaspoon thyme
- 6 small potatoes, peeled and cut in half
- 2 medium carrots, thinly sliced
- 1 broiler-fryer chicken (2 1/2 pounds), cut up
- 1/2 pound mushrooms, sliced

Arrange bacon on paper towel on microproof plate. Place in oven. Cover with paper towel. Set recipe number 132. Touch START. *(Oven cooks: micro, HI, 5 minutes.)*

At Pause, remove from oven; crumble bacon and set aside. Combine soup, wine, onion, garlic, parsley, bouillon, and seasonings; set aside. Place potatoes and carrots in 3-quart microproof and heatproof casserole. Arrange chicken on top, skin-side down, with thickest parts toward outside of casserole. Pour soup mixture over top. Cover with casserole lid and place in oven. Touch START. *(Oven cooks: micro/convec, 320°F, 30 minutes.)*

At Pause, rearrange chicken, bringing bottom pieces to top, skin-side up. Sprinkle with bacon and mushrooms. Cover. Touch START. *(Oven cooks: micro/convec, 320°F, 30 minutes.)*

4 to 6 servings

Recipe No. 133 ⊞

Chicken Wings Parmesan

Cooking Time: 14 minutes

- 6 chicken wings
- 10 buttery crackers
- 1/4 cup grated Parmesan cheese
- 3 tablespoons minced parsley
- 1 teaspoon garlic powder
- 1/8 teaspoon pepper
- 1/2 teaspoon paprika
- 1/2 teaspoon salt
- 1/4 cup butter or margarine, melted

Place wire rack in lower position. Set recipe number 133. Touch START. *(Oven preheats: convec, 350°F.)* Meanwhile, cut chicken wings in half, discarding tips. Rinse wings, pat dry with paper towels and set aside. Mix crackers in blender or food processor to fine crumbs. Pour into bowl. Add all remaining ingredients except melted butter and blend well. Dip chicken in melted butter, then roll in crumbs, coating evenly. Arrange chicken pieces, skin-side up, in spoke pattern in 9-inch round microproof and heatproof pie plate with largest portions of wings toward rim.

At 350°F, place in oven on wire rack. Touch START. *(Oven cooks: micro/convec, 350°F, 14 minutes.)* Serve hot.

2 to 4 servings

⊞ *Recipe can be increased. See "Quantity", page 12.*

Recipe No. 134

Chicken Sukiyaki

Cooking Time: 13 minutes

- 1/2 cup soy sauce
- 1/2 cup chicken broth
- 1/4 cup dry sherry
- 2 tablespoons sugar
- 2 chicken breasts (1/2 pound each), skinned, boned, and cut into 1/2-inch slices
- 1 pound spinach, stems removed
- 1/2 pound bean sprouts
- 1/4 pound pea pods
- 1/2 cup sliced celery
- 1 medium onion, thinly sliced
- 1 medium bunch green onions, cut into 3-inch strips
- 6 small mushrooms, sliced

Combine soy sauce, broth, sherry, and sugar in 2-cup glass measure; stir until sugar is dissolved. Place in oven. Set recipe number 134. Touch START. *(Oven cooks: micro, HI, 2 minutes.)*

At Pause, remove from oven. Combine remaining ingredients in 3-quart microproof casserole; toss lightly. Pour sauce mixture over chicken mixture. Cover with casserole lid and place in oven. Touch START. *(Oven cooks: micro, HI, 4 minutes.)*

At Pause, stir. Cover. Touch START. *(Oven cooks: micro, HI, 3 minutes.)*

At Pause, stir. Cover. Touch START. *(Oven cooks: micro, HI, 4 minutes.)*

Pass additional soy sauce at table.

4 servings

Recipe No. 135 ⊞

Chicken à la King

Cooking Time: 7 minutes

- ¼ cup butter or margarine
- 3 tablespoons all-purpose flour
- 1 can (10¾ ounces) cream of mushroom soup, undiluted
- ¼ cup milk
- 2 teaspoons chicken bouillon granules
- Pinch pepper
- 2 cups cubed cooked chicken or turkey
- ½ cup peas
- 4 to 6 English muffins, split and toasted

Place butter in 1-quart glass measure. Place in oven. Set recipe number 135. Touch START. *(Oven cooks: micro, HI,* 1 *minute.)*

At Pause, add flour, 1 tablespoon at a time, stirring constantly until smooth. Blend in soup, milk, bouillon, and pepper. Cover with plastic wrap. Place in oven. Touch START. *(Oven cooks: micro, HI,* 1 *minute.)*

At Pause, stir. Touch START. *(Oven cooks: micro, HI,* 1 *minute.)*

At Pause, add chicken and peas. Cover. Place in oven. Touch START. *(Oven cooks: micro, HI,* 4 *minutes.)* Spoon over English muffins and serve.

4 to 6 servings

Recipe No. 136

Chicken Noodle Bake

Cooking Time: 13 minutes

- 3 cups cubed cooked chicken
- 1½ cups broken uncooked narrow egg noodles
- 1 cup chicken stock
- ½ cup milk
- ½ teaspoon salt
- ⅛ teaspoon pepper
- 1 cup (4 ounces) shredded Cheddar cheese
- ½ cup sliced stuffed green olives

Combine chicken, uncooked noodles, stock, milk, salt, and pepper in 2-quart microproof casserole and mix lightly. Cover with casserole lid. Place in oven. Set recipe number 136. Touch START. *(Oven cooks: micro,* 70, 5 *minutes.)*

At Pause, stir. Touch START. *(Oven cooks: micro,* 70, 5 *minutes.)*

At Pause, blend in cheese and olives. Cover. Place in oven. Touch START. *(Oven cooks: micro, HI,* 3 *minutes.)* Serve immediately.

4 to 6 servings

Recipe No. 137

Chicken Liver Canton

Cooking Time: 17 minutes

- ½ pound chicken livers, rinsed and drained
- ½ cup sliced celery
- ¼ cup chopped onion
- 3 tablespoons butter or margarine, divided
- 1 envelope (1¾ ounces) mushroom gravy mix
- 1 can (16 ounces) Chinese vegetables
- 1 can (8 ounces) sliced water chestnuts, drained
- 1 tablespoon soy sauce

Cut liver into bite-size pieces; discard membranes; set aside. Combine celery, onion, and 1 tablespoon butter in 3-quart microproof casserole. Cover with casserole lid and place in oven. Set recipe number 137. Touch START. *(Oven cooks: micro, HI,* 4 *minutes.)*

At Pause, stir in gravy mix. Add Chinese vegetables, water chestnuts, and soy sauce; stir until gravy mix is dissolved. Cover. Touch START. *(Oven cooks: micro, HI, 7 minutes.)*

At Pause, remove from oven; set aside. Place liver and remaining 2 tablespoons butter in 4-cup glass measure. Place in oven. Cover with waxed paper. Touch START. *(Oven cooks: micro,* 50, 4 *minutes.)*

At Pause, remove from oven; drain. Carefully stir liver into vegetable mixture. Cover and place in oven. Touch START. *(Oven cooks: micro, HI, 2 minutes.)*

Let stand, covered, 5 minutes. Serve over hot rice and sprinkle with chow mein noodles.

4 to 6 servings

Recipe No. 138

Turkey with Cornbread Stuffing

Approximate Cooking Time: 1 hour 15 minutes

- ½ cup diced onions
- ½ cup diced celery
- 2 tablespoons butter or margarine
- 2 cups diced mushrooms
- 1 cup chicken stock, turkey stock, or bouillon
- 2 cups cornbread stuffing mix
- 1 10- to 12-pound turkey, cleaned, rinsed, and patted dry
- Vegetable oil
- Paprika

Combine onion, celery, and butter in 3-quart microproof bowl. Cover with plastic wrap. Place in oven. Set recipe number 13. Touch START. *(Oven cooks: micro, HI, 4 minutes.)*

At Pause, stir in mushrooms. Cover. Place in oven. Touch START. *(Oven cooks: micro, HI, 3 minutes.)*

Add stock and stuffing mix and blend lightly, adding more liquid if mixture seems too dry. Spoon stuffing into cavity of turkey. Tuck in wings and tie legs together with string. Rub outside with oil and sprinkle with paprika. Set microproof roasting rack in shallow microproof and heatproof baking dish. Place turkey, breast-side up, on rack. Place in oven on ceramic tray. Set recipe number 138. Touch START. *(Oven cooks: micro/convec, 350°F, 15 minutes.)*

At Pause, rotate dish one-half turn. Touch START. *(Oven cooks: micro/convec, 350°F, 15 minutes.)*

At Pause, baste turkey with drippings. Turn breast-side down. Place in oven. Touch START. *(Oven cooks: micro/convec, 350°F, 15 minutes.)*

At Pause, insert probe into fleshy part of thigh. Plug in probe. Touch START. *(Oven cooks: micro/convec, 350°F, to 170°F.)* Tent turkey with aluminum foil and let stand 15 minutes before serving.

8 to 10 servings

Recipe No. 139

Turkey with Nut Stuffing

Approximate Cooking Time: 1 hour 15 minutes

- 1 turkey (12 pounds), neck and giblets removed
- 1 cup chicken broth
- ½ cup butter or margarine
- 2 medium stalks celery, thinly sliced
- 1 large onion, chopped
- 10 cups day-old bread crumbs or ½-inch cubes
- 1 cup coarsely chopped walnuts or pecans
- ¼ cup chopped parsley
- 1 teaspoon poultry seasoning
- ½ teaspoon salt

Rinse turkey in cool water and pat dry; set aside. Place broth and butter in 3-quart microproof casserole. Add celery and onion. Cover and place in oven. Set recipe number 139. Touch START. *(Oven cooks: micro, HI, 5 minutes.)*

At Pause, remove from oven. Add bread crumbs, nuts, parsley, poultry seasoning, and salt; stir lightly. Stuff neck opening with part of stuffing. Secure neck skin with strong wooden toothpicks or skewers. Stuff cavity with remaining stuffing. Tie legs together with strong string; tie wings to body. Place turkey, breast-side up, on microproof roasting rack in large baking dish. Place in oven. Touch START. *(Oven cooks: micro/convec, 350°F, 30 minutes.)*

At Pause, turn over; drain. Touch START. *(Oven cooks: micro/convec, 350°F, 15 minutes.)*

At Pause, baste with pan juices. Rotate pan one-quarter turn. Insert temperature probe in fleshy part of thigh. Plug in probe. Touch START. *(Oven cooks: micro/convec, 350°F, to 170°F.)*

Remove from oven. Cover with aluminum foil. Let stand 10 minutes before carving.

6 to 8 servings

Recipe No. 140

Breast of Turkey Jardinière

Cooking Time: 25 minutes

- 1 medium carrot, cut into thin 2″ strips
- 1 celery stalk, cut into thin 2″ strips
- 1 small onion, cut into thin 2″ strips
- 1 very small potato, cut into thin 2″ strips
- 1 tablespoon minced parsley
- 2 tablespoons butter or margarine
- Salt and pepper to taste
- ½ turkey breast (3 to 4 pounds), boned and skinned (if desired)
- Paprika

Arrange carrot, celery, onion, potato, and parsley close together in microproof and heatproof casserole just large enough to accommodate all ingredients. Dot with butter. Season lightly with salt and pepper. Cover with casserole lid. Place in oven. Set recipe number 2. Touch START. *(Oven cooks: micro, HI, 5 minutes.)* Remove dish from oven. Set aside.

Set recipe number 140. Touch START. *(Oven preheats: convec, 350°F.)* Set turkey breast on vegetables. Sprinkle with paprika. Cover.

At 350°F, place in oven. Touch START. *(Oven cooks: micro/convec, 350°F, 10 minutes.)*

At Pause, rotate dish one-half turn. Touch START. *(Oven cooks: micro/convec, 350°F, 10 minutes.)* Serve immediately.

1 to 2 servings

Recipe No. 141

Glazed Turkey Legs

Cooking Time: 21½ minutes

- ⅓ cup honey
- 1 teaspoon grated lemon peel
- 1 teaspoon lemon juice
- 1 teaspoon cornstarch
- ¼ teaspoon bottled brown sauce
- 2 turkey legs (2½ to 3 pounds)

Stir honey, lemon peel, lemon juice, cornstarch, and brown sauce in small microproof bowl until cornstarch is dissolved. Place in oven. Set recipe number 34. Touch START. *(Oven cooks: micro, HI, 1½ minutes.)* Remove glaze from oven. Set aside.

Place wire rack in lower position. Set recipe number 141. Touch START. *(Oven preheats: convec, 350°F.)* Place turkey legs in 10-inch round or 9-inch microproof and heatproof square casserole.

At 350°F, place in oven on wire rack. Touch START. *(Oven cooks: micro/convec, 350°F, 10 minutes.)*

At Pause, brush with glaze. Turn turkey over and brush again with glaze. Touch START. *(Oven cooks: micro/convec, 350°F, 10 minutes.)* Serve immediately.

2 to 4 servings

This is one of several recipes that use the preset functions of another recipe for part of the cooking sequence. Set recipe number 34 first. At the end of that sequence, set recipe number 141.

Recipe No. 142

Roast Duckling

Approximate Cooking Time: 45 minutes

1 4- to 5-pound duckling
1 teaspoon salt
¼ teaspoon pepper
1 small onion, quartered
Leaves from 2 to 3 celery stalks
Orange Sauce (page 179)

Set recipe number 142. Touch START. *(Oven preheats: convec, 400°F.)* Meanwhile, rinse duckling thoroughly in cool water; pat dry. Sprinkle cavity with salt and pepper. Set onion and celery leaves inside cavity. Tie legs and wings together with string. Prick skin around leg and wing joints with fork. Arrange duckling, breast-side down, on rack in microproof and heatproof baking dish.

At 400°F, place in oven on ceramic tray. Touch START. *(Oven cooks: micro/convec, 400°F, 15 minutes.)*

At Pause, pour off excess fat. Turn duckling over and prick entire surface with fork to allow fat to drain. Insert probe in breast close to leg. Place in oven. Plug in probe. Touch START. *(Oven cooks: micro/convec, 400°F, to 170°F; micro/convec, 400°F, 20 minutes.)* Serve with Orange Sauce.

2 to 4 servings

Recipe No. 143

Roast Raspberry Duckling

Approximate Cooking Time: 55 minutes

1 duckling (4 pounds), giblets removed
1 carrot, peeled and cut into chunks
1 medium onion, cut into quarters
1 jar (10 ounces) raspberry jelly
¼ cup raspberry liqueur
2 tablespoons fresh lemon juice

Rinse duckling in cool water and pat dry. Place carrot and onion pieces in body cavity. Secure neck skin with wooden toothpicks or skewers. Tie legs together with string; tie wings to body. Pierce skin all over to allow fat to drain. Place duckling, breast-side up, on microwave roasting rack in 12×7-inch microproof and heatproof baking dish; set aside.

Remove ceramic tray and place wire rack in lower position. Set recipe number 143. Touch START. *(Oven preheats: convec, 400°F.)*

At 400°F, place duckling in oven. Touch START. *(Oven cooks: micro/convec, 400°F, 15 minutes.)*

Meanwhile, combine remaining ingredients in small bowl and stir until smooth.

At Pause, turn duckling over. Insert temperature probe. Plug in probe. Brush duck with glaze. Touch START. *(Oven cooks: micro/convec, 400°F, to 170°F.)*

At Pause, remove probe. Turn duckling over. Baste. Place in oven. Touch START. *(Oven cooks: convec, 400°F, 10 minutes.)*

2 servings

Roast Duckling with Orange Sauce (page 179) →

Poivre
Oranges, Sugar, Lemons.
Lemoene, Suiker, Suurlemoen.
Vervaardig in RSA

Recipe No. 144

Cornish Hens with Wild Rice Dressing

Approximate Cooking Time: 32 minutes

- ¾ cup chopped onion
- ¼ cup butter or margarine
- 1 package (10 ounces) frozen white and wild rice, thawed
- ½ cup coarsely chopped mushrooms
- 2 Cornish hens (1½ pounds each)
- Salt
- Paprika

Combine onion and butter in 1-quart microproof bowl. Set recipe number 13. Touch START. *(Oven cooks: micro, HI, 4 minutes.)*

At Pause, stir in rice and mushrooms. Cover with plastic wrap. Place in oven. Touch START. *(Oven cooks: micro, HI, 3 minutes.)* Stir and set aside.

Place wire rack in lower position. Set recipe number 144. Touch START. *(Oven preheats: convec, 450°F.)* Rinse hens and pat dry with paper towel. Sprinkle cavities with salt and stuff with dressing. Tie legs with string. Place hens breast-side up in microproof and heatproof baking dish. Sprinkle with paprika.

At 450°F, place in oven. Touch START. *(Oven cooks: micro/convec, 350°F, 15 minutes.)*

At Pause, turn hens over and sprinkle with paprika. Insert temperature probe into fleshy part of thigh or breast. Plug in probe. Touch START. *(Oven cooks: micro/convec, 350°F, about 10 minutes to 170°F.)* Remove from oven. Cover with aluminum foil. Let stand 5 minutes before serving. Remove string. Serve breast side up.

2 servings

Recipe No. 145

Heavenly Cornish Hens

Cooking Time: 20 minutes

- 2 Cornish hens (1½ pounds each)
- ¼ cup melted butter
- ½ teaspoon paprika
- ½ teaspoon salt
- ⅛ teaspoon pepper
- ⅛ teaspoon garlic powder

Split hens lengthwise; remove backbones. Rinse hens in cool water and pat dry. Mix butter and remaining ingredients in small bowl. Brush over hens. Set hens, breast-side up, in round or oval microproof and heatproof baking dish, with thickest portion of hens toward outside of dish.

Place wire rack in upper position. Set recipe number 145. Touch START. *(Oven preheats: convec, 450°F.)*

At Pause, place in oven. Touch START. *(Oven cooks: micro/convec, 350°F, 10 minutes.)*

At Pause, baste hens with drippings. Turn hens over and baste again. Touch START. *(Oven cooks: micro/convec, 350°F, 10 minutes.)* Serve immediately.

4 servings

At the Wharf

Any way you prefer to cook fish or shellfish will be easy and quick with this oven. There are well-defined techniques for whichever method you choose: microwave for poaching or steaming; micro/convection for baking; and convection for searing at high temperatures. No matter what the method, one thing is certain: seafood never tasted as fresh and good. Salmon Ring (page 137), Mountain Trout (page 134), Tuna-Mushroom Patties (page 138), and Scampi (page 131) will be favorites. For best results, prepare seafood just before serving. When planning a fish dinner, have all ingredients at hand before you start to cook.

Shrimp and Mountain Trout are shown arranged for cooking. Au gratin dishes are especially nice, as used for the trout, but any oval microproof and heatproof dish is fine (top left). Breaded Fish Fillets (page 137) are cooked by the convection method in a metal pan on the wire rack, lower position (top right). Shellfish cooks so quickly that arrangement is especially important for even doneness. Correct arrangements for lobster tails and clams are illustrated (above left and above right).

Converting Your Recipes

Seafood is delicate, with no muscle or connective tissue that needs tenderizing by a lengthy cooking process. Gentle cooking is required. The microwave method treats seafood with the necessary speed and gentleness that preserves moisture. Little or no evaporation occurs because no hot air is present to dry the surface. Shrimp should be cooked until it just turns pink (and no water is needed). Fish needs only enough cooking time to turn opaque and will toughen if overcooked.

For fish steaks with heat-seared flavor and appearance, or for fish that is coated with your favorite mix of crumbs or crackers and seasoning, use a preheated oven (450°F is best) and the convection method. Remove the ceramic tray and place the wire rack in the upper position. Do not cover. No alterations are necessary to suit a conventional seafood recipe to this oven. Simply consult the Guides or find a similar recipe to help you determine the cooking time, and be conservative! Remember how quickly seafood cooks and that there's no way to rescue overcooked food. Look to these tips for additional clues to seafood success.

- ☐ Seafood can be steamed in its own natural juice; little or no liquid should ever be required.
- ☐ Cook fish covered unless it is coated with crumbs, which seal in the juices.
- ☐ Fish is done when the flesh becomes opaque and barely flakes with a fork.
- ☐ Shellfish is done when flesh is opaque and just firm.
- ☐ Shellfish come in their own cooking containers which respond well to the microwave method. Clam and mussel shells open before your eyes. Shrimp, crab, and lobster shells turn pink.
- ☐ To remove seafood odors from the oven, combine 1 cup water with lemon juice and a few cloves in a small bowl. Set in oven and cook (micro) on HI for several minutes.

Using the Defrosting Guide

1. For automatic defrosting instructions, see "From Freezer to Table — Fast," pages 37-42.
2. Use the microwave method.
3. Remove wrapping and place fish on microproof dish.
4. To prevent the outer edges from drying out or beginning to cook, remove fish from oven before it has completely thawed.
5. Finish defrosting under cold running water, separating fillets.

Using the Cooking Guide

1. Defrost seafood fully; then cook.
2. Remove original wrapping. Rinse under cold running water.
3. Place seafood in baking dish selected to meet needs of the cooking method you plan to use. Place thick edges of fillets and steaks and thick ends of shellfish toward the outer edge of the dish.
4. Cover dish.
5. Test often during the cooking period to avoid overcooking.
6. Method and time are the same for seafood in the shell or without the shell.

COOKING GUIDE — SEAFOOD AND FISH

Food	Micro Control	Time (in minutes)	Probe Method	Standing Time (in minutes)	Special Notes
Fish fillets, 1 lb. ½ inch thick, 2 lbs.	HI HI	4 - 5 7 - 8	140° 140°	4 - 5 4 - 5	12 × 7-inch microproof dish, covered.
Fish steaks, 1 inch thick, 1 lb.	HI	5 - 6	140°	5 - 6	12 × 7-inch microproof dish, covered.
Whole fish 8 - 10 oz. 1½ - 2 lbs.	 HI HI	 3½ - 4 5 - 7	 170° 170°	 3 - 4 5	Appropriate shallow microproof dish.
Crab legs 8 - 10 oz. 16 - 20 oz.	 HI HI	 3 - 4 5 - 6		 5 5	Appropriate shallow microproof dish, covered. Turn once.
Shrimp, scallops 8 oz. 1 lb.	 70 70	 3 - 4 5 - 7			Appropriate shallow microproof dish, covered. Rearrange halfway.
Snails, clams, oysters, 12 oz.	70	3 - 4			Shallow microproof dish, covered. Rearrange halfway.
Lobster tails 1: 8 oz. 2: 8 oz. each 3: 8 oz. each	 HI HI HI	 3 - 4 5 - 6 9 - 11		 5 5 5	Shallow microproof dish. Split shell to reduce curling.

For a delicious preparation alternate for lobster tails, see Lobster Suprême, page 130.

DEFROSTING GUIDE — SEAFOOD

Food	Amount	Micro Control	Time (in minutes)	Standing Time (in minutes)	Special Notes
Fish fillets	1 lb 2 lbs.	30 30	4 - 6 5 - 7	4 - 5 5	Carefully separate fillets under cold water.
Fish steaks	1 lb.	30	4 - 6	5	Carefully separate steaks under cold running water.
Whole fish	8 - 10 oz. 1½ - 2 lbs.	30 30	4 - 6 5 - 7	5 5	Shallow dish, shape of fish determines size. Should be icy when removed. Finish at room temperature. Cover head with aluminum foil.
Lobster tails	8 oz.	30	5 - 7	5	Remove from package to baking dish.
Crab legs	8 - 10 oz.	30	3 - 4	5	Break apart.
Crab meat	6 oz.	30	4 - 5	5	Defrost in package on dish. Break apart.
Shrimp	1 lb.	30	3 - 4	5	Remove from package to dish. Spread loosely in baking dish and rearrange during thawing as necessary.
Scallops	1 lb.	30	6 - 8	5	Defrost in package if in block; spread out on baking dish if in pieces. Turn over and rearrange during thawing as necessary.
Oysters	12 oz.	30	3 - 4	5	Remove from package to dish. Turn over and rearrange during thawing as necessary.

Recipe No. 146 ⊞

Crab Florentine

Cooking Time: 30½ minutes

1 package (10 ounces) frozen chopped spinach
½ cup chopped onions
3 tablespoons butter or margarine
6 eggs, beaten
1 cup cream
3 tablespoons dry white wine
¼ teaspoon salt
⅛ teaspoon pepper
⅛ teaspoon cayenne
6 ounces chopped crabmeat, rinsed and drained
¼ cup grated Parmesan cheese

Place unopened package of spinach upright on microproof plate. Set recipe number 258. Place plate in oven on ceramic tray. Touch START. *(Oven cooks: micro, HI, 2½ minutes.)*

At Pause, turn spinach package on its side. Touch START. *(Oven cooks: micro, HI, 2 minutes.)*

At Pause, remove spinach from oven. Set aside. Combine onion and butter in 2-quart microproof bowl. Cover with plastic wrap. Place in oven on ceramic tray. Touch START. *(Oven cooks: micro, HI, 3 minutes.)* Let cool slightly. Add eggs, cream, wine, salt, pepper, and cayenne and mix well.

Place wire rack in lower position. Set recipe number 146. Touch START. *(Oven preheats: convec, 330°F.)* Meanwhile, drain spinach well and squeeze dry. Blend into onion-eggs mixture. Stir in crab. Turn into microproof and heatproof au gratin or baking dish and sprinkle with cheese.

At 330°F, place in oven on wire rack. Touch START. *(Oven cooks: micro/convec, 330°F, 8 minutes.)*

At Pause, rotate dish one-quarter turn. Touch START. *(Oven cooks: micro/convec, 330°F, 10 minutes; stands: 0, 5 minutes.)*

6 to 8 servings

⊞ *Recipe can be increased. See "Quantity", page 12.*

Recipe No. 147

Crab Imperial

Cooking Time: 12 minutes

½ cup chopped onions
2 tablespoons butter or margarine
1½ cups light cream
1 cup sliced mushrooms
3 tablespoons all-purpose flour
3 tablespoons dry white wine
¼ teaspoon salt
⅛ teaspoon pepper
2 egg yolks, lightly beaten
1½ cups crabmeat chunks

Place onion and butter in 2-quart glass measure. Place in oven. Set recipe number 147. Touch START. *(Oven cooks: micro, HI, 3 minutes.)*

At Pause, add cream, mushrooms, flour, wine, salt, and pepper; blend well. Touch START. *(Oven cooks: micro, HI, 5 minutes.)*

At Pause, blend in egg yolks. Touch START. *(Oven cooks: micro, HI, 2 minutes.)*

At Pause, add crabmeat; blend well. Touch START. *(Oven cooks: micro, 70, 2 minutes.)*

Serve in au gratin dishes, individual custard cups, ramekins, or shells.

4 to 6 servings

Recipe No. 148

Lobster Suprême

Cooking Time: 7½ minutes

2 8-ounce lobster tails
2 tablespoons butter or margarine, melted
Clarified Butter (page 178)
Lemon wedges

Place wire rack in lower position. Set recipe number 148. Touch START. *(Oven preheats: convec, 450°F.)* Split each lobster tail through top shell and carefully remove meat, leaving small end attached to shell and setting meat on top of shell. Place lobster in microproof and heatproof baking dish. Brush meat with melted butter.

At 450°F, place in oven on wire rack. Touch START. *(Oven cooks: micro/convec, 450°F, 7½ minutes.)* Serve immediately with Clarified Butter and lemon wedges.

2 servings

Recipe No. 149 ⊞

Scampi

Cooking Time: 5 minutes

- 3 tablespoons vegetable oil
- 2 large cloves garlic, minced
- 3 tablespoons minced parsley
- 2 tablespoons dry white wine
- 1/8 teaspoon paprika
- 3/4 pound large shrimp, shelled, deveined, and butterflied, tails intact
- Juice of 1/2 medium lemon
- Salt and pepper to taste

Combine oil and garlic in oval microproof baking dish just large enough to hold all ingredients. Place in oven. Set recipe number 149. Touch START. *(Oven cooks: micro, HI, 1 minute.)*

At Pause, add parsley, wine, and paprika. Touch START. *(Oven cooks: micro, HI, 1 minute.)*

At Pause, add shrimp, lemon juice, salt, and pepper; stir to coat well. Arrange shrimp with tails toward center of dish. Cover with waxed paper. Touch START. *(Oven cooks: micro, HI, 1½ minutes.)*

At Pause, stir. Cover. Touch START. *(Oven cooks: micro, HI, 1½ minutes.)*

Garnish with parsley.

2 servings

Recipe No. 150

Shrimp Veracruz

Cooking Time: 12 minutes

- 1 large onion, cut into chunks
- 1 large green pepper, seeded and cut into chunks
- 2 cloves garlic, crushed
- 2 tablespoons vegetable oil
- 1 can (8 ounces) tomato sauce
- 1/4 cup dry white wine
- 1/2 teaspoon oregano
- 1/2 teaspoon salt
- 1/4 teaspoon cumin
- Dash hot pepper sauce
- 1 pound jumbo shrimp, shelled and deveined

Combine onion, green pepper, garlic, and oil in shallow oval microproof baking dish. Place in oven. Set recipe number 150. Touch START. *(Oven cooks: micro, HI, 3 minutes.)*

At Pause, stir through several times. Add tomato sauce, wine, oregano, salt, cumin, and hot pepper sauce. Touch START. *(Oven cooks: micro, HI, 5 minutes.)*

At Pause, add shrimp. Spoon sauce over shrimp. Touch START. *(Oven cooks: micro, HI, 2 minutes.)*

At Pause, stir. Cover. Touch START. *(Oven cooks: micro, HI, 2 minutes.)*

Garnish with parsley, and serve over hot rice or noodles.

4 servings

Recipe No. 151

Shrimp Chow Mein

Cooking Time: 22 minutes

- 1 medium onion, chopped
- 1 cup sliced celery
- 1 green pepper, seeded and cut into thin strips
- 2 tablespoons butter or margarine
- 1 pound fresh bean sprouts, or 1 can (16 ounces) bean sprouts, drained
- 1 can (8 ounces) sliced water chestnuts, drained
- 8 to 10 ounces cooked deveined shelled shrimp
- ½ cup sliced mushrooms
- 2 tablespoons chopped pimiento
- 3 tablespoons cornstarch
- 3 tablespoons soy sauce
- 1 cup water
- 2 teaspoons chicken bouillon granules

Combine onion, celery, green pepper, and butter in 2-quart microproof casserole. Cover with casserole lid and place in oven. Set recipe number 151. Touch START. *(Oven cooks: micro, HI,* 10 *minutes.)*

At Pause, remove from oven. Add bean sprouts, water chestnuts, shrimp, mushrooms, and pimiento; set aside. Dissolve cornstarch in soy sauce in 4-cup glass measure. Add water and bouillon; blend well. Place soy sauce mixture in oven. Touch START. *(Oven cooks: micro, HI,* 3 *minutes.)*

At Pause, stir. Touch START. *(Oven cooks: micro, HI,* 3 *minutes.)*

At Pause, remove from oven. Stir sauce into shrimp mixture. Cover and place in oven. Touch START. *(Oven cooks: micro, HI,* 6 *minutes.)*

Stir through before serving over hot rice, topped with chow mein noodles.

5 to 6 servings

Recipe No. 152

Shrimp Creole

Cooking Time: 15 minutes

- 4 green onions, thinly sliced
- ½ cup chopped green pepper
- ¼ cup chopped celery
- 1 clove garlic, minced
- 2 tablespoons butter or margarine
- 1 can (16 ounces) whole tomatoes, drained and chopped
- 1 can (6 ounces) tomato paste
- 2 teaspoons parsley flakes
- 1 teaspoon salt
- ¼ teaspoon cayenne
- 1 package (10 ounces) frozen cooked shrimp, thawed

Combine onions, green pepper, celery, garlic, and butter in 2-quart microproof casserole. Cover with casserole lid and place in oven. Set recipe number 152. Touch START. *(Oven cooks: micro, HI,* 3 *minutes.)*

At Pause, add remaining ingredients except shrimp; blend well. Cover. Touch START. *(Oven cooks: micro,* 80, 5 *minutes.)*

At Pause, add shrimp; blend well. Cover. Touch START. *(Oven cooks: micro,* 80, 3 *minutes.)*

At Pause, stir. Cover. Touch START. *(Oven cooks: micro,* 80, 4 *minutes.)*

Stir before serving over hot rice.

4 to 6 servings

Lobster Supreme (page 130), →
Coquilles St. Jacques (page 134)

Recipe No. 153

Coquilles St. Jacques

Cooking Time: 17 minutes

- 2 shallots, finely minced
- 4 tablespoons butter or margarine, divided
- 1 pound scallops, rinsed and drained
- 1/3 cup dry white wine
- 1/4 teaspoon salt
- 1/8 teaspoon pepper
- 1/2 cup cream
- 3 tablespoons all-purpose flour, divided
- Minced parsley

Combine shallots and 2 tablespoons butter in 9-inch microproof pie plate or quiche dish. Place in oven. Set recipe number 153. Touch START. *(Oven cooks: micro,* 90, 3 *minutes.)*

At Pause, add scallops, wine, salt, and pepper to dish. Place in oven. Touch START. *(Oven cooks: micro,* 50, 7 *minutes.)*

At Pause, drain scallops, reserving liquid. Transfer liquid to small microproof bowl. Blend in cream and 2 tablespoons flour. Place in oven. Touch START. *(Oven cooks: micro, HI,* 3 *minutes.)*

At Pause, stir. Touch START. *(Oven cooks: micro, HI,* 1½ *minutes.)*

Stir in remaining butter and flour. Set recipe number 227. Touch START. *(Oven cooks: micro, HI,* 1½ *minutes.)*

At Pause, stir. Touch START. *(Oven cooks: micro, HI,* 1 *minute.)*

Divide scallops among individual dishes. Spoon sauce over. Sprinkle with parsley and serve.

4 servings

Recipe No. 154

Mountain Trout

Cooking Time: 9 minutes

- 2 8-ounce trout
- 1/4 cup dehydrated onion flakes
- 2 tablespoons hot water
- 2 tablespoons dry white wine
- 2 tablespoons butter or margarine, melted, divided
- 6 mushrooms, sliced
- 2 tablespoons slivered almonds
- 2 tablespoons chopped parsley
- Salt and pepper to taste

Place wire rack in lower position. Set recipe number 154. Touch START. *(Oven preheats: convec,* 400°*F.)* Meanwhile, rinse trout and pat dry. Arrange in oval microproof and heatproof baking dish. Combine onion and water in small bowl and set aside. Sprinkle cavity and surface of trout with wine. Pour 1 tablespoon butter inside cavity. Add mushrooms, almonds, and parsley to onion mixture and blend well. Spread remaining butter over trout. Divide half of mixture evenly between cavities, sprinkling remainder over tops. Season with salt and pepper.

At 400°F, place in oven on wire rack. Touch START. *(Oven cooks: micro/convec,* 400°*F,* 9 *minutes.)* Serve immediately.

2 servings

Salmon Ring (page 137), Parsley New Potatoes (page 168), and Broccoli (Guide, page 151) →

Recipe No. 155

Stuffed Bass

Approximate Cooking Time: 19½ minutes

- 1 bass (2 pounds)
- ¼ cup chopped onion
- 2 tablespoons butter or margarine
- ¾ cup dry bread crumbs
- ½ cup chopped mushrooms
- 2 tablespoons minced parsley
- 1 large egg, beaten
- 1 tablespoon lemon juice
- 1 teaspoon salt
- ⅛ teaspoon pepper
- 1 tablespoon bottled brown sauce
- 1 tablespoon water

Rinse bass well in cold water and pat dry; set aside. Place onion and butter in 1½-quart microproof bowl. Place in oven. Set recipe number 155. Touch START. *(Oven cooks: micro, HI, 2 minutes.)*

At Pause, remove from oven. Add remaining ingredients except brown sauce and water; blend well. Spoon stuffing into cavity of bass. Place on oval microproof platter or in 12×7-inch microproof baking dish. Combine brown sauce and water; brush over bass.

Place in oven. Insert temperature probe into meatiest part of fish, parallel to spine and close to probe receptacle. Cover dish tightly with plastic wrap, but wrap loosely around probe to vent. Plug in probe. Touch START. *(Oven cooks: micro, HI, to 170°F; stands: 0, 5 minutes.)*

4 servings

Recipe No. 156

Poached Salmon

Cooking Time: 12 minutes

- 2 cups water
- 1 medium stalk celery, cut into chunks
- ½ medium lemon, sliced
- ½ medium onion, sliced
- 3 tablespoons vinegar
- 2 tablespoons lemon juice
- 1½ teaspoons salt
- 6 whole cloves
- 1 bay leaf
- 4 salmon, swordfish, halibut, or other fish steaks (6 to 8 ounces each)
- Parsley sprigs

Combine all ingredients except fish and parsley in 2-quart microproof casserole. Cover with casserole lid and place in oven. Set recipe number 156. Touch START. *(Oven cooks: micro, HI, 7 minutes.)*

At Pause, add fish; spoon liquid over top. Cover. Touch START. *(Oven cooks: micro, HI, 5 minutes.)*

Carefully turn fish over. Let stand, covered, 5 minutes. Transfer to serving platter. Garnish with parsley. Serve hot or chilled.

4 servings

Recipe No. 157

Halibut Steaks

Cooking Time: 16 minutes

- 2 tablespoons dry white wine
- 1 tablespoon fresh lemon juice
- 1 tablespoon olive oil
- ¼ teaspoon salt
- ⅛ teaspoon pepper
- 2 ¾-pound halibut steaks (¾- to 1-inch thick)

Combine wine, lemon juice, olive oil, salt, and pepper in shallow dish. Add fish, turning several times to coat. Cover and marinate in refrigerator 3 hours, turning once or twice.

Remove ceramic tray. Place wire rack in

upper position. Set recipe number 157. Touch START. *(Oven preheats: convec, 450°F.)* Set fish on aluminum foil or broiling pan; reserve marinade.

At 450°F, place in oven. Touch START. *(Oven cooks: convec, 450°F, 8 minutes.)*

At Pause, turn fish over and brush with marinade. Touch START. *(Oven cooks: convec, 450°F, 8 minutes.)*

2 servings

Recipe No. 158

Salmon Ring

Cooking Time: 12 minutes

- Paprika
- 1 can (16 ounces) red salmon, skin and bones discarded
- 1 cup soft bread crumbs
- 3/4 cup finely chopped celery
- 2 large eggs, lightly beaten
- 3 tablespoons minced green onion
- 2 tablespoons mayonnaise
- Pinch dillweed

Butter 6-cup microproof ring mold; sprinkle with paprika; set aside. Combine all ingredients; blend well. Turn into prepared mold, spreading evenly. Place in oven. Set recipe number 158. Touch START. *(Oven cooks: micro, HI, 7 minutes; 20, 5 minutes.)* Unmold onto serving platter.

4 to 6 servings

Recipe No. 159

Breaded Fish Fillets

Cooking Time: 12 minutes

- 1 1/2 pounds fish fillets about 1/2-inch thick
- 3/4 cup crushed corn flakes
- 2 tablespoons dried parsley
- 1/4 teaspoon salt
- 1/8 teaspoon pepper
- 1 egg, beaten

Remove ceramic tray. Place wire rack in lower position. Set recipe number 159. Touch START. *(Oven preheats: convec, 400°F.)* Meanwhile, rinse fillets with cold water and pat dry. Combine corn flakes, parsley, salt, and pepper. Dip each fillet in beaten egg, then roll in corn flake mixture, covering completely. Arrange in metal pan.

At 400°F, place in oven on wire rack. Touch START. *(Oven cooks: convec, 400°F, 12 minutes.)* Serve immediately.

4 servings

Recipe No. 160 ⊞

Fillet of Fish Amandine

Cooking Time: 10 minutes

- 1/2 cup slivered almonds
- 1/4 cup butter or margarine
- 1 pound fish fillets
- 1 tablespoon lemon juice
- 1 teaspoon chopped parsley
- 1/2 teaspoon salt
- 1/4 teaspoon dillweed
- 1/8 teaspoon pepper

Place almonds and butter in 8-inch microproof and heatproof baking dish. Place wire rack in lower position. Place dish in oven on wire rack. Set recipe number 160. Touch START. *(Oven preheats: convec, 350°F.)* Meanwhile, rinse fillets in cool water and pat dry.

At 350°F, add fillets to dish, turning to coat with butter. Roll up fillets and place on almonds. Sprinkle with lemon juice, parsley, salt, dillweed, and pepper. Place in oven on wire rack. Touch START. *(Oven cooks: micro/convec, 350°F, 10 minutes.)*

Spoon almonds and sauce on fillets and serve. Garnish with lemon wedges, parsley sprigs, or paprika.

2 to 3 servings

⊞ *Recipe can be increased. See "Quantity", page 12.*

Recipe No. 161 ⊞

Fillet of Fish Mediterranean

Cooking Time: 11 minutes

- 1 pound fish fillets
- 2 tablespoons butter or margarine
- 2 tablespoons dry white wine
- ½ teaspoon lemon juice
- 1 medium tomato, peeled and cut into cubes
- 2 green onions, thinly sliced
- ½ cup sliced mushrooms
- ½ teaspoon salt

Arrange fillets in 8-inch round or oval microproof baking dish with thickest parts toward outside of dish. Dot with butter. Combine wine and lemon juice; pour over fillets. Sprinkle with remaining ingredients. Place in oven. Cover with waxed paper. Set recipe number 161. Touch START. *(Oven cooks: micro, HI, 8 minutes; stands: 0, 3 minutes.)*

2 servings

⊞ *Recipe can be increased. See "Quantity", page 12.*

Recipe No. 162

Tuna-Mushroom Patties

Cooking Time: 9½ minutes

- 2 tablespoons milk
- 1 can (10¾ ounces) cream of celery soup, undiluted, divided
- 2 cans (6½ ounces each) tuna, drained
- ½ cup dry bread crumbs
- ½ cup chopped mushrooms
- 1 large egg, beaten
- 2 tablespoons instant minced onion
- ¼ teaspoon white pepper
- 2 tablespoons minced parsley

Combine milk and half of the soup in 2-cup glass measure; blend well; set aside. Combine remaining soup, tuna, bread crumbs, mushrooms, egg, onion, and pepper. Shape into 6 patties, using about ½ cup mixture for each. Place in shallow microproof baking dish. Place in oven. Cover with waxed paper. Set recipe number 162. Touch START. *(Oven cooks: micro, HI, 8 minutes.)*

At Pause, remove from oven. Place milk mixture in oven. Touch START. *(Oven cooks: micro, HI, 1½ minutes.)*

Stir and pour over tuna patties. Sprinkle with parsley before serving.

6 servings

COOKING GUIDE — CONVENIENCE SEAFOOD*

Food	Programming Method	Programming Setting	First Cook Time	Second Cook Time	Special Notes
Fish sticks frozen, (12)	micro/convec	400°	5 min. turn over	change to convec 400° 4-5 min.	Lower position. Preheat. Foil-lined microproof and heatproof baking dish.
Shrimp or crab newburg, frozen 6½ oz.	micro	HI	4-6		Slit pouch, place on plate. Flex pouch to mix halfway through cooking time.
Scallops or fish kabobs, 7 oz.	micro/convec	400°	5 min. turn over	change to convec 400° 4-5 min.	Lower position. Preheat. Foil-lined microproof and heatproof baking dish.
Tuna casserole, frozen, 16 oz.	micro	HI	4-6		Remove from package to 1-quart microproof casserole. Stir once during cooking.

* Due to the tremendous variety in convenience food products available, times given here should be used only as guidelines. We suggest you cook food for the shortest recommended time and then check for doneness. Be sure to check the package for microwave and oven (convec) instructions.

A Continental Flair

What is a quiche but a delicious combination of dairy products in their best form? Once you have tried the delightful recipes here — Sausage and Leek Quiche (page 142), Chili-Cheese Quiche (page 141), and the "first" quiche, Quiche Lorraine (page 142), are just a few — you will soon begin to substitute your own fillings. They are so easy to make with this oven, perfect every time. The micro/convection method shines as the microwaves cook the filling and the hot air crisps the shell and browns the top. French-chef proficiency will be yours, too, with Spinach Soufflé (page 145).

But attractive food and preparation ease, not elegance, are the true story of this chapter. The microwave method offers many traditional egg dishes, like Sunny-Side-Up Eggs (page 147), and Cheddar and Onion Egg (page 147). Plain and simple breakfast fare, including scrambled and poached eggs is also included. You can create your own omelet for breakfast or a light meal anytime. For some fun, though, try the convection method and our delicious and unusually-shaped Mushroom Omelet (page 146).

Quiches are placed on the wire rack, lower position, and cooked the micro/convection way. Quiche Lorraine (page 142) can be the basis for a great, out-of-the-ordinary brunch (above left). When you see that soufflé rise, you'll wonder why it was never so easy before. Spinach Soufflé (page 145) and other soufflés are set on the wire rack in oven bottom position (above right).

Converting Your Recipes

When eggs and cheese are the primary ingredients, the rule is that it is better to undercook than overcook. They cook so quickly that 15 seconds or less can make the difference between fluffy perfection and a rubbery disaster. Such care is exercised with all food but it is especially important here, just as it is in conventional cooking. Egg cookery is eye cookery: you simply must watch what's happening!

Soufflé recipes can be adapted easily: just follow the same format as Cheese Soufflé (page 145), using the same number of eggs and amount of liquid. Tips on other cheese and egg dishes:

- ☐ Undercook eggs slightly and allow standing time to complete cooking. Eggs become tough when overcooked. Always check doneness to avoid overcooking.
- ☐ Cover poaching or baking eggs to trap steam and assure even cooking.
- ☐ Eggs are usually cooked by the microwave method at 60 or 70.
- ☐ If you want a soft yolk, remove the egg from oven before whites are completely cooked. A brief standing time allows whites to set without overcooking yolks.
- ☐ Add ⅛ to ¼ teaspoon vinegar to the water when poaching eggs to help the white coagulate.
- ☐ Cook bacon and egg combinations micro on HI, since most of the microwaves are attracted to the bacon because of its high fat content.
- ☐ Omelets and scrambled eggs should be stirred at least once during cooking. Fondues and sauces profit from occasional stirring during the cooking time.
- ☐ Cheese melts quickly and makes an attractive topping for casseroles and sandwiches.
- ☐ Cook cheese dishes by microwave method on 70 or a lower setting for short periods of time to avoid separation and toughening.

COOKING GUIDE — CONVENIENCE EGGS AND CHEESE*

Food	Amount	Programming Method	Programming Setting	Time (in minutes)	Special Notes
Omelet, frozen	10 oz.	Micro	HI	4 - 5	Use microproof plate.
Egg substitute	8 oz.	Micro	30	4 - 6	Turn carton over after 1 minute. Open carton after 1½ minutes. Stir every 30 seconds until smooth.
Soufflés: Corn, frozen	12 oz.	convec		follow package directions	
Cheese, frozen	12 oz.	convec		follow package directions	
Spinach, frozen	12 oz.	convec		follow package directions	
Welsh rabbit, frozen	10 oz.	Micro	HI	6 - 7	Use 1½-quart microproof caserole, covered. Stir during cooking time.

*Due to the tremendous variety in convenience food products available, times given here should be used only as guidelines. We suggest you cook food for the shortest recommended time and then check for doneness. Be sure to check the package for microwave and oven (convec) instructions.

Recipe No. 163

Chili-Cheese Quiche

Cooking Time: 27½ minutes

- 3 tablespoons butter or margarine
- 1 cup thinly sliced green onions, divided
- 1 can (4 ounces) diced green chilies
- 1 jar (2 ounces) diced pimiento
- 1 cup whipping cream or half-and-half
- ½ teaspoon salt
- ⅛ teaspoon pepper
- ⅛ teaspoon cumin
- 4 eggs, lightly beaten
- 2½ cups shredded Monterey Jack cheese, divided
- 1 prebaked Basic Pie Crust (page 184)
- ½ cup (2 ounces) shredded Cheddar cheese
- ¼ teaspoon paprika

Place butter in 4-cup glass measure. Place in oven. Set recipe number 163. Touch START. *(Oven cooks: micro, HI, 1 minute.)*

At Pause, stir in half of onion. Touch START. *(Oven cooks: micro, HI, 1½ minutes.)* Add chilies and pimiento. Set aside to cool.

Place wire rack in lower position. Set recipe number 166. Touch START. *(Oven preheats: convec, 350°F.)* Meanwhile, combine cream, salt, pepper, and cumin in large bowl. Blend in eggs and 2 cups Monterey Jack cheese. Spread onion-pimiento mixture over crust. Slowly pour custard over top. Sprinkle with Cheddar cheese, paprika, remaining Monterey Jack cheese, and remaining onion.

At 350°F, place in oven on wire rack. Touch START. *(Oven cooks: micro/convec, 350°F, 7½ minutes.)*

At Pause, rotate dish one-half turn. Touch START. *(Oven cooks: micro/convec, 350°F, 7½ minutes; stands: 0, 10 minutes.)* Cut into wedges and serve.

6 to 8 servings

Recipe No. 164

Shirred Eggs

Cooking Time: 4½ minutes

- 1 teaspoon butter or margarine
- 2 eggs
- 1 tablespopon cream
- Salt and pepper to taste

Place butter in microproof ramekin or small microproof cereal bowl. Place in oven. Set recipe number 164. Touch START. *(Oven cooks: micro, HI, 30 seconds.)*

At Pause, break eggs carefully into ramekin. Pierce yolks carefully with toothpick. Add cream and cover tightly with plastic wrap. Touch START. *(Oven cooks: micro, 30, 3 minutes; stands 0, 1 minute.)*

1 serving

This is one of several recipes that use the preset functions of another recipe for part of the cooking sequence. Set recipe number 163 first. At the end of that sequence, set recipe number 166.

Recipe No. 165

Sausage and Leek Quiche

Cooking Time: 38½ minutes

1½ pounds leeks, white and tender part of leaves, well rinsed, drained, and finely chopped
⅓ cup butter or margarine
½ pound bulk pork sausage
1 cup half-and-half
3 egg yolks
1 egg
½ teaspoon salt
⅛ teaspoon pepper
1 prebaked Basic Pie Crust (page 184)
Paprika

Combine leeks and butter in 2-quart microproof bowl. Cover with plastic wrap. Place in oven. Set recipe number 165. Touch START. *(Oven cooks: micro, HI, 5 minutes.)*

At Pause, stir. Cover. Touch START. *(Oven cooks: micro, HI, 5 minutes.)*

At Pause, stir. Cover and set aside. Place sausage in another 2-quart microproof bowl. Cover with plastic wrap. Place in oven. Touch START. *(Oven cooks: micro, HI, 2 minutes.)*

At Pause, stir. Cover. Touch START. *(Oven cooks: micro, HI, 1½ minutes.)* Remove sausage from bowl with slotted spoon and set aside to drain well on paper towels.

Place wire rack in lower position. Set recipe number 166. Touch START. *(Oven preheats: convec, 350°F.)* Meanwhile, beat half-and-half, egg yolks, egg, salt, and pepper in medium bowl. Stir in leeks. Spoon mixture into crust, spreading evenly. Crumble sausage over top and sprinkle with paprika.

At 350°F, place quiche in oven on wire rack. Touch START. *(Oven cooks: micro/convec, 350°F, 7½ minutes.)*

At Pause, rotate dish one-half turn. Touch START. *(Oven cooks: micro/convec, 350°F, 7½ minutes; stands: 0, 10 minutes.)*

6 to 8 servings

Recipe No. 166

Quiche Lorraine

Cooking Time: 36¼ minutes

10 slices bacon
1½ cups (6 ounces) shredded Swiss cheese
½ cup thinly sliced green onions
1 prebaked Basic Pie Crust (page 184)
1 tall can evaporated milk or evaporated skim milk
4 eggs
¼ teaspoon salt
¼ teaspoon nutmeg
Pinch ground red pepper

Arrange 5 slices bacon on paper towel-lined microproof plate. Cover with 2 sheets paper towels and arrange second layer of bacon on top. Cover with paper towel. Place in oven on ceramic tray. Set recipe number 118. Touch QUANTITY. Touch 2. Touch 5. Touch START.* *(Oven cooks: micro, HI, 11¼ minutes.)* Remove bacon from oven. Separate from paper towels, crumble, and set aside.

Place wire rack in lower position. Set recipe number 166. Touch START. *(Oven preheats: convec, 350°F.)* Meanwhile, sprinkle bacon, cheese, and onion over crust, reserving 1 teaspoon of each. Beat milk, eggs, salt, nutmeg, and red pepper in 1-quart bowl. Carefully pour into pie shell. Sprinkle top with reserved bacon, cheese, and onion.

At 350°F, place in oven on wire rack. Touch START. *(Oven cooks: micro/convec, 350°F, 7½ minutes.)*

At Pause, rotate dish one-half turn. Touch START. *(Oven cooks: micro/convec, 350°F, 7½ minutes; stands: 0, 10 minutes.)* Cut into wedges and serve.

6 to 8 servings

**This procedure sets the oven to cook at 2½ times the original Recipe No. 118 program for 4 slices bacon. This is one of several recipes that use the preset functions of another recipe for part of the cooking sequence. Set recipe number 118 first. At the end of that sequence, set recipe number 166.*

Quiche Lorraine, Sausage and Leek Quiche →

Recipe No. 167

Eggs Benedict

Cooking Time: 2 minutes

2 English muffins, split and toasted
4 slices ham, about 1/4-inch thick
4 poached eggs (page 146)
1 cup Hollandaise Sauce (page 178)

Set muffin halves on microproof serving plate and top each with ham slice. Set recipe number 167. Touch START. *(Oven cooks: micro, HI, 2 minutes.)*

Top each with poached egg and hot Hollandaise Sauce. Serve immediately.

4 servings

To reheat Hollandaise Sauce before serving, cook on 30, 2 minutes, stirring once.

Recipe No. 168

Mexican Scrambled Eggs

Cooking Time: 9 1/2 minutes

2 tablespoons butter or margarine
1 can (4 ounces) diced green chilies
1 large tomato, peeled, coarsely chopped, and drained
2 tablespoons dried minced onion
6 eggs
6 tablespoons milk
1/8 teaspoon garlic powder
Salt and pepper to taste
1 cup (4 ounces) shredded Cheddar cheese
Chopped parsley

Place butter in microproof dish or pie plate. Place in oven. Set recipe number 168. Touch START. *(Oven cooks: micro, HI, 1 minute.)*

At Pause, swirl butter to coat bottom. Add chilies, tomato, and onion. Cover with plastic wrap. Touch START. *(Oven cooks: micro, HI, 2 minutes.)*

At Pause, beat eggs, milk, garlic powder, salt, and pepper in medium bowl until well blended. Pour over tomato mixture. Touch START. *(Oven cooks: micro,* 80, 5 *minutes.)* During cooking time, stir outer edge of egg mixture toward center several times.

At Pause, sprinkle with cheese. Touch START. *(Oven cooks: micro,* 80, 1 1/2 *minutes.)* Sprinkle with parsley.

3 to 4 servings

You can substitute 1/2 cup chopped green pepper for chilies. Cook on HI 1 minute before adding to butter.

Recipe No. 169

Cheesed Ham and Eggs

Cooking Time: 12 minutes

1/4 cup butter or margarine
1/4 cup all-purpose flour
2 cups milk
1 cup (4 ounces) shredded Cheddar cheese
2 teaspoons Worcestershire sauce
1 1/2 teaspoons prepared mustard
6 hard-cooked eggs
1 cup diced cooked ham
4 to 6 slices bread, toasted

Place butter in 1 1/2-quart microproof casserole. Place in oven. Set recipe number 169. Touch START. *(Oven cooks: HI, 1 minute.)*

At Pause, blend in flour. Set aside. Place milk in 1-quart measure. Place in oven. Touch START. *(Oven cooks: HI, 2 minutes.)*

At Pause, blend milk into flour mixture. Place in oven. Touch START. *(Oven cooks: micro,* 80, 5 *minutes.)*

At Pause, stir in cheese, Worcestershire sauce, and mustard, and stir until mixture is smooth. Carefully stir in eggs and ham. Place in oven. Touch START. *(Oven cooks: micro,* 50, 4 *minutes.)* Serve on toast.

4 to 6 servings

Recipe No. 170

Cheese Soufflé

Cooking Time: 54 minutes

- 1 teaspoon butter
- 1/4 cup grated Parmesan cheese
- 1/4 cup butter or margarine
- 1/4 cup all-purpose flour
- 1/2 teaspoon dry mustard
- 1/2 teaspoon salt
- 1/4 teaspoon pepper
- 1 cup milk, warmed
- 1 1/2 cups (6 ounces) shredded Cheddar cheese
- 6 eggs, separated
- 1/2 teaspoon cream of tartar

Coat bottom and sides of 2-quart soufflé dish with 1 teaspoon butter. Sprinkle with Parmesan cheese, rotating dish to cover evenly and letting excess cheese remain in bottom. Refrigerate.

Place 1/4 cup butter in 2-quart microproof bowl. Place in oven. Set recipe number 230. Touch START. *(Oven cooks: micro, HI, 1 1/2 minutes.)*

At Pause, stir in flour, mustard, salt, and pepper. Slowly stir in milk. Place in oven. Touch START. *(Oven cooks: micro, HI, 1 1/2 minutes.)*

At Pause, stir through. Touch START. *(Oven cooks: micro, HI, 1 minute.)*

Add Cheddar cheese and stir until melted. Beat yolks until smooth and lemon-colored. Add to cheese mixture and blend thoroughly. Set aside.

Remove ceramic tray. Place wire rack in oven bottom position. Set recipe number 170. Touch START. *(Oven preheats: convec, 330°F.)* Meanwhile, beat egg whites in large bowl until foamy. Add cream of tartar and continue beating until stiff but not dry. Stir one-third of whites into cheese mixture. Gently fold in remaining whites. Turn into prepared soufflé dish.

At 330°F, place dish in oven. Touch START. *(Oven cooks: convec, 330°F, 50 minutes.)* Serve immediately.

6 servings

This is one of several recipes that use the preset functions of another recipe for part of the cooking sequence. Set recipe number 230 first. At the end of that sequence, set recipe number 170.

Recipe No. 171

Spinach Soufflé

Cooking Time: 59 minutes

- 1 package (10 ounces) frozen chopped spinach
- 1 teaspoon butter
- 1/4 cup grated Parmesan cheese
- 1/4 cup butter or margarine
- 1/4 cup all-purpose flour
- 1 clove garlic, minced
- 1/2 teaspoon salt
- 1/4 teaspoon dry mustard
- 1/4 teaspoon pepper
- 1 cup milk
- 1 1/2 cups shredded Cheddar cheese
- 6 eggs, separated
- 1/2 teaspoon cream of tartar

Set unopened package of spinach on microproof plate. Place in oven on ceramic tray. Set recipe number 209. Touch START. *(Oven cooks: micro, HI, 6 minutes.)* Set spinach aside.

Coat bottom and sides of 2-quart soufflé dish with 1 teaspoon butter. Sprinkle with Parmesan cheese, rotating dish to cover evenly and letting excess cheese remain on bottom. Refrigerate.

Place 1/4 cup butter in 2-quart glass measure or microproof bowl. Place in oven on ceramic tray. Touch START. *(Oven cooks: micro, HI, 1 minute.)*

At Pause, stir in flour, garlic, salt, mustard, and pepper. Slowly blend in milk, mixing until smooth. Place in oven. Touch START. *(Oven cooks: micro, HI, 1 minute.)*

At Pause, stir. Touch START. *(Oven cooks: micro, HI, 1 minute.)* Add Cheddar cheese and stir until melted. Set aside.

Remove ceramic tray. Place wire rack in oven bottom position. Set recipe number 171. Touch START. *(Oven preheats: convec, 350°F.)* Meanwhile, drain spinach well and stir into cheese mixture. Beat egg yolks in small bowl until smooth and lemon-colored. Add to spinach mixture and blend well. Beat egg whites in large bowl until foamy. Add cream of tartar and continue beating until stiff peaks form. Stir one-third of whites into spinach mixture. Gently fold in remaining whites. Turn into prepared soufflé dish.

At 350°F, place dish in oven. Touch START. *(Oven cooks: convec, 350°F, 50 minutes.)* Serve immediately.

5 servings

Recipe No. 172

Mushroom Omelet

Cooking Time: 12½ minutes

1 cup sliced mushrooms
¼ cup thinly sliced green onions
2 tablespoons butter or margarine
4 eggs, beaten
3 tablespoons milk
2 tablespoons butter or margarine, melted
¼ teaspoon dillweed
Salt and pepper to taste

Combine mushrooms, onions, and butter in 1-quart glass measure. Place in oven. Set recipe number 227. Touch START. *(Oven cooks: micro, HI, 1½ minutes.)*

At Pause, stir. Touch START. *(Oven cooks: micro, HI, 1 minute.)* Set dish aside.

Remove ceramic tray. Place wire rack in upper position. Set recipe number 172. Touch START. *(Oven preheats: convec, 450°F.)* Meanwhile, beat eggs and milk in mixing bowl. Pour melted butter into 9-inch metal pie plate. Add egg mixture.

At 450°F, place in oven on wire rack. Touch START. *(Oven cooks: convec, 450°F, 10 minutes.)* (Eggs will form a basket.)

Spoon mushrooms into egg basket. Sprinkle with dill. Season with salt and pepper. Serve immediately.

4 servings

This is one of several recipes that use the preset functions of another recipe for part of the cooking sequence. Set recipe number 227 first. At the end of that sequence, set recipe number 172.

Recipe No. 173

Poached Egg

Cooking Time: 3½ minutes

¼ cup water
¼ teaspoon vinegar
Pinch salt
1 large egg

Place water, vinegar, and salt in 6-ounce microproof custard cup. Place in oven. Set recipe number 173. Touch START. *(Oven cooks: micro, HI, 1½ minutes.)*

At Pause, carefully break egg into hot liquid. Carefully pierce yolk in several places with toothpick. Cover with waxed paper. Touch START. *(Oven cooks: micro, 50, 1 minute; stands: 0, 1 minute.)*

1 serving

Recipe No. 174 ⊞

Scrambled Egg

Cooking Time: 2½ minutes

1 large egg
2 tablespoons low-fat milk
6 tablespoons (1½ ounces) shredded Monterey Jack or Cheddar cheese
Salt and pepper to taste

Break egg into small microproof bowl. Add milk; mix well with fork. Add cheese, salt, and pepper; blend well. Place in oven. Cover with waxed paper. Set recipe number 174. Touch START. *(Oven cooks: micro, 60, 1 minute.)*

At Pause, stir. Cover. Touch START. *(Oven cooks: micro, 60, 1½ minutes.)*

Stir before serving.

1 serving

⊞ *Recipe can be increased. See "Quantity", page 12.*

Recipe No. 175

Sunny-Side-Up Eggs

Cooking Time: 8 minutes

1 tablespoon butter or margarine
2 large eggs
Salt and pepper to taste

Remove ceramic tray. Place wire rack in upper position. Set recipe number 175. Touch START. *(Oven preheats: convec, 450°F.)* Place butter in shallow aluminum foil baking pan.

At 450°F, place in oven on wire rack. Touch START. *(Oven cooks: convec, 450°F, 1 minute.)*

At Pause, break eggs into pan. Season with salt and pepper. Place in oven on wire rack. Touch START. *(Oven cooks: convec, 450°F, 7 minutes.)*

1 to 2 servings

Recipe No. 176 ⊞

Cheddar and Onion Egg

Cooking Time: 3 minutes

1 teaspoon butter or margarine
1 green onion, thinly sliced
1 large egg
1 heaping tablespoon shredded Cheddar cheese

Combine butter and onion in microproof custard cup. Place in oven. Set recipe number 176. Touch START. *(Oven cooks: micro, HI, 1 minute.)*

At Pause, carefully break egg into custard cup. Carefully pierce yolk in several places with toothpick. Sprinkle with cheese. Cover with waxed paper. Touch START. *(Oven cooks: micro, 60, 1 minute; stands: 0, 1 minute.)*

1 serving

⊞ *Recipe can be increased. See "Quantity", page 12.*

The Farmers Market

Vegetables and the microwave method were made for each other, or so you'll think when you sit down to dinner with a couple of these side dishes on the table. Because very little water (sometimes none at all) is used in cooking, vegetables retain their bright, fresh color, and are full of flavor. What's more, they don't lose a bit of their vitamin-filled wholesomeness. Whether it's as simple as Green Beans Italiano (page 167), as up-to-date as Ratatouille (page 162), or as unique as Potato Kugel (page 163) and Barley-Rice Casserole (page 155), you'll find the just-right answer to "I wonder what goes with...?" among these recipes. Frozen and canned vegetables are also better when reheated by the microwave method. Finally, you'll find good use for the convection method with many interesting potato recipes.

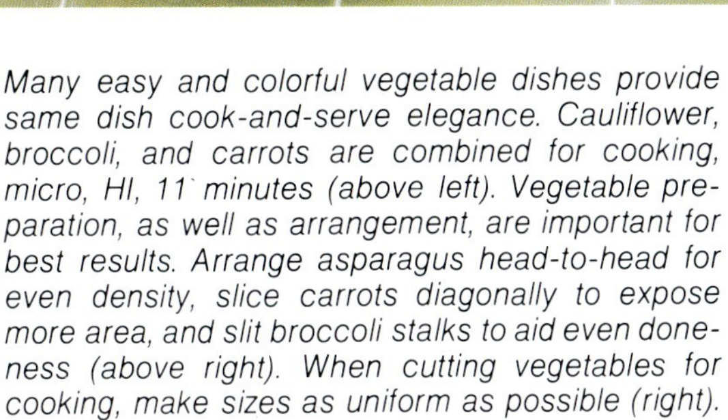

Many easy and colorful vegetable dishes provide same dish cook-and-serve elegance. Cauliflower, broccoli, and carrots are combined for cooking, micro, HI, 11 minutes (above left). Vegetable preparation, as well as arrangement, are important for best results. Arrange asparagus head-to-head for even density, slice carrots diagonally to expose more area, and slit broccoli stalks to aid even doneness (above right). When cutting vegetables for cooking, make sizes as uniform as possible (right).

← *Mushroom-Pimiento Rice (page 156), Corn-on-the-Cob (page 166)*

Converting Your Recipes

Vegetables are best when eaten at the crisp stage, tender but resistant to the bite. However, if you prefer a softer texture, increase water and cooking time. To adapt a conventional recipe to the microwave oven, find a similar recipe in the chapter and check the vegetable cooking guides. The following tips will give you additional help in adapting or creating your own recipes.

- ☐ Check doneness after the shortest recommended cooking times. Add more cooking time to suit individual preferences.
- ☐ When using the temperature probe, a small amount of liquid should be added. Insert probe into the center of the vegetable dish and set at 150°F.
- ☐ If necessary, frozen vegetables may be used in recipes calling for fresh vegetables. It is not necessary to thaw frozen vegetables before cooking.
- ☐ Freeze small portions of your favorite vegetable dishes in boilable plastic pouches. If you use metal twist ties, be sure to replace with string or rubber band before cooking. Cut a steam vent in pouch and reheat on microproof plate.
- ☐ To prevent boiling over of vegetable dishes with cream sauces, use a dish large enough to allow for bubbling. Use 60 or 70.
- ☐ Celery, onions, green peppers, and carrots need to be partially cooked before adding to a casserole. In general, you should partially cook all vegetables before combining with already cooked meats, fish, or poultry.
- ☐ To cook mashed potatoes, cube potatoes. Add a small amount of water. Cook, tightly covered, until soft. Season and mash.
- ☐ To reheat mashed potatoes, set at 80, stirring once during cooking time.
- ☐ Pasta, rice, and cereals are best when added to other ingredients, as in vegetable, meat, or cheese casseroles. While the oven can cook them separately, there's no advantage. It is wise to reheat them in the oven, however. You add no water and they are like fresh cooked. Cook, micro, 80, 3 to 4 minutes for 1 cup (cooked), 5 to 6 minutes for 2 cups, etc. Cover tightly.
- ☐ Grits or other hot cereals are interesting side dishes for brunch, cooked in individual bowls. Cook, micro, HI, 6 to 7 minutes for ⅓ cup grits (uncooked); 1 to 2 minutes for ⅓ cup quick oatmeal. Follow package directions for liquid.

Using the Cooking Guide

1. All fresh or frozen vegetables are cooked and reheated on HI.
2. Choose a wide, shallow dish so vegetables can be spread out.
3. Add ¼ cup water for each ½ to 1 pound fresh vegetables. Do not add water for washed spinach, corn on the cob, squash, baking potatoes, or eggplant.
4. Cover all vegetables tightly.
5. Stir once during cooking time.
6. Pouches of frozen vegetables require steam vents. Slit pouch and cook on microproof dish.
7. Frozen vegetables without sauces can be cooked in their cartons without water. Remove waxed paper or foil wrapping before placing carton in oven. (Remove frozen-in-sauce vegetables if packaged in cartons rather than pouches. Place in 1½-quart microproof casserole. Add liquid before cooking as package directs.)
8. After cooking, allow all vegetables to stand, covered, for 2 to 3 minutes.

COOKING GUIDE — VEGETABLES

Food	Amount	Fresh Vegetable Preparation	Time (in minutes)	Water	Standing Time (in minutes)	Special Notes
Artichokes 3½" in diameter	Fresh: 1 2 Frozen: 10 oz.	Wash thoroughly. Cut tops off each leaf. Slit pouch	7 - 8 11 - 12 5 - 6	¼ cup ½ cup	2 - 3 2 - 3	When done, a leaf peeled from whole comes off easily.
Asparagus spears and cut pieces	Fresh: 1 lb. Frozen: 10 oz.	Wash thoroughly. Snap off tough base and discard.	2 - 3 7 - 8	¼ cup None	None 2 - 3	Stir or rearrange once during cooking time.
Beans: green, wax, French-cut	Fresh: 1 lb. Frozen: 6 oz.	Remove ends. Wash well. Leave whole or break in pieces.	12 - 14 7 - 8	¼ cup None	2 - 3 None	Stir once or rearrange as necessary.
Beets	4 medium	Scrub beets. Leave 1" of top on beet.	16 - 18	¼ cup	None	After cooking, peel. Cut or leave whole.
Broccoli	Fresh, whole 1 - 2½ lbs. Frozen, whole Fresh, chopped 1 - 1½ lbs. Frozen, chopped 10 oz.	Remove outer leaves. Slit stalks.	9 - 10 8 - 10 9 - 10 8 - 9	¼ cup ¼ cup ¼ cup None	3 3 2 2	Stir or rearrange during cooking time.
Brussels sprouts	Fresh: 1 lb. Frozen: 10 oz.	Remove outside leaves if wilted. Cut off Stems. Wash.	8 - 9 6 - 7	¼ cup None	2 - 3 None	Stir or rearrange once during cooking time.
Cabbage	½ medium head, shredded 1 medium head, wedges	Remove outside wilted leaves.	5 - 6 13 - 15	¼ cup ¼ cup	2 - 3 2 - 3	Rearrange wedges after 7 minutes.
Carrots	4: sliced or diced 6: sliced or diced 8: tiny, whole Frozen: 10 oz.	Peel and cut off tops. Fresh young carrots cook best.	7 - 9 9 - 10 8 - 10 8 - 9	1 Tb. 2 Tbs. 2 Tbs. None	2 - 3 2 - 3 2 - 3 None	Stir once during cooking time.
Cauliflower	1 medium, in flowerets 1 medium, whole Frozen: 10 oz.	Cut tough stem. Wash. Remove outside leaves. Remove core.	7 - 8 8 - 9 8 - 9	¼ cup ½ cup ½ cup	2 - 3 3 3	Stir after 5 minutes. Turn over once. Stir after 5 minutes.
Celery	2½ cups, 1" slices	Clean stalks thoroughly.	8 - 9	¼ cup	2	
Corn: kernel	Frozen: 10 oz.		5 - 6	¼ cup	2	Stir halfway through cooking time.
On the cob	1 ear 2 ears 3 ears 4 ears	Husk. Cook no more than 4 at a time.	3 - 4 6 - 7 9 - 10 11 - 12	None None None None	2 2 2 2	Place in microproof dish. Add ¼ cup water. Cover with plastic wrap. After cooking, let stand, covered, 2 minutes.
Eggplant	1 medium, sliced 1 medium, whole	Wash and peel. Cut into slices or cubes. Pierce skin.	5 - 6 6 - 7	2 Tbs.	3	Place on microproof rack.
Greens: collard, kale, etc.	Fresh: 1 lb. Frozen: 10 oz.	Wash. Remove wilted leaves or tough stem.	6 - 7 7 - 8	None None	2 2	

COOKING GUIDE — VEGETABLES

Food	Amount	Fresh Vegetable Preparation	Time (in minutes)	Water	Standing Time (in minutes)	Special Notes
Mushrooms	Fresh: ½ lb. sliced	Add butter.	2 - 4		2	Stir halfway through cooking time.
Okra	Fresh: ½ lb. Frozen: 10 oz.	Wash thoroughly. Leave whole or cut in thick slices.	3 - 5 7 - 8	¼ cup None	2 2	
Onions	1 lb., tiny whole 1 lb., medium to large	Peel. Add 1 Tb. butter. Peel and quarter. Add 1 Tb. butter.	6 - 7 7 - 9	¼ cup ¼ cup	3 3	Stir once during cooking time.
Parsnips	4 medium, quartered.	Peel and cut.	8 - 9	¼ cup	2	Stir once during cooking time.
Peas: green	Fresh: 1 lb. Fresh: 2 lbs. Frozen: 6 oz.	Shell peas. Rinse well.	7 - 8 8 - 9 5 - 6	¼ cup ½ cup None	2 2 - 3 None	Stir once during cooking time.
Peas and onions	Frozen: 10 oz.		6 - 8	2 Tbs.	2	
Pea pods	Frozen: 6 oz.		3 - 4	2 Tbs.	3	
Potatoes, sweet 5 - 6 oz. ea.	1 2 4 6	Wash and scrub well. Pierce with fork. Place on rack or paper towel in circle, 1" apart.	4 - 4½ 6 - 7 8 - 10 10 - 11	None None None None	3 3 3 3	
Potatoes, white baking 6 - 8 oz. ea.	1 2 3 4 5	Wash and scrub well. Pierce with fork. Place on rack or paper towel in circle, 1" apart.	4 - 6 6 - 8 8 - 12 12 - 16 16 - 20	None None None None	3 3 3 3	
boiling	3	Peel potatoes, cut in quarters.	12 - 16	½ cup	None	Stir once during cooking time.
Rutabaga	Fresh: 1 lb. Frozen: 10 oz.	Wash well. Remove tough stems or any wilted leaves.	6 - 7 7 - 8	None None	2 2	Stir once during cooking time.
Spinach	Fresh: 1 lb. Frozen: 10 oz.	Wash well. Remove tough stems. Drain.	6 - 7 7 - 8	None None	2 2	Stir once during cooking time.
Squash, acorn or butternut	1 - 1½ lbs. whole	Scrub. Pierce with fork.	10 - 12	None		Cut and remove seeds to serve.
Spaghetti squash	2 - 3 lbs.	Scrub, pierce with fork. Place on rack.	6 per lb.	None	5	Serve with butter. Parmesan cheese, or spaghetti sauce.
Turnips	4 cups cubed	Peel, wash.	9 - 11	¼ cup	3	Stir after 5 minutes.
Zucchini	3 cups sliced	Wash; do not peel. Add butter.	7 - 8		2	Stir after 4 minutes.

Special Tips about Potatoes

- ☐ If you like your baked potatoes with a crisp skin, they can be prepared using the micro/convection method.
- ☐ Place wire rack in lower position and preheat to 400°F. Cook, micro/convec, at 400°F 9 to 10 minutes for 1 or 2 potatoes, 14 to 15 minutes for 4 potatoes.
- ☐ For sweet potatoes, allow 11 to 12 minutes for 1, 12 to 13 minutes for 2.

* Due to the tremendous variety in convenience food products available, times given here should be used only as guidelines. We suggest you cook food for the shortest recommended time and then check for doneness. Be sure to check the package for microwave and oven (convec) instructions.

COOKING GUIDE — CONVENIENCE VEGETABLES*

Food	Programming Method	Programming Setting	Time (in minutes)	Special Notes
Au gratin vegetables, frozen, 11½ oz.	micro	70	10 - 12 min.	Microproof and heatproof loaf dish, covered.
Onion Rings, 9 oz.	convec	follow package directions		Remove ceramic tray. Upper position. Preheat. Cookie sheet or foil tray.
Potatoes, Country-cut fries, 1 lb.	convec	follow package directions		Remove ceramic tray. Upper position. Preheat. Cookie sheet or foil tray.
French fries, 1 lb.	convec	follow package directions		Remove ceramic tray. Upper position. Preheat. Cookie sheet or foil tray.
Instant mashed, 4 servings	micro	HI	5 - 6 min.	Follow package directions. Reduce liquid by 1 tablespoon.
Stuffed potatoes, 12 oz. (2)	micro/convec	400°	10 - 12 min.	Lower position. Place in oven during preheat. Microproof and heatproof container.
Tater tots, 1 lb.	convec	follow package directions		Remove ceramic tray. Upper position. Preheat. Cookie sheet or foil tray.
Vegetable crêpes, 6½ oz.	micro/convec	300°	7 - 8 min.	Lower position. Heatproof paper tray.
Vegetable soufflé, 12 oz.	micro	HI	12 - 15 min.	Transfer to microproof paper tray.
Vegetables, frozen in pouch, 10 - 12 oz.	micro	HI	5 - 8 min.	Slit pouch. Place on microproof and heatproof plate. Flex halfway through cooking time to mix.

COOKING GUIDE — RICE

Food	Amount Uncooked	Water	Minutes to Full Boil HI	Micro Control	Time (minutes)	Standing Time (minutes)	Special Notes
Short-grain	1 cup	2 cups	4 - 5	50	13 - 15	5	3-quart casserole
Long-grain	1 cup	2 cups	4 - 5	50	15 - 17	5	3-quart casserole
Wild rice	1 cup	3 cups	6 - 7	50	35 - 40	5	3-quart casserole
Brown rice	1 cup	3 cups	6 - 7	50	40	5	3-quart casserole
Quick-cooking	1 cup	1 cup	3 - 4	HI	0	5	1-quart casserole.

COOKING/DEFROSTING GUIDE — CONVENIENCE RICE AND PASTA

Food	Amount	Micro Control Setting	Time (in minutes)	Special Notes
Rice, cooked refrigerated	1 cup	80	1½	Use covered microproof bowl. Let stand 2 minutes, stir.
Cooked, frozen	1 cup 2 cups	80 80	2 - 3 3 - 4	
Pouch, frozen	11 oz.	80	6 - 8	Slit Pouch
Fried rice, frozen	10 oz.	HI	5 - 7	Use covered microproof casserole. Stir twice. Let stand 5 minutes.
Spanish rice, canned	12 oz.	HI	4 - 6	Use covered microproof casserole. Stir twice. Let stand 3 minutes.
Lasagna, frozen	21 oz.	70	follow package directions	Use covered microproof casserole. Let stand, covered, 5 minutes.
Macaroni and beef, frozen	11 oz.	HI	follow package directions	Use covered microproof casserole. Stir twice.
Macaroni and cheese, frozen	10 oz.	HI	follow package directions	Use covered microproof casserole. Stir twice.
Spaghetti and meatballs, frozen	14 oz.	HI	follow package directions	Use covered microproof casserole. Stir twice.

Using the Blanching Guide

The microwave oven can be a valuable and appreciated aid in preparing fresh vegetables for the freezer. (The oven is *not* recommended for canning.) Some vegetables don't require any water at all and, of course, the less water used the better. You'll have that "fresh picked" color and flavor for your produce. Here are some tips in preparing vegetables for blanching.

- ☐ Choose young, tender vegetables.
- ☐ Clean and prepare for cooking according to Cooking Guide.
- ☐ Measure amounts to be blanched; place by batches in microproof casserole.
- ☐ Add water according to Guide.
- ☐ Cover and cook on HI for time indicated in Guide.
- ☐ Stir vegetables halfway through cooking.
- ☐ Let vegetables stand, covered, 1 minute after cooking.
- ☐ Place vegetables in ice water at once to stop cooking. When vegetables feel cool, spread on towel to absorb excess moisture.
- ☐ Package in freezer containers or pouches. Seal, label, date, and freeze quickly.

BLANCHING GUIDE — VEGETABLES

Food	Amount	Water	Approximate Time (in minutes)	Casserole Size
Asparagus (cut in 1-inch pieces)	4 cups	¼ cup	4½	1½ quart
Beans, green or wax (cut in 1-inch pieces)	1 pound	½ cup	5	1½ quart
Broccoli (cut in 1-inch pieces)	1 pound	⅓ cup	6	1½ quart
Carrots (sliced)	1 pound	⅓ cup	6	1½ quart
Cauliflower (cut in florets)	1 head	⅓ cup	6	2 quart
Corn (cut from cob)	4 cups	none	4	1½ quart
Corn-on-the-cob (husked)	6 ears	none	5½	1½ quart
Onions (quartered)	4 medium	½ cup	3 - 4½	1 quart
Parsnips (cubed)	1 pound	¼ cup	2½ - 4	1½ quart
Peas (shelled)	4 cups	¼ cup	4½	1½ quart
Snow peas	4 cups	¼ cup	3½	1½ quart
Spinach (washed)	1 pound	none	4	2 quart
Turnips (cubed)	1 pound	¼ cup	3 - 4½	1½ quart
Zucchini (sliced or cubed)	1 pound	¼ cup	4	1½ quart

Recipe No. 177

Spanish Rice

Cooking Time: 44 minutes

- 1/4 cup butter or margarine
- 1/2 cup chopped onions
- 1/4 cup chopped green pepper
- 1/4 cup chopped celery
- 1 cup long-grain rice
- 1 cup water
- 1 cup tomato sauce
- 1 can (14 1/2 ounces) tomatoes, drained and chopped
- 1 can (4 ounces) diced green chilies (optional)

Place butter in 3-quart microproof and heatproof casserole. Place in oven. Set recipe number 177. Touch START. *(Oven cooks: micro, HI, 1 minute.)*

At Pause, add onion, green pepper, and celery; cover. Place in oven. Touch START. *(Oven cooks: micro, HI, 3 minutes.)*

At Pause, stir in rice, water, tomato sauce, tomatoes, and chilies. Cover with casserole lid. Place in oven on ceramic tray. Touch START. *(Oven cooks: micro/convec, 350°F, 30 minutes; stands: 0, 10 minutes.)* Fluff rice with fork and serve immediately.

6 to 8 servings

Recipe No. 178

Barley-Rice Casserole

Cooking Time: 50 minutes

- 1/2 cup butter or margarine
- 1/2 pound mushrooms, sliced
- 2 celery stalks, chopped
- 1 medium onion, chopped
- 1 cup long-grain rice
- 1 cup barley
- 1 envelope onion soup mix
- 2 cans (10 3/4 ounces each) beef broth or beef stock
- 1 soup can water

Combine butter, mushrooms, celery, and onion in 3-quart microproof and heatproof casserole. Cover with casserole lid. Place in oven on ceramic tray. Set recipe number 178. Touch START. *(Oven cooks: micro, HI, 5 minutes.)*

At Pause, stir in rice and barley; cover. Place in oven. Touch START. *(Oven cooks: micro, HI, 5 minutes.)*

At Pause, add soup mix, broth, and water; cover. Place in oven. Touch START. *(Oven cooks: micro, HI, 20 minutes.)*

At Pause, stir. Place in oven. Touch START. *(Oven cooks: micro/convec, 300°F, 20 minutes.)* Let stand, covered, about 15 minutes, or until all remaining liquid is absorbed.

8 servings

Recipe No. 179

All Seasons Rice

Cooking Time: 17 minutes

- 2 cups chicken or beef broth
- 1 cup long-grain rice
- 1/4 cup minced onion
- 2 tablespoons minced parsley

Combine all ingredients in 3-quart microproof casserole. Cover with casserole lid and place in oven. Set recipe number 179. Touch START. *(Oven cooks: micro, HI, 12 minutes; stands: 0, 5 minutes.)*

4 servings

Recipe No. 180

Chinese Fried Rice

Cooking Time: 8 minutes

- 2 tablespoons butter or margarine
- 3 cups cooked rice
- 1½ tablespoons soy sauce
- 3 large eggs
- 1 tablespoon water
- ¼ teaspoon sugar
- ¼ cup thinly sliced green onions

Place butter in 3-quart microproof casserole. Place in oven. Set recipe number 180. Touch START. *(Oven cooks: micro, HI, 1 minute.)*

At Pause, add rice and soy sauce; blend well. Beat eggs, water, and sugar until blended; pour into center of rice. Cover with casserole lid. Touch START. *(Oven cooks: micro,* 70, 3 *minutes.)*

At Pause, stir in onions. Cover with casserole lid. Touch START. *(Oven cooks: micro,* 70, 4 *minutes.)*

Stir before serving.

4 to 6 servings

Recipe No. 181

Mushroom-Pimiento Rice

Cooking Time: 19 minutes

- 12 mushrooms (about ½ pound)
- 6 shallots (about 12 ounces), minced
- 3 tablespoons butter or margarine
- 2½ cups chicken broth
- 1¼ cups long-grain rice
- 1 jar (4 ounces) pimientos, drained and diced
- Salt and pepper to taste

Mince mushroom stems. Cut caps into ⅛-inch thick slices; set aside. Combine minced stems, shallots, and butter in 3-quart microproof casserole. Place in oven. Set recipe number 181. Touch START. *(Oven cooks: micro,* 90, 2 *minutes.)*

At Pause, stir. Touch START. *(Oven cooks: micro,* 90, 2 *minutes.)*

At Pause, stir in broth and rice. Cover with casserole lid. Touch START. *(Oven cooks: micro,* 90, 10 *minutes.)*

At Pause, add mushroom caps. Cover. Touch START. *(Oven cooks: micro, HI,* 5 *minutes.)*

Add pimientos; blend well. Cover and let stand until all liquid is absorbed. Season with salt and pepper before serving.

6 to 8 servings

Recipe No. 182 ⊞

Rice Pilaf

Cooking Time: 23 minutes

- 2 cups water
- 1 cup long-grain rice
- ¼ cup chopped green pepper
- ¼ cup chopped onion
- ¼ cup instant minced onion
- 2 tablespoons butter or margarine
- 2 teaspoons chicken bouillon granules

Combine all ingredients in 2-quart microproof casserole. Cover with casserole lid and place in oven. Set recipe number 182. Touch START. *(Oven cooks: micro, HI,* 5 *minutes;* 50, 13 *minutes; stands:* 0, 5 *minutes.)*

Stir through before serving.

4 servings

⊞ *Recipe can be increased.* *See "Quantity", page 12.*

Recipe No. 183

Chicken Noodles au Gratin

Cooking Time: 15 minutes

- 1½ cups broken uncooked thin egg noodles
- 1 cup chicken broth
- ½ cup milk
- ½ teaspoon salt
- ⅛ teaspoon pepper
- 2 to 3 cups coarsely chopped cooked chicken or turkey
- 1 cup (4 ounces) shredded Cheddar cheese
- ¼ cup sliced stuffed green olives

Combine noodles, broth, milk, salt, and pepper in 2-quart microproof casserole; stir lightly. Cover with casserole lid and place in oven. Set recipe number 183. Touch START. *(Oven cooks: micro,* 70, 5 *minutes.)*

At Pause, stir in chicken, cheese, and olives. Cover. Touch START. *(Oven cooks: micro,* 70, 5 *minutes.)*

At Pause, stir. Cover. Touch START. *(Oven cooks: micro,* 20, 5 *minutes.)*

4 to 6 servings

Recipe No. 184

Noodles and Cheese

Cooking Time: 11 minutes

- ¼ cup butter or margarine
- ⅓ cup slivered almonds
- 2 cups (8 ounces) shredded Swiss cheese
- ½ cup milk
- 1 large egg, lightly beaten
- 1 teaspoon parsley flakes
- ¼ teaspoon pepper
- ¼ teaspoon nutmeg
- 3 cups cooked wide egg noodles

Place butter and almonds in 1½-quart microproof casserole. Place in oven. Set recipe number 184. Touch START. *(Oven cooks: micro, HI,* 1 *minute.)*

At Pause, add remaining ingredients except noodles; blend well. Add noodles; toss until separated and evenly coated. Cover with casserole lid. Touch START. *(Oven cooks: micro, HI,* 4 *minutes.)*

At Pause, stir. Cover. Touch START. *(Oven cooks: micro, HI,* 4 *minutes; stands:* 0, 2 *minutes.)*

4 to 6 servings

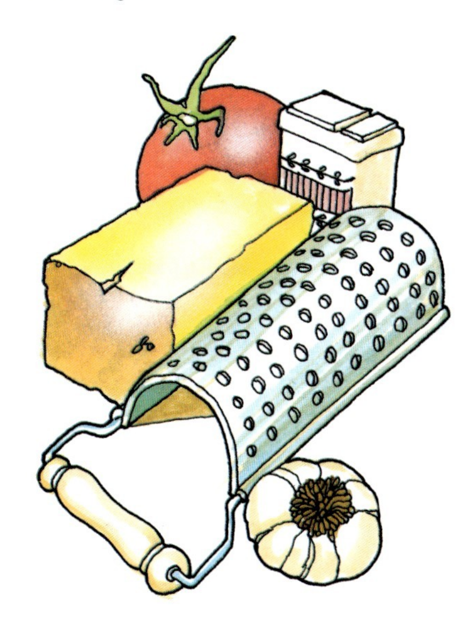

Recipe No. 185

San Francisco Dish

Cooking Time: 17 minutes

- 1 tablespoon beef bouillon granules
- 2½ cups hot water
- 1 medium onion, sliced
- 2 tablespoons butter or margarine
- 1 cup long-grain rice
- ½ cup broken uncooked spaghetti (1-inch pieces)

Dissolve bouillon in hot water; set aside. Place onion and butter in 3-quart microproof casserole. Cover with casserole lid and place in oven. Set recipe number 185. Touch START. *(Oven cooks: micro, HI,* 2 *minutes.)*

At Pause, add rice, spaghetti, and bouillon; stir lightly. Cover. Touch START. *(Oven cooks: micro, HI,* 15 *minutes.)*

Let stand 5 minutes before serving.

5 servings

Recipe No. 186

Casserole Italiano

Cooking Time: 25 minutes

- 1 pound lean ground beef
- 1½ cups spaghetti sauce
- 1½ cups water
- 1 can (16 ounces) green beans, drained
- 1 package (7 ounces) uncooked elbow macaroni
- 2 tablespoons onion flakes
- 1 tablespoon sugar
- 1 teaspoon Italian seasoning
- ½ teaspoon salt
- ⅛ teaspoon pepper
- 1 clove garlic, minced
- 1 cup (4 ounces) shredded mozzarella cheese

Crumble beef into 3-quart microproof casserole. Place in oven. Set recipe number 186. Touch START. *(Oven cooks: micro, HI, 3 minutes.)*

At Pause, remove from oven. Stir to break up beef; drain. Add remaining ingredients except cheese; blend well. Cover with casserole lid and place in oven. Touch START. *(Oven cooks: micro, HI, 12 minutes.)*

At Pause, stir. Cover. Touch START. *(Oven cooks: micro,* 60, 10 *minutes.)*

Sprinkle with cheese. Cover and let stand 10 minutes before serving.

6 to 8 servings

Recipe No. 187

Stroganoff Casserole

Preset Cooking Time: 27 minutes

- 1 pound lean ground beef
- ¼ cup chopped onion
- 2 cloves garlic, minced
- 3 cups (4 ounces) uncooked medium-width egg noodles
- 1 cup sliced mushrooms
- 1 can (13¾ ounces) beef broth
- ⅛ teaspoon pepper
- 1 container (8 ounces) dairy sour cream
- 2 tablespoons chopped parsley

Combine beef, onion, and garlic in 2-quart microproof casserole. Place in oven. Set recipe number 187. Touch START. *(Oven cooks: micro, HI, 3 minutes.)*

At Pause, stir. Touch START. *(Oven cooks: micro, HI, 2 minutes.)*

At Pause, stir in noodles, mushrooms, broth, and pepper. Cover with casserole lid. Touch START. *(Oven cooks: micro,* 50, 11 *minutes.)*

At Pause, stir. Cover. Touch START. *(Oven cooks: micro,* 50, 11 *minutes.)*

Remove from oven. Let stand 5 minutes. Blend in sour cream and sprinkle with parsley before serving.

6 servings

Recipe No. 188

Macaroni and Cheese Vegetable Medley

Cooking Time: 25 minutes

- 1½ cups hot water
- 1 cup uncooked elbow macaroni
- 1 package (10 ounces) frozen chopped broccoli
- 1 package (10 ounces) frozen sliced carrots
- 4 tablespoons butter or margarine
- ½ cup milk
- 1 tablespoon cornstarch
- ½ teaspoon salt
- ¼ teaspoon pepper
- ¼ teaspoon garlic powder
- ¼ teaspoon dry mustard
- 2 cups (8 ounces) shredded Cheddar cheese

Combine hot water, macaroni, broccoli, and carrots in 2-quart microproof casserole. Dot with butter. Cover with casserole lid and place in oven. Set recipe number 188. Touch START. *(Oven cooks: micro,* 70, 7 *minutes.)*

At Pause, stir. Cover. Touch START. *(Oven cooks: micro,* 70, 8 *minutes.)*

At Pause, combine milk, cornstarch, salt, pepper, garlic powder, and dry mustard. Stir until cornstarch is dissolved. Stir into macaroni mixture. Blend in cheese. Cover. Touch START. *(Oven cooks: micro,* 70, 5 *minutes; stands:* 0, 5 *minutes.)*

Let stand until all liquid is absorbed.

6 to 8 servings

This is one of several recipes that use the preset functions of another recipe for part of the cooking sequence. Set recipe number 214 first. At the end of that sequence, set recipe number 189.

Recipe No. 189

Zucchini Soufflé

Cooking Time: 1 hour 5 minutes

- 1 teaspoon butter
- ¼ cup grated Parmesan cheese
- ½ cup butter
- 1 pound young, tender zucchini, shredded
- 3 green onions or 1 medium onion, finely chopped
- 2 cloves garlic, minced
- ¼ cup dry white wine
- 3 tablespoons minced parsley
- 1 tablespoon fresh lemon juice
- Pinch nutmeg
- Salt and pepper to taste
- 1 jar (2 ounces) pimientos, finely diced
- 6 eggs, separated
- 2 tablespoons grated Parmesan cheese
- ½ teaspoon cream of tartar

Coat bottom and sides of 2-quart soufflé dish with 1 teaspoon butter. Sprinkle with ¼ cup Parmesan cheese, rotating dish to cover evenly and letting excess cheese remain on bottom. Refrigerate.

Combine ½ cup butter, zucchini, green onions, and garlic in 2-quart microproof bowl. Place in oven. Set recipe number 214. Touch START. *(Oven cooks: micro, HI,* 4 *minutes.)*

At Pause, add wine, parsley, lemon juice, nutmeg, salt, and pepper. Place in oven. Touch START. *(Oven cooks: micro, HI,* 6 *minutes.)* Add pimientos and mix well. Set aside to cool.

Remove ceramic tray. Place wire rack in oven bottom position. Set recipe number 189. Touch START. *(Oven preheats: convec, 350°F.)* Meanwhile, beat egg yolks with 2 tablespoons Parmesan cheese until thick and lemon colored. Blend in zucchini mixture. Beat egg whites in large bowl until foamy. Add cream of tartar and continue beating until stiff. Stir one-third of egg whites into zucchini mixture. Gently fold in remaining whites. Turn into prepared soufflé dish.

At 350°F, place in oven. Touch START. *(Oven cooks: convec, 350°F,* 55 *minutes.)* Serve immediately.

6 servings

Recipe No. 190 ⊞

Stuffed Tomatoes

Cooking Time: 18 minutes

1 package (10 ounces) frozen chopped spinach
4 medium-size firm tomatoes
1 cup (4 ounces) shredded mozzarella cheese, divided
¼ cup finely minced onions
¼ cup grated Parmesan cheese
½ teaspoon salt
⅛ teaspoon pepper
2 tablespoons minced parsley

Set unopened package of spinach on microproof plate. Place in oven. Set recipe number 190. Touch START. *(Oven cooks: micro, HI, 5 minutes; stands: 0, 5 minutes.)*

At Pause, drain spinach well; squeeze dry. Transfer to large bowl and set aside.

Slice ½-inch piece off top of each tomato. Carefully hollow out centers, discarding seeds and leaving ½-inch shell. Chop pulp finely and add to spinach. Invert shells on paper towels to drain. Add ½ cup mozzarella cheese, onion, Parmesan cheese, salt, and pepper to spinach mixture and blend well. Spoon evenly into tomato shells. Sprinkle with remaining mozzarella and parsley. Arrange in 8-inch round microproof and heatproof baking dish. Place wire rack in lower position. Place dish in oven on wire rack. Touch START. *(Oven cooks: micro/convec, 350°F, 8 minutes.)* Serve immediately.

4 servings

⊞ *Recipe can be increased. See "Quantity", page 12.*

Recipe No. 191

Asparagus Casserole

Cooking Time: 10 minutes

20 saltine crackers, crushed
1 can (15 ounces) asparagus pieces
¾ pound Cheddar cheese, shredded, divided
4 hard-cooked eggs, chopped, divided
½ cup milk
1 can (10¾ ounces) cream of mushroom soup, undiluted

Place wire rack in lower position. Set recipe number 191. Touch START. *(Oven preheats: convec, 350°F.)* Meanwhile, sprinkle half of cracker crumbs into 1½-quart microproof and heatproof casserole. Drain asparagus, reserving 3 tablespoons liquid. Arrange half of cheese, asparagus, and eggs over top. Repeat layering. Combine milk, soup, and reserved liquid in small bowl and blend well. Pour over top.

At 350°F, place in oven on wire rack. Touch START. *(Oven cooks: micro/convec, 350°F, 10 minutes.)* Serve hot.

6 to 8 servings

Broccoli, spinach, or zucchini can be substituted for asparagus.

Twice Baked Potatoes (page 164), Delightful Yams (page 164) →

Recipe No. 192

Stuffed Zucchini Boats

Cooking Time: 14 minutes

- 4 medium zucchini
- 1 cup (4 ounces) shredded Monterey Jack cheese
- 1 cup (4 ounces) shredded Cheddar cheese
- ¾ cup cornbread stuffing mix
- ¼ cup chopped onion
- 1 clove garlic, minced
- 2 tablespoons chopped parsley, divided
- ⅛ teaspoon pepper
- ⅛ teaspoon oregano
- 1 egg, lightly beaten
- ¼ cup grated Parmesan cheese

Place wire rack in lower position. Set recipe number 192. Touch START. *(Oven preheats: convec, 350°F.)* Meanwhile, cut zucchini in half lengthwise. Scoop out pulp, leaving ¼-inch shell. Dice pulp. Transfer to large bowl. Add Monterey Jack and Cheddar cheese, stuffing mix, onion, garlic, 1 tablespoon parsley, pepper, oregano, and egg and mix lightly. Fill zucchini shells evenly with mixture. Sprinkle with Parmesan cheese and remaining parsley. Arrange in oval microproof and heatproof dish just large enough for zucchini.

At 350°F, place in oven on wire rack. Touch START. *(Oven cooks: micro/convec, 350°F, 14 minutes.)* Serve immediately.

4 to 6 servings

Dried bread crumbs can be substituted for stuffing mix. Add ¼ teaspoon salt and cook as above.

Recipe No. 193

Ratatouille

Cooking Time: 46 minutes

- 1 eggplant (about 1½ pounds), peeled or unpeeled
- Salt
- ½ cup olive oil
- 2 medium onions, thinly sliced
- 2 cloves garlic, minced
- 1 green pepper, sliced into thin strips
- 4 zucchini (about 1 pound), cut into ¼-inch slices
- ¼ cup chopped parsley
- ½ teaspoon pepper
- ½ teaspoon basil leaves, crumbled
- ½ teaspoon oregano, crumbled
- ½ pound mushrooms, sliced
- 3 large tomatoes, peeled, seeded, and cut into wedges
- ¼ cup grated Parmesan cheese

Cut eggplant into 1-inch cubes. Transfer to colander and sprinkle with salt. Let stand 30 to 45 minutes. Rinse with cold water and drain. Combine oil, onions, garlic, and green pepper in 4-quart microproof and heatproof casserole. Cover with casserole lid. Place in oven. Set recipe number 193. Touch START. *(Oven cooks: micro, 90, 6 minutes.)*

At Pause, stir through several times. Add eggplant, zucchini, parsley, pepper, basil, and oregano and toss lightly. Cover. Place in oven on ceramic tray. Touch START. *(Oven cooks: micro/convec, 350°F, 20 minutes.)*

At Pause, stir in mushrooms and tomatoes. Cover. Place in oven. Touch START. *(Oven cooks: micro/convec, 350°F, 10 minutes.)*

At Pause, sprinkle casserole with cheese. Place in oven, uncovered. Touch START. *(Oven cooks: micro/convec, 350°F, 10 minutes.)* Serve hot.

6 to 8 servings

⊞ *Recipe can be increased.* *See "Quantity", page 12.*

Recipe No. 194

Scalloped Potatoes

Cooking Time: 19 minutes

- 4 medium red potatoes (about 1 pound), peeled and cut into 1/8-inch slices
- 3 tablespoons all-purpose flour
- 1 teaspoon salt
- 1 teaspoon garlic powder
- 1/8 teaspoon pepper
- 1 cup milk
- 2 tablespoons butter or margarine
- Paprika

Arrange half of potatoes in 1 1/2-quart microproof and heatproof casserole. Combine flour, salt, garlic powder, and pepper. Sprinkle half of mixture over potatoes. Repeat layering. Pour milk into 2-cup glass measure. Place in oven. Set recipe number 194. Touch START. *(Oven cooks: micro, HI, 2 minutes.)*

At Pause, pour milk over potatoes. Dot with butter and sprinkle with paprika. Cover with casserole lid. Place in oven. Touch START. *(Oven cooks: micro, HI, 10 minutes.)*

At Pause, remove cover. Touch START. *(Oven cooks: micro/convec, 350°F, 7 minutes.)* Serve immediately.

4 servings

For Scalloped Potatoes au Gratin, follow above recipe and sprinkle 3/4 cup shredded Cheddar cheese over each layer of potatoes.

Recipe No. 195 ⊞

Easy Country Fries

Cooking Time: 30 minutes

- 1/4 cup dehydrated onion flakes
- 1/8 teaspoon salt
- 1/2 teaspoon pepper
- 1/2 teaspoon paprika
- 2 pounds potatoes
- 1/2 cup butter or margarine, divided

Place wire rack in lower position. Set recipe number 195. Touch START. *(Oven preheats: convec, 350°F.)* Meanwhile, mix onion, salt, pepper, and paprika in small bowl. Rinse potatoes and pat dry (do not peel). Cut evenly into 1/4-inch slices. Arrange one-third of potatoes in 8-inch square microproof and heatproof baking dish. Sprinkle with one-third of onion mixture. Dot with one-third of butter. Repeat layering twice, ending with butter and onion mixture. Cover with plastic wrap.

At 350°F, place in oven on wire rack. Touch START. *(Oven cooks: micro/convec, 350°F, 20 minutes.)*

At Pause, remove cover. Rotate dish one-half turn. Touch START. *(Oven cooks: micro/convec, 350°F, 10 minutes.)* Serve immediately.

4 to 6 servings

Recipe No. 196

Potato Kugel

Cooking Time: 55 minutes

- 2 medium onions, cut into eighths
- 3 eggs
- 1 1/2 teaspoons salt
- 1/2 teaspoon baking powder
- 1/4 teaspoon pepper
- 5 medium potatoes, peeled and shredded
- 1/2 cup matzo meal
- 2 tablespoons vegetable oil, divided

Combine onions, eggs, salt, baking powder, and pepper in 2-quart bowl. Add potatoes and mix well. Blend in matzo meal. Stir in 1 tablespoon oil.

Remove ceramic tray. Place wire rack in lower position. Set recipe number 196. Touch START. *(Oven preheats: convec, 350°F.)* Meanwhile, coat 8-inch square baking dish with remaining oil. Pour in potato mixture.

At 350°F, place in oven on wire rack. Touch START. *(Oven cooks: convec, 350°F, 55 minutes.)* Serve immediately.

6 servings

If you prefer, all-purpose flour can be substituted for matzo meal.

Recipe No. 197

Twice-Baked Potatoes

Cooking Time: 22 minutes

- **4 baking potatoes**
- **½ cup butter or margarine, softened**
- **½ cup dairy sour cream**
- **½ teaspoon salt**
- **Pinch pepper**
- **4 teaspoons crumbled cooked bacon (optional)**

Place wire rack in lower position. Wash potatoes, pat dry, and pierce with fork several times. Arrange in circle on wire rack, spacing about 1 inch apart. Set recipe number 213. Touch START. *(Oven cooks: micro, HI, 6 minutes.)*

At Pause, turn potatoes over. Touch START. *(Oven cooks: micro, HI, 6 minutes.)* Remove potatoes from oven. Let stand several minutes.

Remove ceramic tray. Set recipe number 197. Touch START. *(Oven preheats: convec, 400°F.)* Meanwhile, remove ¼-inch horizontal slice from top of each potato. Carefully scoop pulp into medium bowl, keeping shells intact. Blend butter, sour cream, salt, and pepper into potato pulp and beat with electric mixer until smooth. Spoon mixture evenly into shells, mounding slightly in center (or pipe in with pastry bag). Arrange potatoes on heatproof platter.

At 400°F, place in oven on wire rack. Touch START. *(Oven cooks: convec, 400°F, 10 minutes.)* Sprinkle with bacon and serve immediately. Pass extra sour cream, if desired.

8 servings

Recipe No. 198

Delightful Yams

Cooking Time: 18 minutes

- **1 can (40 ounces) yams, well drained**
- **¼ cup fresh orange juice**
- **1 tablespoon cornstarch**
- **½ cup firmly-packed brown sugar**
- **¼ cup butter or margarine, melted**
- **1 orange, peeled and cubed**
- **½ cup coarsely chopped walnuts**
- **1 tablespoon grated orange peel**
- **1½ cups miniature marshmallows**

Place wire rack in upper position. Set recipe number 198. Touch START. *(Oven preheats: convec, 450°F.)* Meanwhile, arrange yams in 1½-quart round microproof and heatproof baking dish or quiche dish. Mix orange juice and cornstarch in medium bowl until cornstarch is completely dissolved. Blend in brown sugar and butter. Add orange, walnuts, and peel. Pour over yams.

At 450°F, place in oven. Touch START. *(Oven cooks: micro/convec, 450°F, 15 minutes.)*

At Pause, arrange about 1¼ cups marshmallows around rim of dish. Mound remaining marshmallows in center. Return dish to oven. Touch START. *(Oven cooks: micro/convec, 450°F, 3 minutes.)* Serve immediately.

6 servings

Recipe No. 199

Cabbage

Cooking Time: 8 minutes

- **½ medium head cabbage, shredded**
- **¼ cup water**

Place cabbage in 1-quart microproof casserole. Add water. Cover with casserole lid and place in oven. Set recipe number 199. Touch START. *(Oven cooks: micro, HI, 4 minutes.)*

At Pause, stir. Cover. Touch START. *(Oven cooks: micro, HI, 2 minutes; stands: 0, 2 minutes.)*

Drain before serving.

4 servings

Recipe No. 200

Carrots

Cooking Time: 10 minutes

1 pound carrots, peeled and thinly sliced
2 tablespoons water

Place carrots in 1-quart microproof casserole. Add water. Cover with casserole lid and place in oven. Set recipe number 200. Touch START. *(Oven cooks: micro, HI, 5 minutes.)*

At Pause, stir. Cover. Touch START. *(Oven cooks: micro, HI, 5 minutes.)*

Let stand 2 to 3 minutes. Drain before serving.

4 servings

Recipe No. 201

Canned Vegetables

Cooking Time: 2½ minutes

1 can (8 ounces) canned vegetables, drained

Pour vegetables into 1-quart microproof casserole. Cover with casserole lid and place in oven. Set recipe number 201. Touch START. *(Oven cooks: micro, 80, 1 minute.)*

At Pause, stir. Cover. Touch START. *(Oven cooks: micro, 80, 1½ minutes.)*

Let stand 2 to 3 minutes before serving.

2 servings

Recipe No. 202 ⊞

Cauliflower

Cooking Time: 11 minutes

1 head cauliflower (1⅓ pounds)
¼ cup water

Remove stem and outer leaves from cauliflower; discard. Rinse well. Break into florets. Place in 1½- to 2-quart microproof casserole. Add water. Cover with casserole lid and place in oven. Set recipe number 202. Touch START. *(Oven cooks: micro, HI, 5 minutes.)*

At Pause, stir. Cover. Touch START. *(Oven cooks: micro, HI, 3 minutes; stands: 0, 3 minutes.)*

Drain before serving.

5 to 6 servings

Recipe No. 203

Carrot-Broccoli Casserole

Cooking Time: 15¾ minutes

1 package (10 ounces) frozen broccoli spears
1 can (10¾ ounces) cream of chicken soup, undiluted
1 cup finely shredded carrots
½ cup dairy sour cream
1 tablespoon all-purpose flour
1 tablespoon minced onion
¼ teaspoon salt
⅛ teaspoon pepper
2 tablespoons butter or margarine
¾ cup herb-seasoned stuffing cubes

Place broccoli in package on microproof plate. Place in oven. Set recipe number 203. Touch START. *(Oven cooks: micro, HI, 3 minutes.)*

At Pause, remove from oven; set aside. Combine soup, carrots, sour cream, flour, onion, salt, and pepper in 1½-quart microproof casserole. Cut broccoli into 1-inch pieces; stir into soup mixture. Cover with casserole lid and place in oven. Touch START. *(Oven cooks: micro, HI, 6 minutes.)*

At Pause, remove from oven. Stir; set aside. Place butter in 2-cup glass measure. Place in oven. Touch START. *(Oven cooks: micro, HI, 45 seconds.)*

At Pause, remove from oven. Add stuffing cubes to butter; blend well. Spoon over broccoli mixture. Place in oven. Touch START. *(Oven cooks: micro, HI, 6 minutes.)*

5 to 6 servings

⊞ *Recipe can be increased. See "Quantity", page 12.*

Recipe No. 204 ⊞

Corn-on-the-Cob

Cooking Time: 9 minutes

2 unhusked ears of corn (about 7 ounces each)
Butter or margarine
Salt to taste

Discard any soiled outer leaves of husks. Soak corn in cold water 5 to 10 minutes to clean and moisten. Drain well; do not dry. Place directly on microwave roasting rack. Place in oven. Set recipe number 204. Touch START. *(Oven cooks: micro, HI, 7 minutes; stands:* 0, 2 *minutes.)*

Serve with butter and salt.

2 servings

Corn can be husked before cooking. Wrap each ear in waxed paper or plastic wrap. Set recipe number and cook as directed above.

⊞ *Recipe can be increased.* *See "Quantity", page 12.*

Recipe No. 205

Corn-Mushroom Scallop

Cooking Time: 14 minutes

1 can (17 ounces) cream-style corn
1/4 pound mushrooms, sliced
1 large egg, lightly beaten
3/4 cup soda-cracker crumbs, divided
1 tablespoon chopped chives
1/4 teaspoon white pepper
2 tablespoons butter or margarine

Combine corn, mushrooms, and egg in 1-quart microproof casserole; blend well. Stir in 1/2 cup cracker crumbs, chives, and pepper. Spread evenly in casserole. Sprinkle with remaining 1/4 cup cracker crumbs. Dot with butter. Place in oven. Set recipe number 205. Touch START. *(Oven cooks: micro, HI,* 9 *minutes; stands:* 0, 5 *minutes.)*

4 servings

Recipe No. 206

Creamed Potato Mix

Cooking Time: 13 minutes

1 package (5 ounces) creamed potato mix

Prepare potato mix (do not boil water) as directed on package in 3-quart round microproof casserole. Place in oven. Cover lightly with waxed paper. Set recipe number 206. Touch START. *(Oven cooks: micro, HI,* 8 *minutes; stands:* 0, 5 *minutes.)*

4 servings

Recipe No. 207

Creamy Cabbage

Cooking Time: 10 minutes

1 medium head cabbage, shredded
1/4 cup water
1 package (3 ounces) cream cheese, cut into cubes
2 tablespoons milk
1/2 teaspoon salt
1/2 teaspoon celery seeds
Dash pepper
Chopped parsley

Place cabbage and water in 2-quart microproof casserole. Cover with casserole lid and place in oven. Set recipe number 207. Touch START. *(Oven cooks: micro, HI,* 5 *minutes.)*

At Pause, stir. Cover. Touch START. *(Oven cooks: micro, HI,* 4 *minutes.)*

At Pause, add remaining ingredients except parsley. Cover. Touch START. *(Oven cooks: micro, HI,* 1 *minute.)*

Stir to combine cream cheese and cabbage. Sprinkle with parsley before serving.

5 to 6 servings

Recipe No. 208 ⊞

Eggplant

Cooking Time: 7 minutes

1 eggplant (1 pound)

Wash eggplant and pierce skin in several places. Place on microwave roasting rack. Place in oven. Set recipe number 208. Touch START. *(Oven cooks: micro, HI, 7 minutes.)*

Let stand 3 minutes before slicing.

4 to 6 servings

Recipe No. 209

Green Beans Amandine

Cooking Time: 9 minutes

½ cup sliced almonds
2 tablespoons butter or margarine
1 package (10 ounces) frozen French cut green beans
Salt and pepper to taste

Place almonds and butter in 1-cup glass measure; set aside. Place beans in package on microproof plate. Place in oven. Set recipe number 209. Touch START. *(Oven cooks: micro, HI, 6 minutes.)*

At Pause, remove from oven; set aside. Place almonds and butter in oven. Touch START. *(Oven cooks: micro, HI, 1 minute.)*

At Pause, stir. Touch START. *(Oven cooks: micro, HI, 1 minute.)*

At Pause, remove from oven. Transfer beans to microproof serving dish. Add almonds, salt, and pepper; toss lightly. Place in oven. Touch START. *(Oven cooks: micro, HI, 1 minute.)*

3 to 4 servings

Recipe No. 210

Green Beans Italiano

Cooking Time: 17½ minutes

3 slices bacon
2 packages (10 ounces each) frozen green beans
1 small onion, thickly sliced
¾ cup Italian dressing

Arrange bacon on paper towel-lined microproof plate. Place in oven. Cover with paper towel. Set recipe number 210. Touch START. *(Oven cooks: micro, HI, 3½ minutes.)*

At Pause, remove from oven. Crumble bacon; set aside. Place beans in packages on microproof plate. Place in oven. Touch START. *(Oven cooks: micro, HI, 5 minutes.)*

At Pause, turn packages over. Touch START. *(Oven cooks: micro, HI, 5 minutes.)*

At Pause, remove from oven. Transfer beans to 1½-quart microproof casserole. Add onion and dressing; blend well. Cover with casserole lid and place in oven. Touch START. *(Oven cooks: micro, HI, 4 minutes.)*

Sprinkle with crumbled bacon before serving.

6 servings

Recipe No. 211

Harvard Beets

Cooking Time: 8 minutes

- 1 can (16 ounces) diced or sliced beets
- ¼ cup sugar
- ¼ cup wine vinegar
- 1 tablespoon cornstarch
- ½ teaspoon salt
- ⅛ teaspoon pepper

Drain beet liquid into 1-cup glass measure. Add water to equal 1 cup liquid; set aside. Combine sugar, vinegar, cornstarch, salt, and pepper in 1-quart microproof casserole; stir until cornstarch is dissolved. Stir in beet-water mixture. Place in oven. Set recipe number 211. Touch START. *(Oven cooks: micro, HI, 1½ minutes.)*

At Pause, stir. Touch START. *(Oven cooks: micro, HI, 1½ minutes.)*

At Pause, add beets; stir to coat. Cover. Touch START. *(Oven cooks: micro, HI, 5 minutes.)*

4 servings

Recipe No. 212

Onions

Cooking Time: 12 minutes

- 1 pound onions, peeled and cut into quarters
- ¼ cup water
- 1 tablespoon butter

Place onions, water, and butter in wide shallow microproof baking dish. Cover with plastic wrap and place in oven. Set recipe number 212. Touch START. *(Oven cooks: micro, HI, 4 minutes.)*

At Pause, stir. Cover. Touch START. *(Oven cooks: micro, HI, 5 minutes; stands: 0, 3 minutes.)*

3 to 4 servings

Recipe No. 213 ⊞

Parsley New Potatoes

Cooking Time: 12 minutes

- 12 new potatoes (1 pound)
- ¼ cup water
- 2 tablespoons butter
- 1 tablespoon minced parsley
- Dash salt and pepper

Cut ½-inch strip around middle of each potato. Place in 2-quart microproof casserole. Add water. Cover with casserole lid and place in oven. Set recipe number 213. Touch START. *(Oven cooks: micro, HI, 6 minutes.)*

At Pause, stir. Cover. Touch START. *(Oven cooks: micro, HI, 6 minutes.)*

Drain. Stir in butter, parsley, salt, and pepper. Serve hot.

4 servings

Recipe No. 214

Peas Francine

Cooking Time: 10 minutes

- 2 cups shelled green peas
- ¼ cup water
- 1 teaspoon sugar
- 3 or 4 large lettuce leaves
- Dash salt and pepper

Combine peas, water, and sugar in 1½-quart microproof casserole. Cover with casserole lid and place in oven. Set recipe number 214. Touch START. *(Oven cooks: micro, HI, 4 minutes.)*

At Pause, stir. Cover with lettuce, overlapping leaves as necessary. Cover. Touch START. *(Oven cooks: micro, HI, 6 minutes.)*

Discard lettuce leaves. Drain peas; stir in salt and pepper. Cover and let stand 2 to 3 minutes before serving.

4 servings

Recipe No. 215 ⊞

Green Peas

Cooking Time: 10 minutes

1 pound peas in shells
1/4 cup water

Shell peas; rinse and drain. Place peas and water in wide, shallow, microproof baking dish. Cover with plastic wrap and place in oven. Set recipe number 215. Touch START. *(Oven cooks: micro, HI, 4 minutes.)*

At Pause, stir. Cover. Touch START. *(Oven cooks: micro, HI, 4 minutes; stands:* 0, 2 *minutes.)*

Drain and serve seasoned with butter and salt, if desired.

2 servings

Recipe No. 216 ⊞

Baked Potatoes

Cooking Time: 9 minutes

2 potatoes (6 ounces each)

Scrub potatoes and rinse well. Pierce at intervals with fork. Place about 1 inch apart on microwave roasting rack. Place in oven. Set recipe number 216. Touch START. *(Oven cooks: micro, HI, 5 minutes.)*

At Pause, turn potatoes over. Touch START. *(Oven cooks: micro, HI, 4 minutes.)*

Let stand 3 minutes before serving.

2 servings

Recipe No. 217

Savory Cauliflower

Cooking Time: 10 1/2 minutes

1 head cauliflower (1 1/3 pounds)
1/4 cup water
1/2 cup mayonnaise
1 tablespoon instant minced onion
1/2 teaspoon dry mustard
1/4 teaspoon salt
4 slices Cheddar cheese
Paprika

Cut cone-shaped section from cauliflower core. Place cauliflower, cut-side up, in 1 1/2-quart microproof casserole. Add water. Cover with plastic wrap and place in oven. Set recipe number 217. Touch START. *(Oven cooks: micro, HI, 5 minutes.)*

At Pause, turn over. Cover. Touch START. *(Oven cooks: micro, HI, 4 minutes.)*

At Pause, remove from oven; drain. Combine mayonnaise, onion, mustard, and salt; spoon over cauliflower. Lay cheese slices on top. Place in oven. Do not cover. Touch START. *(Oven cooks: micro,* 70, 1 1/2 *minutes.)*

Sprinkle with paprika. Let stand 2 minutes before serving.

6 servings

Recipe No. 218

Scalloped Potato Mix

Cooking Time: 19 minutes

1 package (7 ounces) scalloped potato mix

Prepare scalloped potatoes as directed on package in 3-quart microproof casserole. Cover with casserole lid and place in oven. Set recipe number 218. Touch START. *(Oven cooks: micro, HI,* 4 *minutes;* 50, 10 *minutes; stands:* 0, 5 *minutes.)*

Stir through before serving.

6 servings

⊞ *Recipe can be increased. See "Quantity",* *page 12.*

Recipe No. 219

Spinach

Cooking Time: 6 minutes

1 pound spinach, tough stems removed
Salt and pepper to taste

Rinse spinach and drain. Place in wide shallow microproof baking dish. Cover with plastic wrap and place in oven. Set recipe number 219. Touch START. *(Oven cooks: micro, HI, 6 minutes.)*

Let stand 2 minutes before draining. Season with salt and pepper before serving.

2 servings

Recipe No. 220

Spinach Oriental

Cooking Time: 5 minutes

10 ounces spinach, tough stems removed
1 can (8 ounces) sliced water chestnuts, drained
4 green onions, sliced
2 tablespoons vegetable oil
2 tablespoons wine vinegar
2 tablespoons soy sauce
1 teaspoon sugar

Rinse spinach and drain; tear into bite-size pieces. Combine spinach, water chestnuts, and onions in 2-quart microproof casserole. Cover with casserole lid and place in oven. Set recipe number 220. Touch START. *(Oven cooks: micro, HI, 4 minutes.)*

At Pause, remove from oven; drain. Stir, cover, and set aside. Combine oil, vinegar, soy sauce, and sugar in 1-cup glass measure; stir until sugar is dissolved. Place in oven. Touch START. *(Oven cooks: micro, HI, 1 minute.)*

Stir and pour over spinach mixture; toss lightly. Serve immediately.

4 servings

Recipe No. 221 ⊞

Sweet Potatoes

Cooking Time: 5 minutes

1 sweet potato (about 5 ounces)

Scrub potato and rinse well. Pierce at intervals with fork. Place on microwave roasting rack. Place in oven. Set recipe number 221. Touch START. *(Oven cooks: micro, HI, 5 minutes.)*

Let stand 3 minutes before serving.

1 serving

Recipe No. 222

Sweet-Sour Red Cabbage

Cooking Time: 23 minutes

1 head red cabbage (1½ pounds), shredded
1 tart apple, peeled, cored, and diced
5 tablespoons wine vinegar
1 tablespoon butter or margarine
3 tablespoons sugar
1 teaspoon salt

Combine cabbage, apple, vinegar, and butter in 3-quart microproof casserole; blend well. Cover with casserole lid and place in oven. Set recipe number 222. Touch START. *(Oven cooks: micro, HI, 6 minutes.)*

At Pause, stir. Cover. Touch START. *(Oven cooks: micro, HI, 6 minutes.)*

At Pause, stir. Cover. Touch START. *(Oven cooks: micro, HI, 6 minutes.)*

At Pause, add sugar and salt; blend well. Cover. Touch START. *(Oven cooks: micro, HI, 5 minutes.)*

6 servings

⊞ *Recipe can be increased. See "Quantity", page 12.*

Recipe No. 223

Cranberry Carrots

Cooking Time: 13 minutes

1 pound carrots, thinly sliced
2 tablespoons water
1/4 cup butter or margarine
1/4 cup jellied cranberry sauce
Salt to taste

Place carrots and water in 1 1/2- to 2-quart microproof casserole. Cover with casserole lid and place in oven. Set recipe number 223. Touch START. *(Oven cooks: micro, HI,* 10 *minutes.)*

At Pause, remove from oven. Remove carrots from casserole; drain water. Set carrots aside. Place butter and cranberry sauce in casserole. Cover and place in oven. Touch START. *(Oven cooks: micro, HI,* 1 *minute.)*

At Pause, stir in carrots. Season with salt. Touch START. *(Oven cooks: micro, HI,* 2 *minutes.)*

4 servings

Recipe No. 224

Corn and Pepper Pudding

Cooking Time: 24 minutes

2 tablespoons butter or margarine
2 tablespoons chopped green pepper
2 tablespoons chopped pimiento
2 cans (17 ounces each) cream-style corn
2 large eggs, lightly beaten
3 tablespoons all-purpose flour
1 tablespoon instant minced onion
1 teaspoon salt
1/4 teaspoon pepper

Combine butter, green pepper, and pimiento in shallow 1 1/2-quart round or oval microproof baking dish. Place in oven. Set recipe number 224. Touch START. *(Oven cooks: micro,* 90, 2 *minutes.)*

At Pause, stir in remaining ingredients; blend well. Cover with plastic wrap. Touch START. *(Oven cooks: micro,* 70, 9 *minutes.)*

At Pause, stir. Do not cover. Touch START. *(Oven cooks: micro,* 70, 8 *minutes; stands:* 0, 5 *minutes.)*

6 servings

Sauce Sorcery

Sauces are a cinch in your Kenmore Auto Recipe 300 Micro/Convection Oven. They are definitely a microwave success story. For those of us who have slaved over a hot stove with whisk in hand and double boiler at full speed, those days are gone forever. Sauces simply do not stick or scorch as they do when prepared on the stove top. They heat evenly and require less time and attention. You don't have to stir constantly and can simply retire that double boiler. Usually, just an occasional stirring is all that is required to prevent lumping. Sometimes, a quick beating after cooking can be added to make a sauce velvety-smooth. You can measure, mix, and cook all in the same cup, or in the serving pitcher itself! Choose Tarragon Sauce (page 180) or Béarnaise Sauce (page 176) to perk up meat or vegetables, others for desserts. Just try making a sauce the microwave way and you'll turn an ordinary food into an elegant treat.

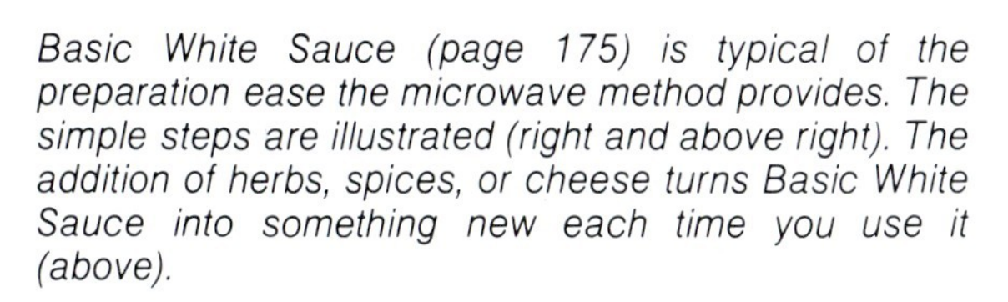

Basic White Sauce (page 175) is typical of the preparation ease the microwave method provides. The simple steps are illustrated (right and above right). The addition of herbs, spices, or cheese turns Basic White Sauce into something new each time you use it (above).

← *Hot Fudge Sauce (page 179) on banana splits, Raspberry Sauce (page 179) on poached pears.*

Converting Your Recipes

All those sauces generally considered too difficult for the average cook are easy in the microwave oven. When looking for a sauce recipe similar to the conventional one you want to convert, find a recipe with a similar quantity of liquid and similar main thickening ingredient such as cornstarch, flour, egg, cheese, or jelly. Read the directions carefully to determine procedure, timing, and micro control setting. Then, when you stir, notice the progress of the sauce, and remove when the right consistency or doneness is reached. Keep notes to help you the next time. The following tips will help:

- ☐ Use a microproof container about twice the volume of ingredients to safeguard against the sauce boiling over — so easy with milk- and cream-based sauces.
- ☐ Sauces and salad dressings with ingredients not sensitive to high heat should be cooked on HI. Basic White Sauce is an example.
- ☐ Bring flour and other starch-thickened mixtures to a boil and remove as soon as thickened. Remember, overcooking will destroy the thickening agent and sauce will be too thin.
- ☐ You will notice that more flour or cornstarch is required in microwave cooking than in conventional cooking to thicken sauces and gravies, since they will not be reduced by evaporation.
- ☐ Stirring quickly two or three times during cooking is sufficient to assure even cooking. Too many stirrings may slow cooking.
- ☐ To reheat sauces: Dessert sauces to 125°F with temperature probe. Main dish sauces, such as gravy or canned spaghetti sauce, to 150°F with temperature probe.
- ☐ When sauces require time to develop flavor or if they contain eggs, which might curdle, they should be cooked slowly, on 50 or even 30. Don't allow delicate egg yolk sauces to boil.
- ☐ You can make your own special sauce by flavoring Basic White Sauce (page 175) as desired. For example, add cheese, cooked mushrooms, cooked onions, your favorite spices, tomato paste, or horseradish.

Recipe No. 225 ⊞

Basic White Sauce

Cooking Time: 7 minutes

- 1 cup milk
- 2 tablespoons butter
- 2 tablespoons all-purpose flour
- Dash white pepper
- Dash nutmeg

Pour milk into 4-cup glass measure. Place in oven. Set recipe number 225. Touch START. *(Oven cooks: micro,* 70, 2 *minutes.)*

At Pause, set milk aside. Place butter in 2-cup glass measure. Place in oven. Touch START. *(Oven cooks: micro, HI,* 1 *minute.)*

At Pause, stir flour into butter. Touch START. *(Oven cooks: micro, HI,* 1 *minute.)*

At Pause, slowly stir milk into flour mixture, blending until smooth. Season with pepper and nutmeg. Place in oven. Touch START. *(Oven cooks: micro, HI,* 3 *minutes.)* Stir through several times. Serve hot.

1 cup

Recipe No. 226

Beef Gravy

Cooking Time: 11 minutes

- ½ cup beef drippings
- ½ cup all-purpose flour
- 4 cups water, heated
- Salt and pepper to taste
- Bottled brown sauce (optional)

Combine drippings and flour in 4-quart microproof casserole and blend well. Place in oven. Set recipe number 226. Touch START. *(Oven cooks: micro, HI,* 30 *seconds.)*

At Pause, stir. Touch START. *(Oven cooks: micro, HI,* 30 *seconds.)*

At Pause, blend in water. Touch START. *(Oven cooks: micro, HI,* 5 *minutes.)*

At Pause, stir. Touch START. *(Oven cooks: micro, HI,* 5 *minutes.)* Season with salt and pepper. Add several drops of brown sauce to deepen color, if desired.

1 quart

Recipe No. 227 ⊞

Lemon Sauce

Cooking Time: 2½ minutes

- ⅔ cup water
- ⅓ cup sugar
- 2 tablespoons cornstarch
- 3 tablespoons fresh lemon juice
- 1 egg yolk
- 1 tablespoon butter or margarine
- 1 teaspoon grated lemon peel
- Pinch salt
- Yellow food coloring (optional)

Combine all ingredients in 1-quart glass measure and blend well. Place in oven. Set recipe number 227. Touch START. *(Oven cooks: micro, HI,* 1½ *minutes.)*

At Pause, stir. Touch START. *(Oven cooks: micro, HI,* 1 *minute.)* Stir briskly until thick and smooth. Serve over pound cake.

about 1 cup

Recipe No. 228 ⊞

Barbecue Sauce

Cooking Time: 8 minutes

- ⅓ cup chopped onion
- 1 clove garlic, minced
- 1 tablespoon butter or margarine
- 1 can (8 ounces) tomato sauce
- 2 tablespoons dark brown sugar
- 2 tablespoons fresh lemon juice
- 1 teaspoon Worcestershire sauce
- ½ teaspoon salt
- ¼ teaspoon paprika
- ¼ teaspoon dry mustard
- ¼ teaspoon pepper
- ⅛ teaspoon ground turmeric

Combine onion, garlic, and butter in 2-quart glass measure. Place in oven. Set recipe number 228. Touch START. *(Oven cooks: micro, HI,* 3 *minutes.)*

At Pause, stir in remaining ingredients. Place in oven. Touch START. *(Oven cooks: micro, HI,* 3 *minutes.)*

At Pause, stir. Touch START. *(Oven cooks: micro, HI,* 2 *minutes.)*

1½ cups

⊞ *Recipe can be increased. See "Quantity", page 12.*

Recipe No. 229

Homemade Spaghetti Sauce

Cooking Time: 23 minutes

- 1 medium onion, sliced
- ¼ cup sliced celery
- 6 medium mushrooms, sliced
- ½ green pepper, sliced into thin strips
- 2 cloves garlic, minced
- 1½ tablespoons vegetable oil
- ½ pound lean ground beef
- 1 can (14 ounces) whole peeled tomatoes, chopped, liquid reserved
- 1 can (6 ounces) tomato paste
- 1 tablespoon chopped parsley
- ½ teaspoon oregano, crumbled

Combine onion, celery, mushrooms, green pepper, garlic, and oil in 2-quart microproof and heatproof casserole. Cover with casserole lid. Place in oven. Set recipe number 229. Touch START. *(Oven cooks: micro, HI, 5 minutes.)*

At Pause, stir in beef. Place in oven. Touch START. *(Oven cooks: micro, HI, 3 minutes.)*

At Pause, stir through several times. Blend in tomatoes with liquid, tomato paste, parsley, and oregano. Cover. Place in oven. Touch START. *(Oven cooks: micro/convec, 350°F, 15 minutes.)*

about 4 cups

Recipe No. 230 ⊞

Apricot Dessert Sauce

Cooking Time: 4 minutes

- 1 cup apricot nectar
- ¼ cup sugar
- 1 tablespoon cornstarch
- 1 teaspoon grated lemon peel
- 3 tablespoons apricot-flavored brandy

Combine apricot nectar, sugar, cornstarch, and lemon peel in 2-cup glass measure; stir until sugar and cornstarch are dissolved. Place in oven. Set recipe number 230. Touch START. *(Oven cooks: micro, HI, 1½ minutes.)*

At Pause, stir. Cover with plastic wrap. Touch START. *(Oven cooks: micro, HI, 1½ minutes.)*

At Pause, add brandy; blend well. Touch START. *(Oven cooks: micro, HI, 1 minute.)*

Stir through several times. Serve warm or chilled over ice cream, rice pudding, tapioca, or pound cake.

1⅓ cups

To make a Lemon Dessert Sauce, substitute ½ cup water for the 1 cup apricot nectar, lemon juice for the brandy, and add 1 egg yolk and 1 tablespoon butter.

Recipe No. 231 ⊞

Béarnaise Sauce

Cooking Time: 1½ minutes

- 4 egg yolks
- 2 teaspoons tarragon vinegar
- 1 teaspoon instant minced onion
- ½ teaspoon chervil
- Dash white pepper
- ½ cup butter or margarine
- 1 teaspoon minced parsley

Combine egg yolks, vinegar, onion, chervil, and pepper in blender or food processor container; set aside. Place butter in 1-cup glass measure. Place in oven. Set recipe number 231. Touch START. *(Oven cooks: micro, HI, 1½ minutes.)*

With blender at high speed, gradually add melted butter through cover opening; process until thick and creamy. Stir in parsley. Serve warm over broiled steak, green vegetables, poached eggs, or fish.

½ cup

⊞ Recipe can be increased. See "Quantity", page 12.

Filet Mignon with Tarragon Sauce (page 180), Carrots with Clarified Butter (page 178) →

Recipe No. 232 ⊞

Clarified Butter

Cooking Time: 2½ minutes

1 cup butter

Place butter in 2-cup glass measure. Place in oven. Set recipe number 232. Touch START. *(Oven cooks: micro,* 20, 2½ *minutes.)*

Let stand 3 to 4 minutes. Skim foam from top. Slowly pour off yellow oil. This is the clarified butter. Discard the leftover impurities. Serve as dipping sauce for steamed clams, crab legs, or shrimp.

⅓ cup

Recipe No. 233 ⊞

Choco-Peanut Butter Sauce

Cooking Time: 3½ minutes

¼ cup milk
1 square (1 ounce) unsweetened chocolate
1 cup sugar
1 tablespoon light corn syrup
⅓ cup peanut butter
¼ teaspoon vanilla

Place milk and chocolate in 4-cup glass measure. Place in oven. Set recipe number 233. Touch START. *(Oven cooks: micro, HI,* 1½ *minutes.)*

At Pause, stir until chocolate is melted. Add sugar and corn syrup; blend well. Touch START. *(Oven cooks: micro, HI,* 2 *minutes.)*

Add peanut butter and vanilla; blend well. Serve hot or chilled over ice cream, cake, or sliced bananas.

1 cup

Recipe No. 234 ⊞

Hollandaise Sauce

Cooking Time: 2 minutes

¼ cup butter
¼ cup light cream
2 egg yolks, well beaten
1 tablespoon lemon juice
½ teaspoon dry mustard
¼ teaspoon salt

Place butter in 4-cup glass measure. Place in oven. Set recipe number 234. Touch START. *(Oven cooks: micro, HI,* 1 *minute.)*

At Pause, remove from oven. Add remaining ingredients. Beat with electric mixer or wire whisk until smooth. Place in oven. Touch START. *(Oven cooks: micro,* 70, 30 *seconds.)*

At Pause, beat until blended. Touch START. *(Oven cooks: micro,* 70, 15 *seconds.)*

At Pause, stir. Touch START. *(Oven cooks: micro,* 70, 15 *seconds.)*

Beat until smooth. Serve immediately over cooked asparagus or broccoli.

¾ cup

If sauce curdles, beat in 1 *teaspoon hot water, and continue beating until smooth.*

To reheat Hollandaise Sauce, cook on 20 *for* 15 *to* 30 *seconds. Stir; let stand* 1 *minute. Repeat until hot.*

Recipe No. 235 ⊞

Hot Fudge Sauce

Cooking Time: 5 minutes

- 1 cup sugar
- 2 squares (1 ounce each) unsweetened chocolate
- ⅓ cup milk
- 3 tablespoons light corn syrup
- 1 large egg, well beaten
- 1 teaspoon vanilla

Combine all ingredients except vanilla in 4-cup glass measure; blend well. Place in oven. Set recipe number 235. Touch START. *(Oven cooks: micro, HI, 2 minutes.)*

At Pause, stir until blended. Touch START. *(Oven cooks: micro, 50, 1½ minutes.)*

At Pause, stir. Touch START. *(Oven cooks: micro, 50, 1½ minutes.)*

Blend in vanilla. Briskly stir with wire whisk until clear and shiny. Refrigerate until cool; sauce will thicken as it stands. Serve over ice cream, chocolate cake, fresh fruit, or as a fondue for dipping pound cake or fresh berries.

1 cup

Recipe No. 236 ⊞

Lemon Butter Sauce

Cooking Time: 1½ minutes

- ½ cup butter
- 2 tablespoons lemon juice
- ⅛ teaspoon salt
- ⅛ teaspoon white pepper

Combine all ingredients in 2-cup glass measure. Place in oven. Set recipe number 236. Touch START. *(Oven cooks: micro, HI, 1½ minutes.)*

Stir sauce. Serve immediately with seafood, hot green vegetables, or Salmon Ring (page 137).

⅔ cup

Recipe No. 237 ⊞

Orange Sauce

Cooking Time: 3 minutes

- ⅔ cup orange juice
- 3 tablespoons fat-free duckling drippings
- 2 tablespoons brown sugar
- 1 tablespoon cornstarch
- 2 teaspoons grated orange peel
- 2 tablespoons orange-flavored liqueur

Combine all ingredients except liqueur in 2-cup glass measure; stir until brown sugar and cornstarch are dissolved. Place in oven. Set recipe number 237. Touch START. *(Oven cooks: micro, HI, 1½ minutes.)*

At Pause, stir. Touch START. *(Oven cooks: micro, HI, 1½ minutes.)*

Stir in liqueur. Serve hot with Roast Duckling (page 124).

1¼ cups

Not having duckling? Any poultry drippings will do. Or, simply increase orange juice by 3 tablespoons and use as a dessert sauce.

Recipe No. 238

Raspberry Sauce

Cooking Time: 6 minutes

- 1 package (10 ounces) frozen raspberries
- 1 teaspoon cornstarch
- 1 tablespoon water

Place raspberries in 1½-quart microproof bowl. Place in oven. Set recipe number 238. Touch START. *(Oven cooks: micro, HI, 3 minutes.)*

At Pause, remove from oven. Break up raspberries with wooden spoon. Press through sieve, discarding seeds, if desired. Return to bowl. Dissolve cornstarch in water; stir into berries. Place in oven. Touch START. *(Oven cooks: micro, HI, 3 minutes.)*

Stir through several times. Serve over angel food cake or ice cream.

1½ cups

Recipe No. 239 ⊞

Strawberry Sauce

Cooking Time: 4 minutes

- 1 pint strawberries, hulled
- 1 cup water
- ½ cup sugar
- 2 tablespoons cornstarch
- 2 tablespoons butter
- ½ cup lemon juice

Set aside a few of the best strawberries for garnish. Force remaining strawberries through food mill, or purée with blender or food processor. Strain to remove seeds; set purée aside. Combine water, sugar, and cornstarch in 4-cup glass measure; stir until sugar and cornstarch are dissolved. Place in oven. Set recipe number 239. Touch START. *(Oven cooks: micro, HI, 2 minutes.)*

At Pause, stir. Cover with plastic wrap. Touch START. *(Oven cooks: micro, HI, 1 minute.)*

At Pause, stir. Cover. Touch START. *(Oven cooks: micro, HI, 1 minute.)*

Add butter; stir until melted. Stir in lemon juice and strawberry purée; blend well. Serve chilled over pound cake, vanilla pudding, custard, or as a parfait sauce.

2½ cups

Recipe No. 240 ⊞

Tarragon Sauce

Cooking Time: 4 minutes

- ½ cup unsalted butter
- ⅓ cup dry white wine
- 2 tablespoons minced fresh tarragon or 2 teaspoons dried tarragon
- 1 tablespoon chopped chives
- 1 tablespoon tarragon vinegar
- ½ teaspoon salt
- ¼ teaspoon pepper
- 3 egg yolks, beaten

Combine all ingredients except egg yolks in 4-cup glass measure; blend well. Place in oven. Set recipe number 240. Touch START. *(Oven cooks: micro, HI, 2 minutes.)*

At Pause, remove from oven. Stir small amount butter mixture into egg yolks; gradually stir yolk mixture into butter mixture. Place in oven. Touch START. *(Oven cooks: micro, 50, 1 minute.)*

At Pause, stir. Touch START. *(Oven cooks: micro, 50, 1 minute.)*

Beat with wire whisk until smooth. Serve immediately with poached eggs, broiled meat, cooked cauliflower, or carrots.

1½ cups

⊞ *Recipe can be increased. See "Quantity", page 12.*

How Sweet It Is!

When the recipe testing for this book began, it began here! The cakes, pies, cookies, candies, and other tempting sweets should capture your delighted interest. And they are all so much fun to make! If you thought candies were too much bother, let the microwave method change your mind: one bowl, no scorching. When you add the convenience provided by automatic, preset control of the power setting and the timing, each recipe will quickly become one of your specialities. The convection method helps you rise to any occasion with an incredible Chocolate Soufflé (page 190), or Pineapple Baked Alaska (page 191). Convection is the choice, too, to keep that cookie jar filled. Finally, the micro/convection method is the wonder that helps you create pies of all kinds. Sweet tooth ready? Go!

Pie shells (Basic Pie Crust, page 184) are prebaked, then filled. Pecan Pie (page 186) is just one of the results possible (above left). Make candy quickly and easily with the microwave method. Do not leave a conventional candy thermometer in the oven (above right). Chocolate Chip Cookies (page 189) are baked by the convection method using a cookie sheet on the wire rack, lower position. The convection method is the only one that permits metal utensils to be used on the wire rack (right).

Converting Your Recipes

The best route to adapting your dessert recipes is to find a recipe here that is similar to the one you want to try. Most puddings can be cooked by either the microwave or micro/convection method. They don't need a water bath and require only occasional stirring. Fruit is microwave territory and needs little or no water. It retains its orchard-ripe color and just-picked flavor. Candies convert readily to the microwave method. The only caution is to compare the amount of any water, milk, or juice that might be called for to a recipe in the book. You may need to reduce such liquids a bit because evaporation is minimal in microwave cooking. Some tips:

- ☐ For even cooking, select fruit of uniform size to be cooked whole.
- ☐ Remove baked custards from the oven when centers are nearly firm. They will set as they cool.
- ☐ To avoid lumping, puddings should be stirred once or twice.
- ☐ Following the recipe for Chocolate Soufflé (page 190) as a guide, you can create your favorite flavor: strawberry, mint, etc. A few drops of food coloring is in order if, for example, you flavor with extracts instead of liqueurs.
- ☐ You can bake pie shells in metal pie plates. But be sure to carefully transfer to a microproof and heatproof pie plate if the recipe for the pie or quiche requires cooking (even partially) by the microwave or micro/convection methods.

GUIDE TO CONVENIENCE DESSERTS*

Food	Programming Method	Programming Setting	Time	Special Notes
Brownies, bar cookies. 12 - 13	micro	30	2 to 3 min.	Original ¾" foil tray, lid removed. Let stand 5 minutes
Cookies, 16 oz.	convec	350°	10 to 12 min.	Remove ceramic tray. Lower position. Preheat. Cookie sheet or foil tray.
Fruit, frozen, 10 oz.	micro	HI	5 to 5½ min.	Slit pouch. On microproof plate. Flex pouch halfway through cooking time to mix.
Fruit turnover, 12½ oz.	convec	follow package directions		Remove ceramic tray. Lower position. Preheat. Metal baking sheet.
Pudding and pie filling mix. 3¼ oz.	micro	HI	6½ to 7 min.	Follow package directions. Stir every 3 minutes.
Cake, frozen 2- or 3-layer	micro	30	2½ - 3 min.	Remove from foil pan to plate. Watch carefully, frosting melts fast. Let stand 5 minutes.
Cheesecake, 17 - 19 oz.	micro	30	4 - 5 min.	Remove from foil pan to plate. Let stand 1 minute.
Coffeecake, whole frozen 10 - 13 oz.	micro	80	1½ - 2 min.	Place on paper plate or towel.
Cupcakes, crumb cakes, (1 or 2)	micro	30	½ - 1 min.	Place on shallow microproof plate.
Doughnuts, (4)	micro	80	35 - 40 sec.	Place on paper plate or towel. Add 15 seconds if frozen.
Fruit pie, 2-crust, 9" 2½ - 3 lbs.	convec	follow package directions		Remove ceramic tray. Lower position. Preheat. Original foil tray.
Orange Danish, refrigerated, 11 oz.	convec	follow package directions		Remove ceramic tray. Lower position. Preheat. Cookie sheet or foil tray.
Pound cake, frozen 10¾ oz.	micro	30	2 min.	Remove from foil pan to plate. Rotate once. Let stand 5 minutes.

* Due to the tremendous variety in convenience food products available, times given here should be used only as guidelines. We suggest you cook food for the shortest recommended time and then check for doneness. Be sure to check the package for microwave and oven (convec) instructions.

COOKING GUIDE — PUDDING AND PIE FILLING MIX

Food	Amount	Time (minutes)	Micro Control	Special Notes
Pudding and pie filling mix	3¼ ounces 5½ ounces	6½ - 7 8 - 10	HI HI	Follow package directions. Stir every 3 minutes. Use 4-cup glass measure.
Egg custard	3 ounces	8 - 10	70	Follow package directions. Stir every 3 minutes. Use 4-cup glass measure.
Tapioca	3¼ ounces	6 - 7	HI	Follow package directions. Stir every 3 minutes. Use 4-cup glass measure.

Recipe No. 241

Apple Pie

Cooking Time: 50 minutes

- Pastry for Basic Pie Crust two-crust pie (right)
- ¾ cup sugar
- ¼ cup all-purpose flour
- ¾ teaspoon cinnamon
- ¼ teaspoon nutmeg
- Pinch salt
- 8 tart medium green apples, peeled, cored, and thinly sliced
- 2 tablespoons butter or margarine
- 1 egg white, lightly beaten

Bake bottom pie crust according to directions for Basic Pie Crust.

Remove ceramic tray. Place wire rack in oven bottom position. Set recipe number 241. Touch START. *(Oven preheats: convec, 400°F.)* Meanwhile, mix sugar, flour, cinnamon, nutmeg, and salt in large bowl. Add apples and toss until coated. Spoon apples into prebaked crust. Dot with butter. Brush rim of crust with egg white. Roll out uncooked dough to ⅛-inch thickness. Drape over fruit, then gently press edges of pastry together with fork to seal. Cut slits in top crust to allow steam to escape. Brush top with remaining egg white.

At 400°F, place in oven on wire rack. Touch START. *(Oven cooks: convec, 400°F, 50 minutes.)* Let cool 5 to 10 minutes before serving.

8 servings

Recipe No. 242

Basic Pie Crust

Cooking Time: 12 minutes

- 1 cup flour
- ½ teaspoon salt
- ⅓ cup shortening
- 2 to 3 tablespoons cold water
- 1 egg, beaten

Remove ceramic tray. Place wire rack in oven bottom position. Set recipe number 242. Touch START. *(Oven preheats: convec, 420°F.)* Meanwhile, mix flour and salt in medium bowl. Cut in shortening using pastry blender or 2 knives until mixture resembles coarse meal. Stir in water, 1 tablespoon at a time, until flour is moistened. Shape dough into ball, then flatten on lightly floured surface. Roll dough into circle about ¼-inch thick and 1½ inches larger than 9-inch microproof and heatproof pie plate or quiche dish. Fit into pie plate and trim, leaving ½-inch overlap. Turn excess dough under to form rolled rim. Flute edges. Pierce crust with fork and brush crust with beaten egg. At 420°F, place in oven. Touch START. *(Oven cooks: convec, 420°F, 12 minutes.)* Let cool.

1 9-inch pie crust

For two-crust pie or 2 one-crust pie shells: Double each ingredient except egg white. Mix as directed. Divide dough in half. For two shells, prepare and cook separately as directed above. For two-crust pie, roll out one half and cook as directed above. Fill as directed in specific recipe. Roll out second half of dough and finish according to recipe directions.

If you are preparing a pie shell for a pie that is cooked by convection only, or for a pie requiring no cooking once the filling is added, you may use a metal pie plate.

Recipe No. 243

Deep Dish Cranapple Pie

Cooking Time: 50 minutes

- 1¼ cups sugar
- ½ cup all-purpose flour
- 8 to 9 tart green apples, peeled, cored, and sliced
- 2 cups fresh or frozen cranberries
- 2 tablespoons butter or margarine
- Pastry for Basic Pie Crust (page 184)
- 1 egg white, mixed with 1 teaspoon water (optional)

Remove ceramic tray. Place wire rack in oven bottom position. Set recipe number 243. Touch START. *(Oven preheats: convec, 400°F.)* Meanwhile, mix sugar and flour in small bowl. Alternate layers of apples, cranberries, and sugar mixture in 8-inch square glass or ceramic baking dish, beginning and ending with apples. Dot with butter. Roll dough out on lightly floured surface into 9-inch square. Fold dough in half. Set over fruit and unfold. Seal to edges of dish. Cut slits in top to allow steam to escape. Brush crust with egg mixture.

At 400°F, place in oven on wire rack. Touch START. *(Oven cooks: convec, 400°F, 50 minutes.)* Serve warm.

8 to 10 servings

Recipe No. 244

Fresh Pear Pie

Cooking Time: 35 minutes

- Pastry for Basic Pie Crust two-crust 9-inch pie (page 184)
- ½ cup sugar
- ⅓ cup all-purpose flour
- ½ teaspoon mace
- 6 to 7 medium-size firm pears, peeled, cored, and sliced
- 1 tablespoon fresh lemon juice
- 2 tablespoons butter or margarine
- 1 egg white, lightly beaten

Bake bottom pie crust according to directions for Basic Pie Crust on page 184.

Place wire rack in lower position. Set recipe number 244. Touch START. *(Oven preheats: convec, 400°F.)* Mix sugar, flour, and mace in large bowl. Add pears and toss until coated. Arrange pears in prebaked crust. Sprinkle with lemon juice and dot with butter. Brush rim of crust with some of the egg white. Roll out dough to ⅛-inch thickness. Drape over fruit, then gently press edges of pastry together with fork to seal. Cut slits in top crust to let steam escape. Brush top with remaining egg white.

At 400°F, place in oven on wire rack. Touch START. *(Oven cooks: micro/convec, 400°F, 30 minutes; stands: 0, 5 minutes.)*

6 to 8 servings

Recipe No. 245

Pecan Pie

Cooking Time: 20 minutes

- 1/4 cup butter or margarine, melted
- 3 eggs, well beaten
- 1 cup sugar
- 3/4 cup light corn syrup
- 2 cups pecan halves
- 1 teaspoon vanilla
- 1 prebaked Basic Pie Crust (page 184)

Place wire rack in lower position. Set recipe number 245. Touch START. *(Oven preheats: convec, 350°F.)* Meanwhile, blend melted butter, eggs, sugar, corn syrup, pecan halves, and vanilla in large bowl. Turn mixture into crust.

At 350°F, place in oven on wire rack. Touch START. *(Oven cooks: micro/convec, 350°F, 5 minutes.)*

At Pause, rotate dish one-half turn. Touch START. *(Oven cooks: micro/convec, 350°F, 5 minutes; stands: 0, 10 minutes.)* Serve warm.

8 servings

Recipe No. 246

Perfect Lemon Meringue Pie

Cooking Time: 15 minutes

- 1/3 cup cornstarch
- 1/2 cup cold water
- 1 3/4 cups sugar, divided
- 1 cup hot water
- 1/4 teaspoon salt
- 5 eggs, separated
- 2 tablespoons butter or margarine
- 1/2 cup fresh lemon juice
- 2 tablespoons finely grated lemon peel
- 1 prebaked Basic Pie Crust (page 184)
- 1/4 teaspoon cream of tartar
- 1/2 teaspoon vanilla

Dissolve cornstarch in cold water in 2-quart microproof bowl. Add 1 1/4 cups sugar, hot water, and salt and blend well. Cover. Place in oven. Set recipe number 12. Touch START. *(Oven cooks: micro, HI, 7 minutes.)*

At Pause, stir through mixture several times. Beat egg yolks in another bowl until thick. Gradually beat into cornstarch mixture. Place in oven. Touch START. *(Oven cooks: micro, HI, 2 minutes.)* Add butter and stir until melted. Blend in lemon juice and peel. Pour into crust. Set aside to cool slightly.

Remove ceramic tray. Place wire rack in lower position. Set recipe number 246. Touch START. *(Oven preheats: convec, 450°F.)* Meanwhile, beat egg whites with cream of tartar in large bowl until foamy. Gradually beat in remaining sugar until whites are stiff and glossy. Blend in vanilla. Spread over cooled filling, sealing to edges.

At 450°F, place in oven on wire rack. Touch START. *(Oven cooks: convec, 450°F, 6 minutes.)* Let cool to room temperature before serving.

6 to 8 servings

Whenever you have pastry dough left over, remember Grandma's trick. Roll out dough, brush with egg white mixture, sprinkle with sugar and cinnamon. Arrange on cookie sheet. Set on wire rack. Cook, convec, at 420°F 10 minutes or until cookie-crisp. Break into pieces for a quick-energy finger food.

This is one of several recipes that use the preset functions of another recipe for part of the cooking sequence. Set recipe number 12 first. At the end of that sequence, set recipe number 246.

Recipe No. 247

Pumpkin Pie

Cooking Time: 55 minutes

- 1½ cups canned or cooked pumpkin
- 1 cup half-and-half
- ½ cup firmly-packed brown sugar
- 2 eggs, beaten
- 1 tablespoon all-purpose flour
- 1 teaspoon cinnamon
- ¼ teaspoon ginger
- ¼ teaspoon nutmeg
- ¼ teaspoon salt
- ⅛ teaspoon ground cloves
- 1 prebaked Basic Pie Crust (page 184)

Remove ceramic tray. Place wire rack in oven bottom position. Set recipe number 247. Touch START. *(Oven preheats: convec, 350°F.)* Meanwhile, mix all ingredients except pie shell in large bowl. Pour into pie shell.

At 350°F, place in oven. Touch START. *(Oven cooks: convec, 350°F, 50 minutes; stands: 0, 5 minutes.)*

8 servings

Recipe No. 248

Angel Food Cake

Cooking Time: 50 minutes

- 1 package (16 ounces) Angel Food Cake mix
- Raspberry Sauce (page 179)

Remove ceramic tray. Place wire rack in oven bottom position. Set recipe number 248. Touch START. *(Oven preheats: convec, 350°F.)* Meanwhile, prepare cake according to package directions. Pour batter into ungreased 10-inch metal tube pan.

At 350°F, place in oven. Touch START. *(Oven cooks: convec, 350°F, 50 minutes.)* Invert pan onto cooling rack (do not remove cake). Cool completely before removing from pan. Serve with Raspberry Sauce.

10 servings

Recipe No. 249

Carrot Cake

Cooking Time: 20 minutes

- 1½ cups all-purpose flour
- 2 teaspoons cinnamon
- 1½ teaspoons baking soda
- 1 teaspoon nutmeg
- ½ teaspoon salt
- 3 cups grated carrots
- 1½ cups sugar
- 1 cup vegetable oil
- 1 cup chopped walnuts
- 3 eggs, beaten

Frosting:

- 1 package (8 ounces) cream cheese, softened
- ½ cup butter or margarine, softened
- ¼ cup chopped walnuts
- 2 teaspoons vanilla
- 3 cups confectioners sugar, sifted

Place wire rack in lower position. Set recipe number 249. Touch START. *(Oven preheats: convec, 350°F.)* Meanwhile, generously grease 10-cup microproof and heatproof Bundt-type pan. Sift together flour, cinnamon, baking soda, nutmeg, and salt. Combine carrots, sugar, oil, nuts, and eggs in large bowl. Add dry ingredients and mix thoroughly. Turn into prepared pan.

At 350°F, place in oven on wire rack. Touch START. *(Oven cooks: micro/convec, 350°F, 15 minutes.)*

At Pause, rotate dish one-half turn. Touch START. *(Oven cooks: micro/convec, 350°F, 5 minutes.)* Let cool in pan in oven.

Invert cake onto serving platter. Beat cream cheese and butter in large bowl. Add nuts and vanilla and blend well. Gradually beat in sugar. Frost cake. Sprinkle with additional chopped walnuts, if desired.

8 to 10 servings

Recipe No. 250

Lemon Chiffon Cake

Cooking Time: 55 minutes

- 2 cups all-purpose flour
- 1½ cups sugar
- 1 tablespoon baking powder
- ½ teaspoon salt
- ½ cup vegetable oil
- ½ cup cold water
- ¼ cup fresh lemon juice
- 6 egg yolks
- 2 tablespoons grated lemon peel, divided
- 9 egg whites
- ½ teaspoon cream of tartar
- Snow White Frosting (page 197)

Remove ceramic tray. Place wire rack in bottom position. Set recipe number 250. Touch START. *(Oven preheats: convec, 350°F.)* Meanwhile, mix flour, sugar, baking powder, and salt in large bowl. Make well in center. Add oil, water, lemon juice, egg yolks, and all but ½ teaspoon lemon peel to well and stir until smooth. Beat egg whites in another bowl until foamy. Add cream of tartar and continue beating until stiff peaks form. Stir ¼ of egg yolk mixture into whites. Gently fold in remaining egg yolk mixture, blending thoroughly. Turn into ungreased 10-inch metal tube pan.

At 350°F, place in oven. Touch START. *(Oven cooks: convec, 350°F, 50 minutes; stands: 0, 5 minutes.)*

Invert cake onto rack and let cool completely. Frost with Snow White Frosting. Sprinkle with ½ teaspoon lemon peel.

8 servings

Recipe No. 251

Party Cake

Cooking Time: 36 minutes

- 2 cups all-purpose flour
- 1¼ cups sugar
- 3½ teaspoons baking powder
- 1 teaspoon salt
- ¼ cup butter or margarine, softened
- ¼ cup shortening
- 1 cup milk
- 1½ teaspoons vanilla
- 3 eggs

Frosting:

- ⅓ cup butter or margarine, softened
- 3 cups confectioners sugar
- 2 tablespoons milk
- 1 tablespoon maraschino cherry juice
- 1 teaspoon vanilla
- 5 drops red food color
- 8 maraschino cherries, drained and chopped

Remove ceramic tray. Place wire rack in lower position. Set recipe number 251. Touch START. *(Oven preheats: convec, 350°F.)* Meanwhile, grease and flour 9×13-inch microproof and heatproof baking dish. Mix flour, sugar, baking powder, and salt in large ~~bowl.~~ Add all remaining ingredients except frosting and beat well. Pour into prepared dish.

At 350°F, place in oven. Touch START. *(Oven cooks: convec, 350°F, 25 minutes; micro/convec, 350°F, 6 minutes; stands: 0, 5 minutes.)* Remove from oven and let cool.

Cream butter with sugar. Add milk, cherry juice, vanilla, and food color and mix until smooth. Stir in chopped cherries. Spread frosting over top of cake. Cut into squares and serve.

16 to 20 servings

If you want to make a two-layer frosted cake, a brown appearance may not be important to you. You can prepare this cake by using micro only. Pour batter into two 8-inch round microproof cake dishes. Cook each layer separately as follows: Cook, micro, 50, 8 minutes. Rotate pan ¼ turn and cook, micro, HI, 1 to 2 minutes or until done. Invert onto rack to cool. Cook second layer.

Recipe No. 252

Pineapple Praline Upside-Down Cake

Cooking Time: 30 minutes

- 1/4 cup butter or margarine, melted
- 1/2 cup firmly-packed brown sugar
- 6 slices canned pineapple, well drained
- 1/4 cup pecan halves
- 6 maraschino cherries
- 1 1/4 cups all-purpose flour
- 1 cup sugar
- 1 teaspoon baking powder
- 3/4 cup milk
- 1/3 cup butter or margarine, melted
- 1 egg, lightly beaten
- 1 teaspoon vanilla

Remove ceramic tray. Place wire rack in lower position. Set recipe number 252. Touch START. *(Oven preheats: convec, 350°F.)* Pour 1/4 cup melted butter into 9-inch round microproof and heatproof baking dish. Add brown sugar, spreading evenly over bottom. Place 1 pineapple slice in center. Surround with remaining slices. Arrange pecans, rounded side down, around outsides of pineapple slices. Place cherry in center of each pineapple slice. Set aside.

Mix flour, sugar, and baking powder in large bowl. Combine milk, 1/3 cup melted butter, egg, and vanilla, and add to flour mixture, blending thoroughly. Carefully pour batter over pineapple slices.

At 350°F, place in oven on wire rack. Touch START. *(Oven cooks: convec, 350°F, 20 minutes; micro/convec, 350°F, 10 minutes.)* Remove from oven and let cool on wire rack for 5 minutes. Turn out onto platter.

8 servings

Recipe No. 253

Chocolate Chip Cookies

Cooking Time: 12 minutes (repeat)

- 1 cup butter or margarine, softened
- 3/4 cup sugar
- 3/4 cup firmly-packed brown sugar
- 2 eggs
- 1 1/2 teaspoon vanilla
- 2 1/2 cups all-purpose flour
- 2 cups semi-sweet chocolate pieces
- 1 cup chopped walnuts
- 1 teaspoon baking soda
- 1 teaspoon salt

Remove ceramic tray. Place wire rack in lower position. Set recipe number 253. Touch START. *(Oven preheats: convec, 370°F.)* Meanwhile, beat butter, sugars, eggs, and vanilla in large bowl. Stir in remaining ingredients. Drop dough by rounded tablespoons onto ungreased baking sheet.

At 370°F, place in oven. Touch START. *(Oven cooks: convec, 370°F, 12 minutes.)* Transfer to wire rack to cool. Repeat with remaining dough, setting recipe number 253 and touching START each time. Store cookies in airtight container.

about 4 dozen

Recipe No. 254

Peanut Butter Cookies

Cooking Time: 14 minutes
(repeat once)

- 1 cup natural-style crunchy peanut butter
- ½ cup butter or margarine, softened
- ½ cup firmly-packed brown sugar
- ½ cup sugar
- 1 egg, beaten
- 1 teaspoon vanilla
- 1½ cups all-purpose flour
- ¾ teaspoon baking soda
- ¼ teaspoon salt

Remove ceramic tray. Place wire rack in lower position. Set recipe number 254. Touch START. *(Oven preheats: convec, 350°F.)* Lightly grease aluminum or metal baking sheet. Combine peanut butter, butter, sugars, egg, and vanilla in large bowl and beat until smooth. Blend in flour, baking soda, and salt. Shape dough into thirty 1-inch balls. Arrange 15 on prepared sheet, spacing 3 inches apart. Flatten into 2-inch rounds using fork in crisscross pattern.

At 350°F, place in oven on wire rack. Touch START. *(Oven cooks: convec, 350°F, 14 minutes.)* Transfer to wire rack to cool. Repeat with remaining dough, setting recipe number 254 and touching START again. Store cookies in airtight container.

30 cookies

Recipe No. 255

Chocolate Soufflé

Cooking Time: 1 hour 14 minutes

- 2 teaspoons butter
- 3 tablespoons confectioners sugar, sifted
- 1 cup milk
- ½ cup sugar
- 2 tablespoons cornstarch
- 2 squares (1 ounce each) unsweetened chocolate
- ¼ cup semi sweet chocolate pieces
- 3 tablespoons butter or margarine
- 1 teaspoon vanilla
- 5 egg yolks
- 8 egg whites (1⅓ cups)
- 1 teaspoon cream of tartar
- 1 tablespoon confectioners sugar

This is one of several recipes that use the preset functions of another recipe for part of the cooking sequence. Set recipe number 230 first. At the end of that sequence, set recipe number 255.

Coat bottom and sides of 2-quart soufflé dish with 2 teaspoons butter. Sprinkle with 3 tablespoons confectioners sugar, rotating dish to cover evenly and letting excess sugar remain in bottom. Refrigerate.

Combine milk, sugar, cornstarch, and chocolate in microproof bowl. Place in oven. Set recipe number 230. Touch START. *(Oven cooks: micro, HI, 1½ minutes.)*

At Pause, stir. Touch START. *(Oven cooks: micro, HI, 1½ minutes.)*

At Pause, stir again. Touch START. *(Oven cooks: micro, HI, 1 minute.)* Add 3 tablespoons butter and vanilla to chocolate mixture and blend thoroughly. Beat egg yolks in another bowl until pale yellow. Gradually beat into chocolate mixture. Let cool to room temperature.

Remove ceramic tray. Place wire rack in bottom position. Set recipe number 255. Touch START. *(Oven preheats: convec, 450°F.)* Meanwhile, beat egg whites in separate bowl with electric mixer until foamy. Add cream of tartar and continue beating until stiff peaks form. Fold in 1 tablespoon confectioners sugar. Stir ⅓ of whites into chocolate mixture. Gently fold in remaining whites. Turn into chilled dish, reaching edges, without handling inside of coated dish.

At 450°F, place in oven. Touch START. *(Oven cooks: convec, 330°F, 70 minutes.)* Serve immediately.

6 to 8 servings

Recipe No. 256

Pineapple Baked Alaska

Cooking Time: 5 minutes

1 small-to-medium pineapple
4 scoops ice cream
8 maraschino cherries
½ cup chopped nuts
4 egg whites
⅓ cup sugar
¼ teaspoon cream of tartar

Cut pineapple in half lengthwise. Carefully hollow out pulp, leaving thick shell. Pour off juice. Cut pulp into bite-size chunks. Fill shell with ice cream, pineapple chunks, cherries, and nuts. Freeze until solid.

Just before serving, remove ceramic tray and place wire rack in lower position. Set recipe number 256. Touch START. *(Oven preheats: convec, 430°F.)* Meanwhile, beat egg whites until soft peaks form. Gradually add sugar and cream of tartar, beating constantly until whites are stiff and glossy. Spread over pineapple filling, covering completely and sealing meringue to edges. Set shell on heatproof plate or oval baking dish.

At 430°F, place in oven on wire rack. Touch START. *(Oven cooks: convec, 430°F, 5 minutes.)* Serve immediately.

4 to 6 servings

Recipe No. 257 ⊞

Crème Caramel

Cooking Time: 17 minutes

⅔ cup sugar, divided
2 tablespoons water
2 cups milk
3 eggs
3 egg yolks
1 teaspoon vanilla

Mix ⅓ cup sugar and water in 1½-quart microproof and heatproof brioche dish or fluted dish. Place in oven. Set recipe number 273. Touch START. *(Oven cooks: micro, HI, 4 minutes.)*

At Pause, carefully tilt dish to coat bottom and sides evenly. Set aside. Place milk in 1-quart glass measure. Place in oven. Touch START. *(Oven cooks: micro, HI, 3 minutes.)* Meanwhile, beat eggs, egg yolks, remaining sugar, and vanilla in 2-quart bowl. Remove milk from oven and slowly pour into egg mixture, beating constantly until smooth. Pour into caramelized dish. Set aside.

Place wire rack in lower position. Set recipe number 257. Touch START. *(Oven preheats: convec, 350°F.)*

At 350°F, place in oven on wire rack. Touch START. *(Oven cooks: micro/convec, 350°F, 10 minutes.)* Remove from oven and let cool completely. To serve, run knife along edge of custard, then invert onto small platter to unmold.

6 to 8 servings

This is one of several recipes that use the preset functions of another recipe for part of the cooking sequence. Set recipe number 273 first. At the end of that sequence, set recipe number 257.

Recipe No. 258 ⊞

Almond Bark

Cooking Time: 7½ minutes

1 cup whole blanched almonds
1 teaspoon butter or margarine
1 pound white chocolate

Line large microproof baking sheet with waxed paper; set aside. Place almonds and butter in 9-inch glass pie plate. Place in oven. Set recipe number 258. Touch START. *(Oven cooks: micro, HI, 2½ minutes.)*

At Pause, stir. Touch START. *(Oven cooks: micro, HI, 2 minutes.)*

At Pause, remove from oven; set aside. Place chocolate in large microproof bowl. Place in oven. Touch START. *(Oven cooks: micro, HI, 3 minutes.)*

Stir almonds into chocolate. Pour onto prepared baking sheet. Spread to desired thickness. Refrigerate until set. Break into pieces, and store in airtight container.

1½ pounds

⊞ *Recipe can be increased. See "Quantity", page 12.*

Recipe No. 259

Applesauce

Cooking Time: 12 minutes

- 6 cups sliced peeled cooking apples
- ½ cup water
- 1 tablespoon lemon juice
- ¼ cup sugar
- ½ teaspoon cinnamon or nutmeg

Place apples, water, and lemon juice in 2-quart microproof casserole. Cover with casserole lid and place in oven. Set recipe number 259. Touch START. *(Oven cooks: micro, HI, 6 minutes.)*

At Pause, stir. Touch START. *(Oven cooks: micro, HI, 6 minutes.)*

Stir in sugar and cinnamon. Serve warm or chilled with pork or as a light dessert.

4 to 6 servings

Recipe No. 260 ⊞

Baked Apples

Cooking Time: 8 minutes

- 2 baking apples (1 pound)
- Lemon juice
- 2 teaspoons slivered almonds
- 2 teaspoons raisins
- 2 teaspoons brown sugar
- ¼ teaspoon cinnamon
- 4 tablespoons water
- 2 teaspoons butter or margarine

Core apples, starting from tops, without cutting all the way through. Remove a thin circle of peel around tops. Sprinkle with lemon juice. Combine almonds, raisins, brown sugar, and cinnamon; mix lightly. Fill apples with mixture. Place each apple in microproof custard cup. Add 2 tablespoons water to each cup. Dot each apple with 1 teaspoon butter. Place in oven. Cover with waxed paper. Set recipe number 260. Touch START. *(Oven cooks: micro, HI, 5 minutes; stands: 0, 3 minutes.)*

2 servings

⊞ *Recipe can be increased. See "Quantity", page 12.*

Recipe No. 261

Bananas Foster

Cooking Time: 4½ minutes

- ¼ cup brown sugar
- 3 tablespoons rum
- 2 tablespoons butter
- 4 small bananas, cut in half lengthwise

Combine sugar, rum, and butter in 1-quart shallow microproof casserole. Cover with casserole lid. Place in oven. Set recipe number 261. Touch START. *(Oven cooks: micro, HI, 1 minute.)*

At Pause, add bananas. Spoon butter mixture over bananas. Cover. Touch START. *(Oven cooks: micro, HI, 1½ minutes.)*

At Pause, turn bananas over. Cover. Touch START. *(Oven cooks: micro, HI, 2 minutes.)*

4 servings

Recipe No. 262

Brownie Mix

Cooking Time: 19 minutes

- 1 package (20 to 24 ounces) brownie mix
- 1 tablespoon confectioners sugar

Remove ceramic tray. Place wire rack in lower position. Set recipe number 262. Touch START. *(Oven preheats: convec, 380°F.)* Meanwhile, butter 8-inch microproof and heatproof pie plate and set aside. Prepare brownie mix according to package directions. Pour into prepared pie plate.

At 380°F, place in oven on wire rack. Touch START. *(Oven cooks: convec, 380°F, 15 minutes.)*

At Pause, rotate pie plate one-half turn. Touch START. *(Oven cooks: micro/convec, 380°F, 4 minutes.)*

Dust with confectioners sugar, cut into squares, and serve.

16 brownies

Recipe No. 263

Snackin' Cake

Cooking Time: 16 minutes

1 package (14 ounces) single-layer cake mix

Remove ceramic tray. Place wire rack in lower position. Set recipe number 263. Touch START. *(Oven preheats: convec, 370°F.)* Prepare cake mix according to package directions. Pour into ungreased 9-inch round microproof and heatproof baking dish.

At 370°F, place in oven. Touch START. *(Oven cooks: micro/convec, 370°F, 8 minutes.)*

At Pause, rotate dish one-half turn. Touch START. *(Oven cooks: convec, 370°F, 8 minutes.)*

Let cool 5 minutes before serving.

1 layer

Recipe No. 264

Chocolate Fudge Frosting

Cooking Time: 3 minutes

- 1/3 cup milk
- 1 1/2 cups sugar
- 1/4 cup butter or margarine, cut into small pieces
- 3/4 cup semi sweet chocolate chips
- 1 teaspoon vanilla
- 1/4 cup chopped nuts
- 1 teaspoon brewed coffee (optional)

Combine milk, sugar, and butter in 4-cup measure. Stir. Place in oven. Set recipe number 264. Touch START. *(Oven cooks: micro, HI, 1 1/2 minutes.)*

At Pause, stir. Touch START. *(Oven cooks: micro, HI, 1 1/2 minutes.)*

Add chocolate chips; beat with electric mixer until smooth. Add vanilla and nuts, and coffee, if desired. Beat until mixture is of spreading consistency. Frosting will thicken as it cools.

1 cup

Recipe No. 265

Chocolate-Cherry Bundt Cake

Cooking Time: 23 minutes

- 1 tablespoon sugar
- 1 package (18 ounces) chocolate cake mix with pudding
- 1 cup cherry pie filling
- 3 eggs
- 3/4 cup water
- 1/4 cup vegetable oil
- 1 teaspoon almond extract

Generously grease 12-cup microproof Bundt-type pan; chill. Sprinkle pan with 1 tablespoon sugar and shake well to coat. Mix remaining ingredients. Carefully pour into prepared pan. Place in oven on ceramic tray. Set recipe number 265. Touch START. *(Oven cooks: micro, 70, 7 minutes.)*

At Pause, rotate pan one-half turn. Touch START. *(Oven cooks: micro, 70, 6 minutes; stands: 0, 10 minutes.)* Invert onto serving platter and let cool completely.

10 to 12 servings

Recipe No. 266

Cranapple Jelly

Cooking Time: 24 minutes

- 4 cups cranapple juice
- 1 package (1 3/4 ounces) powdered fruit pectin
- 4 cups sugar

Combine juice and pectin in 4-quart microproof casserole. Cover with casserole lid and place in oven. Set recipe number 266. Touch START. *(Oven cooks: micro, HI, 7 minutes.)*

At Pause, stir. Cover. Touch START. *(Oven cooks: micro, HI, 5 minutes.)*

At Pause, add sugar; blend well. Do not cover. Touch START. *(Oven cooks: micro, HI, 12 minutes.)*

Skim foam with metal spoon. Pour into hot sterilized jars, and seal.

6 cups

Recipe No. 267

Blueberry Pie

Cooking Time: 15 minutes

- 4 to 4½ cups frozen blueberries, defrosted and drained
- 1 teaspoon grated lemon peel
- ¾ cup sugar
- 3 tablespoons cornstarch
- 1 prebaked Basic Pie Crust (page 184), for single crust pie
- 1 tablespoon lemon juice

Toss blueberries with grated lemon peel. Mix sugar and cornstarch. Sprinkle over blueberries and toss thoroughly. Spoon mixture into crust. Sprinkle with lemon juice.

Place wire rack in lower position. Set recipe number 267. Touch START. *(Oven preheats: convec, 350°F.)*

At Pause, place pie in oven. Touch START. *(Oven cooks: micro/convec, 350°F, 10 minutes.)*

At Pause, rotate dish one-half turn. Touch START. *(Oven cooks: micro/convec, 350°F, 5 minutes.)*

Remove pie from oven. Let cool 15 minutes before serving.

8 servings

Frozen pie crusts can be used. Timing will be the same.

If using fresh blueberries, reduce cornstarch to 2 tablespoons.

Recipe No. 268

Fluffy Tapioca

Cooking Time: 16 minutes

- 2 cups milk
- 3 tablespoons quick-cooking tapioca
- 5 tablespoons sugar, divided
- 1 large egg, separated
- ⅛ teaspoon salt
- 1 teaspoon vanilla
- Apricot Dessert Sauce (page 176)

Combine milk, tapioca, 3 tablespoons sugar, egg yolk, and salt in 2-quart microproof casserole; blend well. Place in oven. Set recipe number 268. Touch START. *(Oven stands: 0, 5 minutes; cooks: micro, HI, 6 minutes.)*

At Pause, beat with wire whisk until well blended. Touch START. *(Oven cooks: micro, 70, 5 minutes.)*

Meanwhile, beat egg white in small mixing bowl with electric mixer until foamy. Gradually beat in remaining 2 tablespoons sugar until soft peaks form.

Stir vanilla into tapioca. Fold egg whites into tapioca a little at a time until just blended. Serve topped with Apricot Dessert Sauce.

5 servings

Recipe No. 269

Golden Apple Chunks

Cooking Time: 8 minutes

- 4 medium cooking apples, peeled, cored, and cut into quarters
- ¼ cup firmly-packed brown sugar
- 1 teaspoon cinnamon
- 2 tablespoons butter or margarine

Place apples in 1-quart microproof casserole. Combine brown sugar and cinnamon; sprinkle over apples. Dot with butter. Cover with casserole lid and place in oven. Set recipe number 269. Touch START. *(Oven cooks: micro, HI, 4 minutes.)*

At Pause, stir. Touch START. *(Oven cooks: micro, HI, 4 minutes.)*

4 servings

You can mix apple chunks, pear chunks, peach quarters, and maraschino cherries for an interesting variation.

Recipe No. 270

Lemon Pineapple Crème

Cooking Time: 6 minutes

- 1 can (8 ounces) crushed pineapple
- ¾ cup sugar, divided
- ⅔ cup water
- 3 tablespoons cornstarch
- 2 large eggs, separated
- 1 package (3 ounces) cream cheese, cut into cubes
- 2 tablespoons lemon juice
- 1 teaspoon grated lemon peel

Combine pineapple, ½ cup sugar, water, and cornstarch in 4-cup glass measure; stir until cornstarch is dissolved. Place in oven. Set recipe number 270. Touch START. *(Oven cooks: micro, HI, 2½ minutes.)*

At Pause, stir. Touch START. *(Oven cooks: micro, HI, 2½ minutes.)*

At Pause, beat egg yolks in small mixing bowl with electric mixer until lemon-colored. Stir into pineapple mixture; stir in cream cheese, lemon juice, and lemon peel. Touch START. *(Oven cooks: micro,* 80, 1 *minute.)*

Beat with electric mixer until blended. Let stand until cool. Beat egg whites in small bowl until frothy. Gradually beat in remaining ¼ cup sugar until soft peaks form. Fold into pudding. Spoon into individual dessert dishes, and chill before serving.

5 to 6 servings

Recipe No. 271

Peanut Brittle

Cooking Time: 10 minutes

- 1 cup sugar
- ½ cup corn syrup
- 1¾ to 2 cups unsalted dry-roasted peanuts
- 1 teaspoon butter or margarine
- 1 teaspoon vanilla
- 1 teaspoon baking soda

Generously grease large microproof baking sheet; set aside. Combine sugar and corn syrup in 2-quart glass measure. Place in oven. Set recipe number 271. Touch START. *(Oven cooks: micro, HI, 4 minutes.)*

At Pause, stir in peanuts with wooden spoon. Touch START. *(Oven cooks: micro, HI, 4 minutes.)*

At Pause, stir in butter and vanilla. Touch START. *(Oven cooks: micro, HI, 2 minutes.)*

Add baking soda; stir until light and foamy. Pour onto prepared baking sheet; spread quickly to edges using back of wooden spoon. As candy cools, stretch into thin sheet using palms of hands. Cool completely before breaking into pieces. Store in airtight container in cool place.

1 pound

Recipe No. 272

Peanut Crispy Bars

Cooking Time: 3½ minutes

- ¼ cup butter or margarine
- 5 cups miniature or 40 regular marshmallows
- ⅓ cup peanut butter
- 5 cups crispy rice cereal
- 1 cup unsalted dry-roasted peanuts, chopped

Lightly grease 12×7-inch baking dish; set aside. Place butter in 3-quart microproof bowl. Place in oven. Set recipe number 272. Touch START. *(Oven cooks: micro, HI, 1 minute.)*

At Pause, add marshmallows. Cover. Touch START. *(Oven cooks: micro, HI, 2½ minutes.)*

Add peanut butter; stir until smooth. Stir in cereal and peanuts. Press warm mixture into prepared baking dish. Cool before cutting into bars.

36 bars

Recipe No. 273

Pudding Mix

Cooking Time: 7 minutes

1 package (3¼ ounces) pudding and pie filling mix
2 cups milk

Place pudding mix in 2-quart microproof bowl. Stir in milk. Place in oven. Set recipe number 273. Touch START. *(Oven cooks: micro, HI, 4 minutes.)*

At Pause, stir. Touch START. *(Oven cooks: micro, HI, 3 minutes.)*

Pour into individual dessert dishes, and chill before serving.

4 servings

Recipe No. 274

Raisin Bread Pudding

Cooking Time: 20½ minutes

4 slices raisin bread, cut into cubes (about 4 cups)
¼ cup raisins
3 large eggs
½ cup firmly-packed brown sugar
1 teaspoon vanilla
Dash salt
2 cups milk
2 tablespoons butter or margarine
Cinnamon or nutmeg

Combine bread and raisins in 2-quart round microproof baking dish; set aside. Combine eggs, brown sugar, vanilla, and salt; beat until well blended; set aside. Combine milk and butter in 2-quart glass measure. Place in oven. Set recipe number 274. Touch START. *(Oven cooks: micro, HI, 4½ minutes.)*

At Pause, remove from oven. Gradually stir egg mixture into milk mixture. Pour over bread and raisins. Sprinkle with cinnamon. Place in oven. Cover with waxed paper. Touch START. *(Oven cooks: micro, 50, 16 minutes.)*

Center may be slightly soft but will set as pudding cools. Serve warm or chilled.

6 servings

Recipe No. 275

Rich Chocolate Fudge

Cooking Time: 20 minutes

4 cups sugar
1 tall can evaporated milk
1 cup butter or margarine
1 package (12 ounces) semisweet chocolate pieces
1 jar (7 ounces) marshmallow creme
1 cup chopped nuts
1 teaspoon vanilla

Butter 9-inch square or 12×7-inch baking dish; set aside. Combine sugar, milk, and butter in 4-quart microproof bowl. Place in oven. Set recipe number 275. Touch START. *(Oven cooks: micro, HI, 10 minutes.)*

At Pause, stir. Touch START. *(Oven cooks: micro, HI, 10 minutes.)*

Stir in chocolate and marshmallow creme; blend well. Stir in nuts and vanilla. Pour into prepared dish. Cool before cutting into squares.

48 squares

Recipe No. 276

Rocky Road Candy

Cooking Time: 5 minutes

1 package (12 ounces) semisweet chocolate pieces
1 package (12 ounces) butterscotch pieces
½ cup butter
1 package (10½ ounces) miniature marshmallows
1 cup chopped nuts

Butter 13×9-inch baking dish; set aside. Combine chocolate, butterscotch, and ½ cup butter in 4-quart microproof bowl. Place in oven. Set recipe number 276. Touch START. *(Oven cooks: micro, 70, 5 minutes.)*

Stir until blended. Stir in marshmallows and nuts. Pour into prepared dish and spread evenly. Refrigerate 2 hours, or until set before cutting into squares.

45 squares

Recipe No. 277

Snow White Frosting

Approximate Cooking Time: 5 minutes

- 1 cup sugar
- ½ cup water
- ¼ teaspoon cream of tartar
- Dash salt
- 2 egg whites
- 1 teaspoon vanilla

Combine sugar, water, cream of tartar, and salt in 2-cup glass measure. Place in oven. Insert temperature probe and plug probe in. Set recipe number 277. Touch START. *(Oven cooks: micro,* 70, *to* 200°*F; holds warm:* 1.)

Beat egg whites in small mixing bowl with electric mixer until soft peaks form. Gradually beat hot syrup into egg whites. Beat in vanilla. Beat 5 minutes, or until thick and fluffy.

1½ to 2 cups

Recipe No. 278

Rhubarb Cobbler

Cooking Time: 26 minutes

- 1 package (20 ounces) frozen rhubarb
- 1 cup sugar
- 1 tablespoon cornstarch
- 2 cups yellow cake mix
- ½ cup coarsely chopped walnuts or pecans
- ¼ cup butter, melted
- 1 teaspoon cinnamon
- Whipped topping

Combine rhubarb, sugar, and ¼ cup water in 2-quart microproof and heatproof casserole. Cover with casserole lid. Place in oven. Set recipe number 269. Touch START. *(Oven cooks: micro, HI,* 4 *minutes.)*

At Pause, stir. Touch START. *(Oven cooks: micro, HI,* 4 *minutes.)* Remove from oven.

Place wire rack in lower position. Set recipe number 278. Touch START. *(Oven preheats: convec,* 350°*F.)* Drain rhubarb, reserving ¼ cup syrup. Add cornstarch to reserved syrup, and stir until cornstarch dissolves. Add cornstarch mixture to rhubarb, and stir until well mixed.

Combine cake mix, nuts, butter, and cinnamon in a separate bowl. Sprinkle evenly over rhubarb.

At 350°F, place in oven. Touch START. *(Oven cooks: micro/convec,* 350°*F,* 13 *minutes.)*

At Pause, rotate dish one-half turn. Touch START. *(Oven cooks: micro/convec,* 350°*F,* 5 *minutes.)*

Remove from oven and let cool. Serve with whipped topping.

6 servings

Cooking Just for You or Two

At one time or another, all of us are faced with the challenge of cooking just for ourselves or ourselves-plus-one. That's what this chapter is all about, and we think you'll be delighted to learn just how well this oven adapts to those situations. If you're like the home economists who have worked on this cookbook, you've probably shied away from doing much elaborate food preparation and chosen a "fast food" solution to many of your it's-just-me meals. Chances are that you just couldn't be bothered with heating a large oven, or dragging some mini-appliance out from under the counter. Now, you have the perfect appliance, always on your countertop, ready when you are. Soon, some of your greatest culinary triumphs will be the result of your new-found enjoyment of cooking "Just for You or Two."

To get you started, we've put together 17 recipes for you among the 300 automatic recipes stored in this oven's computer. But they should be just the beginning for you. You can adapt many of these recipes to suit your fancy, or come up with all-new recipes of your own. For example, substitute well-drained chopped spinach for the mushrooms in our Mushroom Soufflé (page 203), or

Thanks to convenient microwave reheating, you might find yourself saving today's microproof TV dinner containers (or you can buy disposable microproof trays). Then go ahead and try some larger recipes, such as Prime Rib (page 90), and make your own TV dinners (above left). And why not divide Country Vegetable Soup (page 57), into whatever freezer containers you happen to have for easy reheating whenever you like (above right)? An impressive array of new one- or two-serving microproof cookware is available today and it can come right to the table (right).

← *Orange Roughy (page 205)*

prepare a tenderloin steak with a tarragon butter sauce using our Lamb Chops (page 206) sequence. You're not a fan of Chocolate Cake (page 207)? Go ahead, try a spice cake or yellow cake with your favorite frosting.

But automatic cooking is not all there is to the wonders available to you in preparing one or two servings with this oven. By now we hope you're sold on the speed of microwave and micro/convection cooking, and the convenience of countertop convection cooking. The next step is to realize that you can also prepare larger-yield recipes and do some "creative storing" by freezing them in smaller portions for speedy reheating in this oven. Some of our suggestions appear in the photographs on page 199. Here are some other tips.

- ☐ A homemade frozen dinner usually reheats in 5 to 6 minutes on HI. Use care in arranging food on the plate, placing meat, potatoes, and dense vegetables around the outside of the plate. Place rice, noodles, mushrooms, and delicate vegetables in the center of the plate.
- ☐ Use a gravy or a sauce to help meat reheat in a bit less time, while retaining its moisture.
- ☐ When reheating frozen soup, remove the lid and set the container upside down in the microproof serving bowl you plan to use. For an 8-ounce portion, reheat on HI for 5 minutes. Remove container, stir, cover bowl with a paper towel, and continue to reheat on HI for 3 to 5 minutes, or until hot.
- ☐ For the best control, reheat cake slices, sandwiches, and other baked goods on a low power setting. Of course, you can choose to use the convection method to reheat such items if the crispness generally achieved is desirable. Throughout the previous recipe chapters, you will also find many other automatic recipes with one or two servings. Among them are: Italian Meatball Sandwich (page 68), Reuben Sandwich (page 69), Medallions of Veal (page 102), Lamb Shanks for Two (page 103), Liver, Bacon, and Onions (page 109), Chicken Milano (page 118), Lobster Supreme (page 130), Mountain Trout (page 134), Fillet of Fish Amandine (page 137), and Cheddar and Onion Egg (page 147). As you browse through the book, you might want to make a special note of others you want to try.

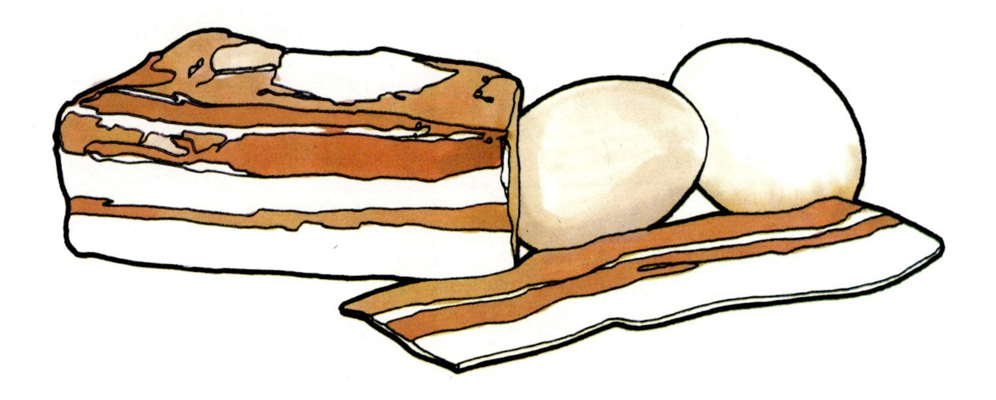

Recipe No. 279

Cheese Enchiladas

Cooking Time: 9½ minutes

- 1 cup shredded Longhorn cheese
- ½ cup shredded Monterey Jack cheese
- 1 carton (4 ounces) dairy sour cream
- ¼ cup chopped green onions
- 2 tablespoons chopped jalapeño peppers (optional)
- ½ teaspoon prepared mustard
- ¼ teaspoon white pepper
- 1½ teaspoons butter
- 1½ teaspoons flour
- ½ cup milk
- 4 ounces grated Cheddar cheese
- 4 flour tortillas
- 1 jar (8 ounces) enchilada sauce, divided
- 1 small avocado, sliced
- ½ cup shredded lettuce
- 1 small tomato, diced

Combine Longhorn and Monterey Jack cheeses and sour cream in 1-quart glass measure. Place in oven. Set recipe number 279. Touch START. *(Oven cooks: micro,* 50, 1 *minute.)*

At Pause, stir cheese mixture. Add green onions, jalapeño peppers, if desired, mustard, and pepper; mix well. Set aside.

Place butter in 2-cup glass measure. Place in oven. Touch START. *(Oven cooks: micro, HI,* 30 *seconds.)*

At Pause, stir in flour and milk. Place in oven. Touch START. *(Oven cooks: micro, HI,* 2 *minutes.)*

At Pause, stir in Cheddar cheese; set aside. Spread one-fourth of the cheese and sour cream mixture on each of the four tortillas. Roll tightly; place in 1-quart shallow microproof casserole. Pour half of the enchilada sauce evenly over tortillas. Spoon Cheddar cheese sauce over enchilada sauce. Place in oven. *(Oven cooks: micro,* 80, 6 *minutes.)*

Serve topped with remaining enchilada sauce, avocado, lettuce, and tomato.

2 servings

Recipe No. 280

Hot Chicken Salad

Cooking Time: 12 minutes

- 1 cup cubed cooked chicken
- ½ cup diced celery
- ¼ cup toasted slivered almonds
- 1 green onion, sliced
- 2 tablespoons grated Parmesan cheese
- 2 tablespoons grated Monterey Jack cheese
- ½ teaspoon dillweed
- ¼ teaspoon Italian herbs
- ¼ teaspoon salt
- ¼ teaspoon freshly ground black pepper
- 1 teaspoon lemon juice
- ½ cup mayonnaise
- 1 tablespoon dry breadcrumbs

Place wire rack in lower position. Set recipe number 280. Touch START. *(Oven preheats: convec,* 350°*F.)* Lightly grease a shallow 1-quart microproof and heatproof casserole. Combine all ingredients except breadcrumbs in 2-quart mixing bowl; mix thoroughly. Spoon salad into prepared casserole. Sprinkle breadcrumbs over salad.

At 350°F, place in oven. Touch START. *(Oven cooks: micro/convec,* 350°*F,* 10 *minutes; stands:* 0, 2 *minutes.)*

1 serving

Recipe No. 281

Sirloin Steak Sandwich

Cooking Time: 4 minutes 10 seconds

- 4 ounces ground sirloin steak
- 1½ teaspoons Worcestershire sauce, divided
- Salt and pepper to taste
- 1 slice Cheddar or Swiss cheese (optional)
- ½ jar (2½ ounces) sliced mushrooms
- 1 crusty hard roll

Place wire rack in upper position. Set recipe number 281. Touch START. *(Oven preheats: convec, 400°F.)* Combine ground sirloin with 1 teaspoon Worcestershire sauce, salt, and pepper. Shape into patty.

At 400°F, place patty on 6-inch round microproof and heatproof plate and place in oven. Touch START. *(Oven cooks: micro/convec, 400°F, 3 minutes.)*

At Pause, turn patty over. Top with cheese slice, if desired, and mushrooms. Sprinkle with remaining ½ teaspoon Worcestershire sauce. Touch START. *(Oven cooks: micro/convec, 400°F, 1 minute.)*

At Pause, remove plate. Place hard roll on wire rack. Touch START. *(Oven cooks: micro, HI, 10 seconds.)* Serve sirloin patty and mushrooms on hard roll.

1 serving

Recipe No. 282

Ham Divan

Cooking Time: 12½ minutes

- 1 teaspoon butter, melted
- 1 teaspoon flour
- ½ cup milk
- ¼ cup dairy sour cream
- 1 egg yolk
- ¼ cup grated Parmesan cheese
- 1 package (10 ounces) frozen broccoli spears, cooked and drained
- ¼ pound ham, thinly sliced deli-style
- 1 teaspoon chopped parsley
- ½ teaspoon rosemary
- ¼ teaspoon paprika

Place melted butter and flour in 2-cup glass measure; stir to blend. Gradually blend in milk. Place in oven. Set recipe number 163. Touch START. *(Oven cooks: micro, HI, 1 minute.)*

At Pause, stir. Touch START. *(Oven cooks: micro, HI, 1½ minutes.)* Remove from oven; stir in sour cream, egg yolk, and Parmesan cheese.

Place wire rack in lower position. Set recipe number 282. Touch START. *(Oven preheats: convec, 350°F.)* Arrange broccoli in 2 buttered individual microproof and heatproof baking dishes. Place ham over broccoli. Top with sauce and sprinkle with parsley, rosemary, and paprika.

At 350°F, place dishes in oven. Touch START. *(Oven cooks: micro/convec, 350°F, 5 minutes.)*

At Pause, turn dishes. Touch START. *(Oven cooks: micro/convec, 350°F, 5 minutes.)* Serve directly from baking dishes or over hot toast points.

2 servings

Recipe No. 283

Beefy Stuffed Potato

Cooking Time: 9½ minutes

- 1 Russet baking potato (8 ounces)
- ½ cup cottage cheese
- 1 tablespoon butter
- 1 teaspoon chopped chives
- Salt and pepper to taste
- 1 package (2½ ounces) dried beef, diced
- 1 teaspoon chopped parsley

Wash potato; prick evenly with fork. Place potato in oven on ceramic tray. Set recipe number 283. Touch START. *(Oven cooks: micro, HI, 6 minutes; stands: 0, 2 minutes.)*

At Pause, cut potato in half lengthwise. Carefully scoop pulp into small mixing bowl, keeping shells intact. Blend cottage cheese, butter, chopped chives, salt, and pepper into potato pulp. Beat with electric mixer until smooth. Stir in dried beef. Spoon mixture evenly into shells.

Place in oven. Touch START. *(Oven cooks: micro, HI, 1½ minutes.)*

Sprinkle with parsley before serving.

1 serving

Recipe No. 284

Mushroom Soufflé

Cooking Time: 34 minutes

- 1½ teaspoons butter, divided
- 2 tablespoons dry breadcrumbs
- 2 tablespoons grated Parmesan cheese
- 1 cup finely chopped mushrooms (about ¼ pound)
- 1 green onion, sliced
- 2 teaspoons chopped parsley
- 1 teaspoon Dijon-style mustard
- 1 tablespoon butter
- 1 tablespoon flour
- Dash salt and pepper
- ¾ cup milk
- 2 eggs, separated
- 1 cup plus 1½ teaspoons shredded sharp Cheddar cheese, divided
- ¼ teaspoon cream of tartar

Coat the bottom and sides of 2-cup soufflé dish with ½ teaspoon butter. Combine dry breadcrumbs and Parmesan cheese. Sprinkle dish with crumb mixture, rotating dish to cover evenly and letting excess remain in bottom. Set aside.

Place remaining 1 teaspoon butter and mushrooms in 1-quart glass measure. Place in oven. Set recipe number 230. Touch START. *(Oven cooks: micro, HI, 1½ minutes.)* Drain off excess liquid.

At Pause, stir in onion, parsley, mustard, 1 tablespoon butter, flour, salt, and pepper. Slowly stir in milk. Place in oven. Touch START. *(Oven cooks: micro, HI, 1½ minutes.)*

At Pause, stir. Touch START. *(Oven cooks: micro, HI, 1 minute.)* Beat egg yolks until smooth and lemon-colored; blend into milk mixture. Stir in 1 cup shredded sharp Cheddar.

Remove ceramic tray. Place wire rack in lower position. Set recipe number 284. Touch START. *(Oven preheats: convec, 350°F.)* Beat egg whites in large bowl until foamy. Add cream of tartar and continue beating until stiff but not dry. Stir one-third of whites into cheese mixture. Gently fold in remaining whites. Turn into prepared soufflé dish. Sprinkle remaining cheese on top.

At 350°F, place in oven. Touch START. Touch START. *(Oven cooks: convec, 350°F, 30 minutes.)* Serve immediately.

2 servings

Recipe No. 285

Stuffed Eggplant Parmigiana

Cooking Time: 22 minutes

- 1 eggplant (1 pound)
- 3 medium tomatoes, peeled, seeded, and chopped
- 1 stalk celery, finely chopped
- 1 green onion, chopped
- ½ cup grated Parmesan cheese
- 1 clove garlic, minced
- 1 teaspoon Italian herbs
- ½ teaspoon freshly ground black pepper
- ¼ teaspoon salt
- 1½ cups (6 ounces) shredded mozzarella cheese, divided
- 1 teaspoon chopped parsley

Wash eggplant, remove stem, and pierce skin in several places. Place in 9-inch round microproof dish. Place in oven. Set recipe number 208. Touch START. *(Oven cooks: micro, HI, 7 minutes.)*

At Pause, remove eggplant from oven. Set recipe number 285. Touch START. *(Oven preheats: convec, 350°F.)* Combine tomatoes, celery, green onion, Parmesan cheese, garlic, Italian herbs, pepper, salt, and half of the mozzarella cheese in 1-quart mixing bowl.

Cut eggplant in half lengthwise; remove seeds. Set halves in 9-inch round microproof and heatproof baking dish. Spoon half of the tomato mixture into each cavity. Sprinkle with remaining mozzarella cheese.

At 350°F, place in oven. Touch START. *(Oven cooks: micro/convec, 350°F, 15 minutes.)* Sprinkle with chopped parsley and serve.

2 servings

Recipe No. 286

Pepper Steak

Cooking Time: 13 minutes

- ½ clove garlic, minced (optional)
- ½ teaspoon freshly ground black pepper
- 1 rib eye steak (8 to 10 ounces), ½-inch thick
- 1 small green pepper, cut into ½-inch squares
- 1 small red pepper, cut into ½-inch squares
- 1 medium onion, sliced
- 1 teaspoon cornstarch
- ¼ cup beef broth
- 2 tablespoons dry red wine
- ½ teaspoon Worcestershire sauce

Sprinkle minced garlic and black pepper over both sides of steak; pound lightly into meat with wooden mallet. Cut meat into 1-inch long strips. Set aside. Place peppers and onion in 1-quart shallow microproof and heatproof casserole. Cover with casserole lid. Place in oven. Set recipe number 9. Touch START. *(Oven cooks: micro, HI, 2 minutes.)*

At Pause, remove casserole. Place steak strips over vegetables. Set aside. Set recipe number 286. Touch START. *(Oven preheats: convec, 400°F.)*

Stir together cornstarch, beef broth, wine, and Worcestershire sauce in 2-cup measure until well blended. Pour broth mixture over steak and vegetables.

At 400°F, place in oven. Touch START. *(Oven cooks: micro/convec, 400°F, 5 minutes.)*

At Pause, turn meat over. Touch START. *(Oven cooks: micro/convec, 400°F, 6 minutes for medium doneness.)* If well-done meat is preferred, add 1 minute to cooking cycle.

Serve with hot rice.

1 serving

Recipe No. 287

Hawaiian Chicken

Cooking Time: 23 minutes

- 2 whole chicken breasts (1 pound each), rinsed and patted dry
- 1 can (8 ounces) pineapple chunks, drained, juice reserved
- 1/4 cup brown sugar
- 2 tablespoons vinegar
- 1 teaspoon soy sauce
- 1/2 teaspoon grated lemon peel
- 1/2 teaspoon grated orange peel
- 2 teaspoons cornstarch
- 1 can (11 ounces) mandarin orange sections, drained

Place chicken in 9-inch round microproof and heatproof baking dish. Set aside. Combine pineapple juice, brown sugar, vinegar, soy sauce, lemon peel, and orange peel in 2-cup glass measure. Add cornstarch and stir until mixture is well blended. Place in oven. Set recipe number 237. Touch START. *(Oven cooks: micro, HI, 1½ minutes.)*

At Pause, stir. Touch START. *(Oven cooks: micro, HI, 1½ minutes.)*. Pour sauce mixture over chicken.

Place wire rack in upper position. Set recipe number 287. Touch START. *(Oven preheats: convec, 370°F.)*

At 370°F, place in oven. Touch START. *(Oven cooks: micro/convec, 370°F, 18 minutes.)*

At Pause, spoon pineapple chunks and orange sections over chicken. Baste with sauce. Touch START. *(Oven cooks: micro/convec, 370°F, 2 minutes.)*

2 servings

Recipe No. 288

Orange Roughy with Vegetables

Cooking Time: 5 minutes

- 2 Orange Roughy or Haddock fillets (4 ounces each)
- 1 small tomato, diced
- 1 green onion, sliced
- 2 tablespoons chopped green pepper
- 2 tablespoons chopped celery
- 2 tablespoons chopped parsley
- 2 tablespoons dry white wine
- Juice of 1 lime
- 2 tablespoons melted butter

Place wire rack in upper position. Set recipe number 288. Touch START. *(Oven preheats: convec, 450°F.)* Place fish fillets in 7×11-inch microproof and heatproof baking dish. Combine tomato, onion, green pepper, celery, and parsley. Spoon vegetables over fillets. Combine wine, lime juice, and melted butter, and pour over vegetables and fish.

At 450°F, place in oven. Touch START. *(Oven cooks: micro/convec, 450°F, 2½ minutes.)*

At Pause, turn dish. Touch START. *(Oven cooks: micro/convec, 450°F, 2½ minutes.)*

2 servings

Recipe No. 289

Salmon in Coquilles

Cooking Time: 12 minutes

- 1 can (7½ ounces) salmon, drained and flaked
- 1 stalk celery, finely chopped
- 1 green onion, thinly sliced
- 1 teaspoon chopped parsley
- ½ teaspoon dillweed
- Juice of ½ lemon
- ¼ cup mayonnaise
- 2 lettuce leaves
- 1 tablespoon melted butter
- ¼ cup soft breadcrumbs

Place wire rack in lower position. Set recipe number 289. *(Oven preheats: convec, 350°F.)* Combine salmon, celery, green onion, parsley, dillweed, lemon juice, and mayonnaise. Place each lettuce leaf in an individual microproof baking dish. Spoon salmon mixture onto lettuce leaves. Stir melted butter into breadcrumbs until well mixed. Sprinkle buttered crumbs over salmon.

At 350°F, place in oven. Touch START. *(Oven cooks: micro/convec, 350°F, 12 minutes.)*

2 servings

Recipe No. 290

Lamb Chops

Cooking Time: 6 minutes

- 2 lamb shoulder blade chops (3½ to 4 ounces each)
- 1 tablespoon lemon juice
- 1 tablespoon dry white wine
- 1 green onion, sliced
- 1 teaspoon chopped parsley
- 1 teaspoon chopped mint
- ⅛ teaspoon thyme
- ⅛ teaspoon rosemary
- ⅛ teaspoon oregano
- ⅛ teaspoon freshly ground black pepper

Set recipe number 290. Touch START. *(Oven preheats: convec, 350°F.)* Place chops in 1-quart shallow microproof and heatproof casserole. Combine lemon juice and white wine, and pour over chops. Combine onion, herbs, and pepper, and sprinkle over chops.

At 350°F, place in oven. Touch START. *(Oven cooks: micro/convec, 350°F, 6 minutes.)*

1 serving

Recipe No. 291

Cheese Broccoli

Cooking Time: 6½ minutes

- 1 package (10 ounces) frozen broccoli spears
- ¼ cup shredded Monterey Jack cheese

Unwrap broccoli; place in shallow 2-cup microproof dish. Cover with plastic wrap. Place in oven. Set recipe number 291. Touch START. *(Oven cooks: micro, HI, 6 minutes.)*

At Pause, sprinkle cheese on broccoli. Touch START. *(Oven cooks: micro, HI, 30 seconds.)*

2 servings

Recipe No. 292

Zucchini, Green Pepper, and Tomato

Cooking Time: 6 minutes

- 1 small zucchini (4 ounces), peeled and cut into 1-inch pieces
- 1 medium tomato (3 ounces), cut into 8 wedges
- 1 small green pepper, cut into 1-inch pieces
- ½ teaspoon lemon pepper seasoning
- 1 tablespoon butter

Place zucchini in individual microproof baking dish. Cover with plastic wrap. Place in oven. Set recipe number 292. Touch START. *(Oven cooks: micro, HI, 2 minutes.)*

At Pause, remove dish from oven. Stir in tomato, green pepper and lemon pepper. Dot with butter. Cover. Place in oven. Touch START. *(Oven cooks: micro, HI, 2 minutes.)*

At Pause, turn. Touch START. *(Oven cooks: micro, HI, 2 minutes.)*

1 serving

Recipe No. 293

Bran Casserole Bread

Cooking Time: 35 minutes

- ⅔ cup warm water (105° to 115°F)
- 2 tablespoons molasses
- ½ cup bran bud cereal
- 1 package active dry yeast
- 1 egg
- 3 tablespoons butter or margarine, melted
- 1 teaspoon salt
- 2 cups all-purpose flour

Generously grease a 1½-quart casserole. Set aside. Combine water, molasses, bran cereal, and yeast in 2-quart mixing bowl. Let stand, without stirring, for 10 minutes. Stir in egg, margarine, and salt and mix well. Blend in 1 cup flour. Gradually stir in enough of the remaining flour to make a soft dough. Transfer to prepared casserole. Cover with towel. Let rise in warm, draft-free area for 40 to 50 minutes or until doubled in bulk.

Remove ceramic tray. Place wire rack in lower position. Set recipe number 293. Touch START. *(Oven preheats: convec, 370°F.)*

At 370°F, place in oven. Touch START. *(Oven cooks: convec, 370°F, 35 minutes.)*

1 loaf

Recipe No. 294

Hot Fruit Compote

Cooking Time: 6 minutes

- 1 can (8½ ounces) pineapple chunks, drained
- 1 apple, cut into chunks
- 1 banana, cut into thick slices
- 5 maraschino cherries, halved
- 1 tablespoon brown sugar
- ¼ teaspoon cinnamon
- Dash nutmeg
- Dash cloves
- 2 tablespoons orange juice concentrate or apple juice concentrate
- 1 teaspoon butter

Combine all ingredients in 2-quart glass measure. Cover with plastic wrap. Place in oven. Set recipe number 294. *(Oven cooks: micro, 50, 2 minutes.)*

At Pause, stir. Cover. Touch START. *(Oven cooks: micro, 50, 2 minutes; stands: 0, 2 minutes.)*

Serve hot for breakfast, or as an accompaniment to ham or pork.

2 servings

Recipe No. 295

Chocolate Cake

Cooking Time: 6 minutes

- ¾ cup all-purpose flour
- ¼ cup cocoa
- ½ teaspoon baking soda
- ¼ cup butter
- ½ cup sugar
- 1 egg
- ⅓ cup milk
- ¼ cup chopped nuts
- ½ teaspoon vanilla

Place wire rack in lower position. Set recipe number 295. Touch START. *(Oven preheats: convec, 350°F.)* Grease a 1-quart shallow microproof and heatproof casserole. Sift together flour, cocoa, and baking soda in small bowl. Cream butter, sugar, and egg in mixing bowl. Add milk to creamed mixture alternately with dry ingredients. Stir in nuts and vanilla. Spoon into prepared casserole.

At 350°F, place in oven. Touch START. *(Oven cooks: micro/convec, 350°F, 6 minutes.)*

Serve with ice cream and hot fudge sauce.

2 servings

Dinner's in the Oven

Dinner's in the oven! Who doesn't look forward to hearing this familiar saying as mealtime approaches? You'll find that just as in conventional cooking you can prepare a whole two- or three-dish meal at the same time in your microwave oven. For the most successful whole meal, it is important to consider the placement of dishes in the oven, the size and shape of the microproof containers, the kinds of food you select, the timing, and the sequence of cooking. This chapter provides you with all the necessary information and step-by-step instructions for organizing your own whole meals. Start by reading the following basic tips on how to approach whole meal planning:

- ☐ Since microwaves enter from the top of the oven, they are primarily attracted to food placed on the wire rack; a smaller amount reaches the ceramic tray. It is logical then to place delicate, quick-cooking food on the ceramic tray and longer cooking food on the wire rack.
- ☐ Whenever the wire rack is not being used, remove it from oven.
- ☐ An ideal procedure for whole-meal cooking is to place two foods with similar cooking times on the wire rack and one shorter-cooking food on the ceramic tray.
- ☐ If all foods require the same cooking time, reverse the location of dishes in the oven halfway through cooking period.
- ☐ While the wire rack can be used in two positions, the upper position is generally best. Use the lower position whenever greater capacity on the top is needed. This does limit the usable space below.
- ☐ Check your cooking dishes to be sure they will fit together on a shelf before filling with food.
- ☐ Often covers with knobs are too high to fit easily when the wire rack is used. Use plastic wrap instead of casserole lids when necessary.
- ☐ All whole-meal cooking is done on HI.

IMPORTANT GUIDELINES FOR TIMING AND PLANNING

- ☐ If all foods take less than 15 minutes individually, add cooking times together and program the menu for the total time.
- ☐ If all foods take 15 to 35 minutes individually, add cooking times together and subtract about 5 minutes.
- ☐ If any one food takes over 35 minutes, all the food can be cooked in the time suggested for food taking the longest time.

The following chart presents five main dishes appearing in the recipe chapters and 12 complementary dishes. There's no need to keep with the particular combinations we've provided. Simply choose any dish from column "A" and complete the menu with any "B" and any "C".

1. Choose a menu from the chart.
2. Review the individual recipe. You may find that an ingredient should be prepared ahead. (Onion is often sautéed as a separate step, for example).
3. Check the dishes to be sure they fit in the oven together. Change the size and type of dish as required. *Be sure you are always thinking microproof.*
4. Place dishes in oven with food from column "A" on the wire rack (it is the most dense and needs to receive the most microwave energy); "B" and "C" are placed on the ceramic tray.
5. Apply the rules in "Important Guidelines for Timing." The approximate cooking time for each recipe follows the recipe title in the menu chart.
6. Most recipes in whole-meal cooking are best stirred or rearranged halfway through cooking time.

A	B	C
One-Step Lasagna (37) (page 95)	Brussels Sprouts (9) (page 151)	Parsley New Potatoes (12) (page 168)
Beef Shanghai (9) (page 96)	Green Beans Amandine (9) (page 167)	Pudding Mix (7) (page 196)
All-American Meatballs (20) (page 95)	Cauliflower (11) (page 165)	All-Seasons Rice (17) (page 155)
Salmon Ring (12) (page 137)	Stuffed Tomatoes (18) (page 160)	Golden Apple Chunks (8) (page 194)
Shrimp Veracruz (12) (page 131)	Carrots (10) (page 165)	Fluffy Tapioca (16) (page 194)

As you continue to enjoy micro/convection cooking, you'll discover many time-saving whole meal techniques on your own. Simply remember that the convection method is similar to your conventional oven, that the micro/convection method gives convection benefits with microwave energy, and that the microwave method uses the "Guidelines" on page 208. Now, here are our seven Whole Meals, preset for extra convenience.

Recipe No. 296

Scrambled Eggs, Bacon, and Sweet Rolls

Cooking Time: 11½ minutes

- 6 large eggs
- ⅓ cup milk
- 2 tablespoons butter, melted
- 6 slices bacon
- 6 sweet rolls

Place wire rack in upper position. Combine eggs, milk, and butter in 1-quart microproof casserole; beat with fork until blended. Cover with casserole lid; set aside. Arrange bacon on paper towel-lined microproof plate. Cover with paper towel; set aside. Arrange rolls on microproof plate; set aside. Arrange egg mixture and bacon in oven as shown in "A." Set recipe number 296. Touch START. *(Oven cooks: micro, HI, 4 minutes.)*

At Pause, stir eggs. Cover. Touch START. *(Oven cooks: micro, HI, 3½ minutes.)*

At Pause, remove eggs from oven. Stir. Cover. Set aside. Add rolls as shown in "B." Touch START. *(Oven cooks: micro, HI, 1 minute; stands: 0, 3 minutes.)*

4 to 6 servings

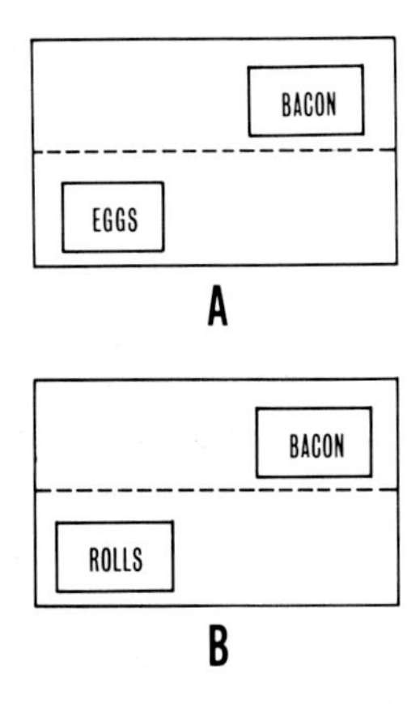

Recipe No. 297

Beef Stew, Garlic Bread, and Pudding

Cooking Time: 13 minutes

- 1 can (24 ounces) beef stew
- ¼ cup butter, melted
- ½ teaspoon garlic powder
- ½ pound French bread, cut into 1-inch thick slices
- 1 package (3¼ ounces) pudding mix
- 2 cups milk

Place wire rack in upper position. Pour stew into 1-quart microproof casserole. Cover with casserole lid; set aside. Combine butter and garlic powder. Brush both sides of bread slices with butter mixture. Reshape into loaf and wrap in paper towels. Place on microproof plate; set aside. Place pudding mix in 1-quart microproof casserole. Stir in milk; set aside. Arrange stew and pudding mixture in oven as shown in "A." Set recipe number 297. Touch START. *(Oven cooks: micro, HI, 5 minutes.)*

At Pause, stir stew and pudding. Cover stew. Touch START. *(Oven cooks: micro, HI, 3½ minutes.)*

At Pause, stir pudding. Place bread in oven as shown in "B." Touch START. *(Oven cooks: micro, HI, 4½ minutes.)*

3 servings

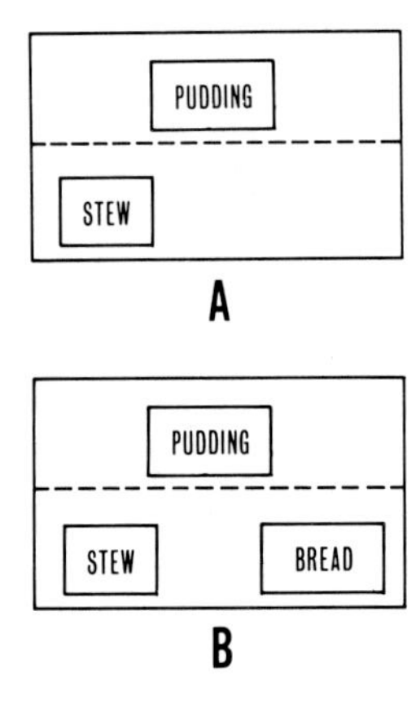

Recipe No. 297 Alternate

Chili, Corn Muffins, and Apple Crisp

Cooking Time: 13 minutes

1 can (24 ounces) chili
3 corn muffins
1 recipe Apple Crisp (below)

Place wire rack in upper position. Pour chili into 1½-quart microproof casserole. Cover with casserole lid; set aside. Wrap corn muffins in paper towels; set aside. Prepare Apple Crisp as directed below. Cover with waxed paper. Arrange chili and Apple Crisp in oven as shown in "A." Set recipe number 297. Touch START. *(Oven cooks: micro, HI, 5 minutes.)*

At Pause, stir chili. Cover. Change position of dishes as shown in "B." Touch START. *(Oven cooks: micro, HI, 3½ minutes.)*

At Pause, stir chili. Cover. Place muffins in oven as shown in "C." Touch START. *(Oven cooks: micro, HI, 4½ minutes.)*

Let Apple Crisp stand 3 minutes before serving.

3 servings

Apple Crisp

4 cups sliced tart apples
½ cup rolled oats
¼ cup butter or margarine
¼ cup all-purpose flour
¼ cup firmly-packed brown sugar
1 teaspoon lemon juice
½ teaspoon cinnamon
⅛ teaspoon nutmeg

Arrange apple slices in 8-inch square microproof baking dish. Combine remaining ingredients; blend well. Crumble over apples.

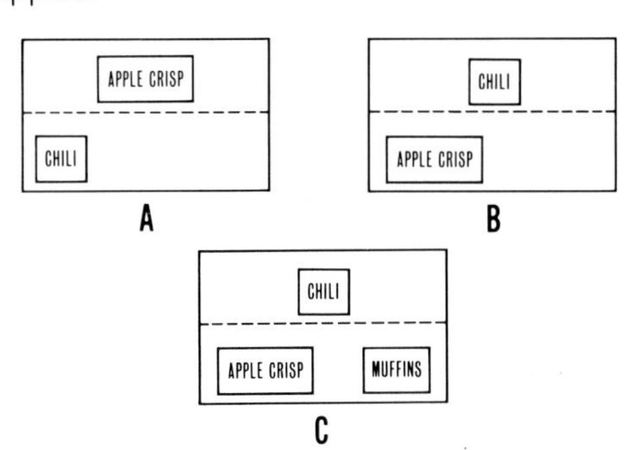

Recipe No. 298

Baked Chicken, Rice, and Asparagus

Cooking Time: 26 minutes

¾ cup corn-flake crumbs
⅓ cup grated Parmesan cheese
1 broiler-fryer chicken (2½ to 3 pounds), quartered
¼ cup butter, melted
1 package (11 ounces) frozen rice in pouch
2 cans (14½ ounces each) asparagus spears, drained

Place wire rack in upper position. Combine corn-flake crumbs and Parmesan cheese. Brush chicken lightly with butter; coat with crumb mixture. Arrange chicken in large microproof baking dish, skin-side up, with thickest parts toward outside of dish. Cover with waxed paper; set aside. Place rice in pouch on small microproof plate; slit pouch; set aside. Place asparagus in 8×4-inch microproof loaf pan. Cover lightly with plastic wrap. Arrange all 3 dishes in oven as shown in "A." Set recipe number 298. Touch START. *(Oven cooks: micro, HI, 10 minutes.)*

At Pause, rotate chicken dish one-half turn. Touch START. *(Oven cooks: micro, HI, 10 minutes.)*

At Pause, rotate rice one-quarter turn. Touch START. *(Oven cooks: micro, HI, 4 minutes.)*

At Pause, remove chicken and asparagus from oven. Rotate rice as shown in "B." Touch START. *(Oven cooks: micro, HI, 2 minutes.)*

3 to 4 servings

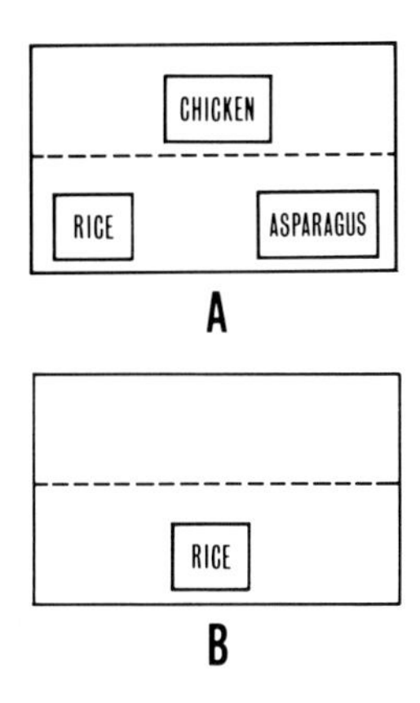

Recipe No. 298 Alternate

Seasoned Pork Chops, Parsley Potatoes, and Mixed Vegetables

Cooking Time: 26 minutes

- 1 envelope ($2\frac{1}{4}$ ounces) seasoned coating mix for pork
- 4 pork chops ($1\frac{1}{4}$ pounds)
- 3 potatoes (5 ounces each), peeled and cut into $\frac{3}{4}$-inch cubes
- $\frac{1}{4}$ cup water
- 1 can (16 ounces) mixed vegetables, drained
- Butter or margarine
- 1 tablespoon chopped parsley

Place wire rack in upper position. Empty coating mix into plastic bag. Shake pork chops, one at a time, in coating mix. Place chops in 12 × 7-inch microproof baking dish. Cover with waxed paper; set aside. Place potatoes and water in 8 × 4-inch microproof loaf pan. Cover with plastic wrap; set aside. Place mixed vegetables in 1-quart microproof casserole. Arrange all 3 dishes in oven as shown in "A." Set recipe number 298. Touch START. *(Oven cooks: micro, HI,* 10 *minutes.)*

At Pause, rotate pork dish one-half turn. Touch START. *(Oven cooks: micro, HI,* 10 *minutes.)*

At Pause, stir potatoes. Cover. Touch START. *(Oven cooks: micro, HI,* 4 *minutes.)*

At Pause, check pork chops. If done, remove from oven. Touch START. *(Oven cooks: micro, HI,* 2 *minutes.)*

Remove all dishes from oven. Stir vegetables. Dot potatoes with butter, and sprinkle with parsley before serving.

3 to 4 servings

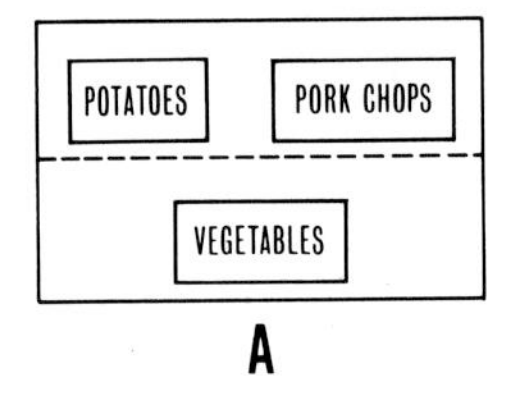

A

Recipe No. 299

Beef & Spaghetti Casserole, Green Peas, and Baked Apple Chunks

Cooking Time: 30 minutes

- 1 package ($7\frac{1}{2}$ ounces) spaghetti meat-noodle main dish mix
- 1 pound lean ground beef
- 4 cups hot water
- 1 package (10 ounces) frozen green peas
- 1 recipe Baked Apple Chunks (below)

Place wire rack in upper position. Prepare meat-noodle mix, adding beef and hot water as directed on package. Place in 2-quart microproof casserole. Cover with casserole lid; set aside. Place peas in 1-quart microproof casserole. Cover with casserole lid; set aside. Prepare Baked Apple Chunks as directed below. Arrange dishes in oven as shown in "A." Set recipe number 299. Touch START. *(Oven cooks: micro, HI,* 20 *minutes.)*

At Pause, stir beef mixture and Baked Apple Chunks. Cover both casseroles. Touch START. *(Oven cooks: micro, HI,* 5 *minutes; stands:* 0, 5 *minutes.)*

4 servings

Baked Apple Chunks

- 4 medium-size tart cooking apples, peeled, cored, and cut into quarters
- $\frac{1}{4}$ cup firmly-packed brown sugar
- 1 teaspoon cinnamon
- 2 tablespoons butter or margarine

Place apples in 8 × 4-inch microproof loaf pan. Combine brown sugar and cinnamon; blend well. Crumble over apples. Dot with butter.

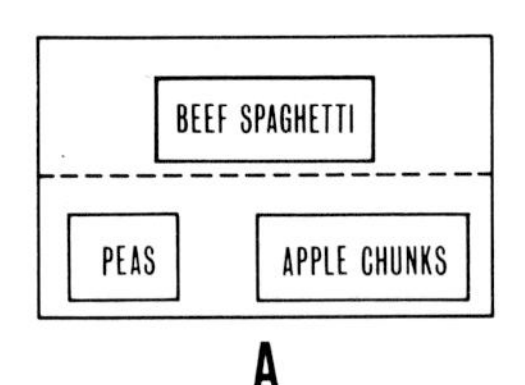

A

Recipe No. 300

Meatloaf, Yellow Squash, and Chocolate Fudge Layer Cake

Cooking Time: 23 minutes

- 1 recipe Meatloaf (opposite)
- 1 recipe Chocolate Fudge Layer Cake (opposite)
- 1 medium yellow squash, peeled and thinly sliced
- 1 tablespoon butter
- ¼ teaspoon salt
- Whipped cream

Place wire rack in upper position. Prepare Meatloaf and Chocolate Fudge Layer Cake as directed below; set aside. Place squash in 8 × 4-inch microproof loaf pan. Cover with plastic wrap. Arrange all 3 dishes in oven as shown in "A." Set recipe number 300. Touch START. *(Oven cooks: micro, HI, 15 minutes.)*

At Pause, rotate meatloaf and cake dishes one-half turn. Stir squash; cover. Touch START. *(Oven cooks: micro, HI, 7 minutes.)*

At Pause, insert toothpick into cake. If toothpick comes out clean, remove cake from oven. Touch START. *(Oven cooks: micro, HI, 1 minute.)*

Stir butter and salt into squash. Let cake stand 3 to 5 minutes. Gently twist glass to remove. Invert cake onto serving plate. Remove waxed paper. Slice and serve topped with whipped cream.

6 servings

Meatloaf

- 1½ pounds lean ground beef
- 2 cups soft bread crumbs
- 1 can (8 ounces) tomato sauce, divided
- ½ cup finely chopped onions
- ¼ cup finely chopped green pepper
- 1 large egg
- 1½ teaspoons salt

Combine beef, bread crumbs, ½ cup tomato sauce, onion, green pepper, egg, and salt; blend well. Pack into 8-inch round microproof baking dish. Insert straight-sided, 2-inch diameter glass, open end up, into center of dish. Pour remaining sauce over beef mixture.

Chocolate Fudge Layer Cake

- 1 package (15 ounces) snacking chocolate fudge cake mix

Prepare cake batter as directed on package. Line bottom of 9-inch round microproof baking dish with waxed paper. Place straight-sided, 2-inch diameter glass, open end up, in center of dish. Pour batter into dish.

A 6-cup microproof Bundt-type pan or ring mold can be substituted for baking dish with glass.

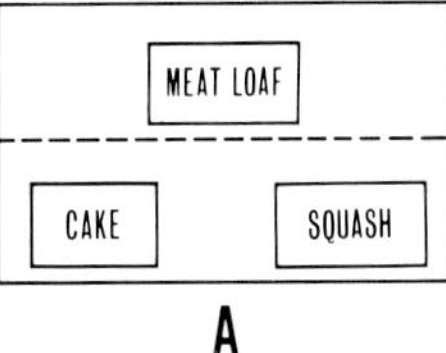

A

Food Preservation For Today

In recent years, supermarkets throughout the country have been adding special sections for dried fruits, mushrooms, vegetables, and similar items at an impressive rate. Because dried foods are so versatile, take up so little storage space, weigh next to nothing, and require no special jars or other equipment, they have caught our fancy, for they fit our mobile lifestyles. Now, with the special dehydration cycle of this oven, dried foods that you prepare yourself are just a few simple steps away. Whether you've been fond of visiting that supermarket section or a health foods store, you'll soon look to your own collection of dried foods for most of your needs. And here's an idea: why not collect unusual jars and colorful ribbons to make gifts for your friends with your own dried fruits, soup mix, or beef jerky? They are sure to be appreciated.

The instructions in the Guide and recipes that follow will generally be all you need for successful dehydration with your Kenmore Auto Recipe 300 Micro/Convection oven. However, you may also want to consult your Use & Care Manual and these tips.

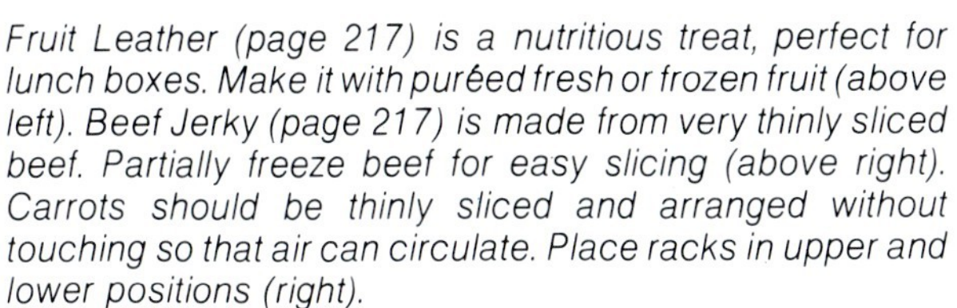

Fruit Leather (page 217) is a nutritious treat, perfect for lunch boxes. Make it with purẽed fresh or frozen fruit (above left). Beef Jerky (page 217) is made from very thinly sliced beef. Partially freeze beef for easy slicing (above right). Carrots should be thinly sliced and arranged without touching so that air can circulate. Place racks in upper and lower positions (right).

← *Dried apples and bananas (page 218), Trail Mix (page 217)*

- ☐ All suggested timings are approximate. Drying times cannot be predicted exactly because the thickness, freshness, sugar content, and other factors of the food vary. For example, hours can be cut from the estimated drying time just by slicing the food thinner, or cutting it into smaller pieces. Apply the dryness tests described in the Guide as well as your judgment.
- ☐ If you prefer chewy fruit, for example, you may want to use less time than recommended. Similarly, if you prefer very crisp fruit, a bit more time should be considered.
- ☐ To help assure even results, cut foods into like sizes and thicknesses.
- ☐ Be imaginative in your use of dehydrated foods. Create your own soup mix by combining dehydrated vegetables with instant bouillon; simmer fruit with your favorite spices for "instant desserts," or serve cucumber chips instead of potato chips! There's no limit to what you can do.
- ☐ Store your dehydrated foods in any clean, airtight jars or in plastic bags that can be tightly sealed (squeeze bags to exhaust as much air as possible before completing the seal). Store in cool area, away from direct light.

Backpacker's Vegetable Soup

1 cup dried carrots
½ cup dried corn kernels
½ cup dried tomatoes
¼ cup dried onions
¼ cup dried mushrooms
¼ cup dried green or red peppers
¼ cup barley
2- 3 tablespoons dry beef or chicken bouillon crystals
½ teaspoon basil
½ teaspoon thyme
½ teaspoon salt
⅛ teaspoon freshly ground black pepper

In 4-cup mixing bowl, combine dried vegetables, barley, bouillon crystals, and herbs. Stir to mix. Store in airtight containers.

To reconstitute: Pour 2 to 2½ cups boiling water over dried vegetables and allow to stand 1 - 2 hours until soft.

You may also make 1 cup of soup at a time. Simply place 2 tablespoons dry soup mix in large mug and fill with boiling water.

Fruit Leather

1½ pounds fresh fruit or defrosted frozen fruit
¼ cup corn syrup
Ground cinnamon, nutmeg, cloves, lemon peel, or orange peel (optional)

Place plastic mesh on dehydration rack and cover with plastic wrap, bringing wrap around sides of rack and secure with tape. If very firm fresh fruit, such as apples, are chosen, cook briefly to soften. Purée fruit in blender. Add corn sryup and process until well mixed. Pour purée onto plastic wrap and spread evenly, leaving a ½-inch border on all sides. Sprinkle with your choice of flavoring in any combination desired. Place mesh on rack in lower position and dehydrate approximately 4 hours.

Beef Jerky

2 pounds lean Flank steak, brisket, or round steak, trimmed of fat
3 tablespoons dry white wine
2 tablespoons soy sauce
2 tablespoons Worcestershire sauce
1 tablespoon sugar
¾ teaspoon salt
½ teaspoon pepper
¼ teaspoon garlic powder
⅛ teaspoon cayenne pepper

Slice beef very thinly against the grain and cut into strips. Combine remaining ingredients and stir until well blended. Stir sliced beef into marinade. Cover and marinate about 1½ hours, stirring once. Remove beef and blot dry with paper towels. Place mesh on both racks and dehydrate for 3 hours. Let cool on paper towels. Store in airtight container.

Trail Mix

1 cup dried banana chips
1 cup dried coconut chips
½ cup chopped dried apples
½ cup chopped dried peaches
½ cup chopped dried apricots
¼ cup chopped dates
¼ cup sesame seeds
¼ cup salted dried sunflower seeds, shelled
½ cup sliced almonds
¼ cup chocolate chips or carob chips

Mix fruit, coconut, seeds, nuts, and chips. Store in airtight containers.

Trail mix is excellent for school lunches and nutritious snacks.

DEHYDRATION
Suggested Preparation and Timing

Food	Preparaton	Pretreatment	Drying Time (approximate)	Dryness Test (when cool)	Special Notes
Fruit					
Apples 3 pounds	Peel, core and slice 1/4 to 3/8" thick.	Dip in lemon juice. Drain and dry.	4-1/2 hours. (5 to 6 hours if in rings). Both racks.	Leathery. No moisture when cut and squeezed.	Sprinkle with cinnamon. Switch racks 1/2 way. By cutting apple slices in half you can shorten dehydration time.
Apple Leather 5 Cooking apples, 1-1/2 pounds. Makes about 2-1/2 cups when puréed	Core & slice apples, place 2 teaspoons ascorbic acid in 6 cups water. Soak apples. Drain water. Cook covered. Microwave on HI 10 minutes. Purée in blender. Add 1 teaspoon lemon juice and 1/4 teaspoon cinnamon.	Line tray with plastic wrap. Tape all four sides. Pour purée on plastic. Tilt to spread. Leave at least 1/2" border.	About 4 hours.	Pliable and leathery.	1 rack - lower position. Roll while still warm
Bananas 3-1/2 pounds before peeling	Peel and slice 1/4 to 3/8" thick crosswise or lengthwise.	Dip in lemon juice. Drain and dry.	5-1/2 hours. Both racks.	Pliable	Sprinkle with cinnamon or ground cloves. Switch racks 1/2 way. Drying will take 1/2 hour more.
Coconut 3-1/2 to 4 cups	Drain milk. Crack shell to remove meat. Trim dark outer skin. Grate or slice thin in processor.	None.	2 hours. Both racks.	Leathery to crisp.	Switch racks 1/2 way. Use in cakes, desserts, granola. Garnish fruit leathers, banana and apple slices. Use plastic wrap on rack if coconut is grated.
Pears 3 pounds	Peel, core and slice 1/4 to 3/8" thick.	Dip in lemon juice. Drain and dry.	4 to 5 hours. Both racks.	Pliable and leathery. No moisture when cut and squeezed.	Switch racks 1/2 way. Timing will increase if pears are thick and in quarters.
Peaches 3 pounds	Peel, core and slice 3/8" thick.	Dip in lemon juice. Drain and dry.	5 to 6 hours. Both racks.	Pliable and leathery. No moisture.	Switch racks 1/2 way. By cutting peach slices in half you can shorten time.
Peach Leather 1-1/4 pounds defrosted frozen peaches, or 1-1/2 pounds fresh sliced peaches. About 2-1/2 cups when puréed	Purée in blender. Add 1/4 cup light corn syrup, 1/8 teaspoon each cinnamon, cloves and ginger.	Line tray with plastic wrap. Tape all four sides. Pour purée on plastic. Tilt to spread. Leave at least 1/2" border.	About 4 hours.	Pliable and leathery.	1 rack - lower position. Roll while still warm
Strawberry Leather 1-1/4 pounds defrosted frozen berries or 1-1/2 pounds fresh berries.	(follow directions for peach leather)				

DEHYDRATION
Suggested Preparation and Timing

Food	Preparaton	Pretreatment	Drying Time	Dryness Test	Special Notes
Vegetable					
Carrots 3 pounds	Peel, slice 1/8 - 1/4" thick or cubed 3/8".	Blanch.	3 hours. Both racks.	Very tough and leathery.	Switch racks 1/2 way. Turn pieces over at 1/2 way point to assure more uniform drying. But not required.
Corn Cut - Frozen 2 pounds	Rinse with cold water & drain well.	None.	2 hours. Both racks	Dry and brittle.	Switch racks 1/2 way.
Cucumbers 2 - 8"	Peel & slice 1/8" thick.	None.	2 hours or until very brittle for chips. Both racks.	Dry, brittle and crisp.	Switch racks 1/2 way. Seedless, or young cucumbers are best. Does not rehydrate well, use for chips, or sprinkle on salads and soups.
Mushrooms 1-1/2 pounds	Clean and trim woody pieces from stem. Slice lengthwise 1/4 - 3/8" thick.	None.	2 hours. Both racks	Very dry and leathery.	Switch racks 1/2 way.
Onions 1-1/2 pounds	Remove root, trim top skin. Slice 1/8" - 3/8" thick.	None.	3 hours at 140°. Both racks.	Very dry, but pliable. Feels like paper.	Switch racks 1/2 way. Dry to brittle to make flakes and powder.
Peas 4 cups	Shell.	Blanch. Rinse with cold water.	3 hours. Both racks.	Brittle and wrinkled.	Switch racks 1/2 way.
Peppers Green or Red 4 medium	Cut in strips. Remove seeds and ribs (may cut in rings — will increase drying time).	None.	2 hours. Both racks.	Tough to brittle.	Switch racks 1/2 way. Make flakes for salads and soups.
Peppers Chili	Wash. Dice or dry whole. Don't remove seeds.	None.	Diced, 1-1/2 hours. Whole, 2 - 2-1/2 hours. Both racks.	Tough to brittle.	Switch racks 1/2 way. Wear gloves while handling hot peppers.
Tomatoes 8 medium	Remove skins. Immerse in boiling water 30-45 seconds, then in cold water. Remove stems. Slice 1/4" thick.	Dry well.	3 to 4 hours. Both racks as needed. Use upper rack for 1 rack.	Dry and brittle.	Switch racks 1/2 way. Chop in blender for salads or soups. Or use the same as steamed tomatoes.
Meat					
Beef Jerky 2 pounds round steak, Flank steak or brisket of beef	Trim all fat. Partially freeze, cut into long narrow strips - across the grain, no more than 1/4" thick.	Use marinade such as a prepared Teriyaki Sauce. Or marinade suggested in ingredients for Beef Jerky.	3 to 3-1/2 hours. Both racks.	No moist spots. Will crack when bent, but not break.	Switch racks 1/2 way. Blot meat with towel to remove oil and moisture from surface. Let cool on paper towel.

Index